The
New Jerusalem

G. K. Chesterton

1st WORLD
LIBRARY
Literary Society

The New Jerusalem

G. K. Chesterton

© 1st World Library – Literary Society, 2004
PO Box 2211
Fairfield, IA 52556
www.1stworldlibrary.org
First Edition

LCCN: 2005901324

Softcover ISBN: 1-4218-1139-1
Hardcover ISBN: 1-4218-1039-5
eBook ISBN: 1-4218-1239-8

Purchase *"The New Jerusalem"*
as a traditional bound book at:
www.1stWorldLibrary.org/purchase.asp?ISBN=1-4218-1139-1

1st World Library Literary Society is a nonprofit
organization dedicated to promoting literacy by:

- Creating a free internet library accessible from any
  computer worldwide.
- Hosting writing competitions and offering book
  publishing scholarships.

The New Jerusalem
contributed by Tim, Ed & Rodney
in support of
1st World Library Literary Society

PREFACE

This book is only an uncomfortably large note-book; and it has the disadvantages, whether or no it has the advantages, of notes that were taken on the spot. Owing to the unexpected distraction of other duties, the notes were published in a newspaper as they were made on the spot; and are now reproduced in a book as they were published in the newspaper. The only exception refers to the last chapter on Zionism; and even there the book only reverts to the original note-book. A difference of opinion, which divided the writer of the book from the politics of the newspaper, prevented the complete publication of that chapter in that place. I recognise that any expurgated form of it would have falsified the proportions of my attempt to do justice in a very difficult problem; but on re-reading even my own attempt in extenso, I am far from satisfied that the proper proportions are kept. I wrote these first impressions in Palestine, where everybody recognises the Jew as something quite distinct from the Englishman or the European; and where his unpopularity even moved me in the direction of his defence. But I admit it was something of a shock to return to a conventional atmosphere, in which that unpopularity is still actually denied or described as mere persecution. It was more of a shock to realise that this most obscurantist of all types of obscurantism is still some-times regarded as a sort of liberalism. To talk of the Jews always as the oppressed and never as the oppressors is simply absurd; it is as if men pleaded for reasonable help for exiled French aristocrats or ruined Irish landlords, and forgot that the French and Irish peasants had any wrongs at all. Moreover, the Jews in the West do not seem so much concerned to ask, as I have done however tentatively here, whether a larger and less local colonial development might really transfer the bulk of Israel to a more independent basis, as simply to demand that Jews shall continue to control other nations as well as their own. It might be worth while for England to take risks to settle the Jewish problem; but not to take risks merely to unsettle the Arab problem, and leave the Jewish problem unsolved.

For the rest, there must under the circumstances be only too many mistakes; the historical conjectures, for they can be no more, are founded on authorities sufficiently recognised for me to be permitted to trust them; but I have never pretended to the knowledge necessary to check them. I am aware that there are many disputed points; as for instance the connection of Gerard, the fiery Templar, with the English town of Bideford. I am also aware that some are sensitive about the spelling of words; and the very proof-readers will sometimes revolt and turn Mahomet into Mohammed. Upon this point, however, I am unrepentant; for I never could see the point of altering a form with historic and even heroic fame in our own language, for the sake of reproducing by an arrangement of our letters something that is really written in quite different letters, and probably pronounced with quite a different accent. In speaking of the great prophet I am therefore resolved to call him Mahomet; and am prepared, on further provocation, to call him Mahound.

G. K. C.

CONTENTS

CHAPTER I

THE WAY OF THE CITIES

It was in the season of Christmas that I came out of my little garden in that "field of the beeches" between the Chilterns and the Thames, and began to walk backwards through history to the place from which Christmas came. For it is often necessary to walk backwards, as a man on the wrong road goes back to a sign-post to find the right road. The modern man is more like a traveller who has forgotten the name of his destination, and has to go back whence he came, even to find out where he is going. That the world has lost its way few will now deny; and it did seem to me that I found at last a sort of sign-post, of a singular and significant shape, and saw for a moment in my mind the true map of the modern wanderings; but whether I shall be able to say anything of what I saw, this story must show.

I had said farewell to all my friends, or all those with my own limited number of legs; and nothing living remained but a dog and a donkey. The reader will learn with surprise that my first feeling of fellowship went out to the dog; I am well aware that I lay open my guard to a lunge of wit. The dog is rather like a donkey, or a small caricature of one, with a large black head and long black ears; but in the mood of the moment there was rather a moral contrast than a pictorial parallel. For the dog did indeed seem to stand for home and everything I was leaving behind me, with reluctance, especially that season of the year. For one thing, he is named after Mr. Winkle, the Christmas guest of Mr.

Wardle; and there is indeed something Dickensian in his union of domesticity with exuberance. He jumped about me, barking like a small battery, under the impression that I was going for a walk; but I could not, alas, take him with me on a stroll to Palestine. Incidentally, he would have been out of place; for dogs have not their due honour in the East; and this seemed to sharpen my sense of my own domestic sentinel as a sort of symbol of the West. On the other hand, the East is full of donkeys, often very dignified donkeys; and when I turned my attention to the other grotesque quadruped, with an even larger head and even longer ears, he seemed to take on a deep shade of oriental mystery. I know not why these two absurd creatures tangled themselves up so much in my train of thought, like dragons in an illuminated text; or ramped like gargoyles on either side of the gateway of my adventure. But in truth they were in some sense symbols of the West and the East after all. The dog's very lawlessness is but an extravagance of loyalty; he will go mad with joy three times on the same day, at going out for a walk down the same road. The modern world is full of fantastic forms of animal worship; a religion generally accompanied with human sacrifice. Yet we hear strangely little of the real merits of animals; and one of them surely is this innocence of all boredom; perhaps such simplicity is the absence of sin. I have some sense myself of the sacred duty of surprise; and the need of seeing the old road as a new road. But I cannot claim that whenever I go out for a walk with my family and friends, I rush in front of them volleying vociferous shouts of happiness; or even leap up round them attempting to lick their faces. It is in this power of beginning again with energy upon familiar and homely things that the dog is really the eternal type of the Western civilisation. And the donkey is really as different as is the Eastern civilisation. His very anarchy is a sort of secrecy; his very revolt is a secret. He does not leap up because he wishes to share my walk, but to follow his own way, as lonely as the wild ass of Scripture. My own beast of burden supports the authority of Scripture by being a very wild ass. I have given him the name of Trotsky, because he seldom trots, but either scampers or stands still. He scampers all over the field when it is necessary to catch him, and stands still when it is really urgent to drive him. He also breaks fences, eats vegetables, and fulfills other functions; between delays and destructions he could ruin a really poor man in a day. I wish this fact were more often remembered, in judging whether really poor men have really been cruel to donkeys. But I assure the reader that I am not cruel to my donkey; the cruelty is all the other way. He kicks the people who try to catch him; and again I am haunted by a dim human parallel. For it seems to me that many of us, in just detestation of the dirty trick of cruelty to animals, have really a great deal of patience with animals; more patience, I fear, than many of us have with human beings. Suppose I had to go out and catch my secretary in a field every morning; and suppose my secretary always kicked me by way of beginning the day's work; I wonder whether that day's work would resume its normal course as if nothing had happened. Nothing graver than these grotesque images and groping speculations would come into my conscious mind just then, though at the back of it there was an indescribable sense of regret and parting. All through my wanderings the dog remained in my memory as a Dickensian and domestic emblem of England; and if it is difficult to take a donkey seriously, it ought to be easiest, at least, for a man who is going to Jerusalem.

There was a cloud of Christmas weather on the great grey beech-woods and the silver cross of the cross-roads. For the four roads that meet in the market-place of my little town make one of the largest and simplest of such outlines on the map of England; and the shape as it shines on that wooded chart always affects me in a singular fashion. The sight of the cross-roads is in a true sense the sign of the cross. For it is the sign of a truly Christian thing; that sharp combination of liberty and limitation which we call choice. A man is entirely free to choose between right and left, or between right and wrong. As I looked for the last time at the pale roads under the load of cloud, I knew that our civilisation had indeed come to the cross-roads. As the paths grew fainter, fading under the gathering shadow, I felt rather as if it had lost its way in a forest.

It was at the time when people were talking about some menace of the end of the world, not apocalyptic but astronomical; and the cloud that covered the little town of Beaconsfield might have fitted in with such a fancy. It faded, however, as I left the place further behind; and in London the weather, though wet, was comparatively clear. It was almost as if Beaconsfield had a domestic day of judgment, and an end of the world all to itself. In a sense Beaconsfield has four ends of the world, for its four corners are named "ends" after the four nearest towns. But I was concerned only with the one called London End; and the very name of it was like a vision of some vain thing at once ultimate and infinite. The very title of London End sounds like the other end of nowhere, or (what is worse) of everywhere. It suggests a sort of derisive riddle; where does London End? As I came up through the vast vague suburbs, it was this sense of London as a shapeless and endless muddle that chiefly filled my mind. I seemed still to carry the cloud with me; and when I looked up, I almost expected to see the chimney-pots as tangled as the trees.

And in truth if there was now no material fog, there was any amount of mental and moral fog. The whole industrial world symbolised by London had reached a curious complication and confusion, not easy to parallel in human history. It is not a question of controversies, but rather of cross-purposes. As I went by Charing Cross my eye caught a poster about Labour politics, with something about the threat of Direct Action and a demand for Nationalisation. And quite apart from the merits of the case, it struck me that after all the direct action is very indirect, and the thing demanded is many steps away from the thing desired. It is

G. K. CHESTERTON

all part of a sort of tangle, in which terms and things cut across each other. The employers talk about "private enterprise," as if there were anything private about modern enterprise. Its combines are as big as many commonwealths; and things advertised in large letters on the sky cannot plead the shy privileges of privacy. Meanwhile the Labour men talk about the need to "nationalise" the mines or the land, as if it were not the great difficulty in a plutocracy to nationalise the Government, or even to nationalise the nation. The Capitalists praise competition while they create monopoly; the Socialists urge a strike to turn workmen into soldiers and state officials; which is logically a strike against strikes. I merely mention it as an example of the bewildering inconsistency, and for no controversial purpose. My own sympathies are with the Socialists; in so far that there is something to be said for Socialism, and nothing to be said for Capitalism. But the point is that when there is something to be said for one thing, it is now commonly said in support of the opposite thing. Never since the mob called out, "Less bread! More taxes!" in the nonsense story, has there been so truly nonsensical a situation as that in which the strikers demand Government control and the Government denounces its own control as anarchy. The mob howls before the palace gates, "Hateful tyrant, we demand that you assume more despotic powers"; and the tyrant thunders from the balcony, "Vile rebels, do you dare to suggest that my powers should be extended?" There seems to be a little misunderstanding somewhere.

In truth everything I saw told me that there was a large misunderstanding everywhere; a misunderstanding amounting to a mess. And as this was the last impression that London left on me, so it was the impression I carried with me about the whole modern problem of Western civilisation, as a riddle to be read or a knot to be untied. To untie it it is necessary to get hold of the right end of it, and especially the other end of it. We must begin at the beginning; we must return to our first origins in history, as we must return to our first principles in philosophy. We must consider how we came to be doing what we do, and even saying what we say. As it is, the very terms we use are either meaningless or something more than meaningless, inconsistent even with themselves. This applies, for instance, to the talk of both sides in that Labour controversy, which I merely took in passing, because it was the current controversy in London when I left. The Capitalists say Bolshevism as one might say Boojum. It is merely a mystical and imaginative word suggesting horror. But it might mean many things; including some just and rational things. On the other hand, there could never be any meaning at all in the phrase "the dictatorship of the proletariat." It is like saying, "the omnipotence of omnibus-conductors." It is fairly obvious that if an omnibus-conductor were omnipotent, he would probably prefer to conduct something else besides an omnibus. Whatever its exponents mean, it is clearly something different from what they say; and even this verbal inconsistency, this mere welter of words, is a sign of the common confusion of thought. It is this sort of thing that made London seem like a limbo of lost words, and possibly of lost wits. And it is here we find the value of what I have called walking backwards through history.

It is one of the rare merits of modern mechanical travel that it enables us to compare widely different cities in rapid succession. The stages of my own progress were the chief cities of separate countries; and though more is lost in missing the countries, something is gained in so sharply contrasting the capitals. And again it was one of the advantages of my own progress that it was a progress backwards; that it happened, as I have said, to retrace the course of history to older and older things; to Paris and to Rome and to Egypt, and almost, as it were, to Eden. And finally it is one of the advantages of such a return that it did really begin to clarify the confusion of names and notions in modern society. I first became conscious of this when I went out of the Gare de Lyon and walked along a row of cafes, until I saw again a distant column crowned with a dancing figure; the freedom that danced over the fall of the Bastille. Here at least, I thought, is an origin and a standard, such as I missed in the mere muddle of industrial opportunism. The modern industrial world is not in the least democratic; but it is supposed to be democratic, or supposed to be trying to be democratic. The ninth century, the time of the Norse invasions, was not saintly in the sense of being filled with saints; it was filled with pirates and petty tyrants, and the first feudal anarchy. But sanctity was the only ideal those barbarians had, when they had any at all. And democracy is the only ideal the industrial millions have, when they have any at all. Sanctity was the light of the Dark Ages, or if you will the dream of the Dark Ages. And democracy is the dream of the dark age of industrialism; if it be very much of a dream. It is this which prophets promise to achieve, and politicians pretend to achieve, and poets sometimes desire to achieve, and sometimes only desire to desire. In a word, an equal citizenship is quite the reverse of the reality in the modern world; but it is still the ideal in the modern world. At any rate it has no other ideal. If the figure that has alighted on the column in the Place de la Bastille be indeed the spirit of liberty, it must see a million growths in a modern city to make it wish to fly back again into heaven. But our secular society would not know what goddess to put on the pillar in its place.

As I looked at that sculptured goddess on that classical column, my mind went back another historic stage, and I asked myself where this classic and republican ideal came from, and the answer was equally clear. The place from which it had come was the place to which I was going; Rome. And it was not until I had reached Rome that I adequately realised the next great reality that simplified the whole story, and even this particular part of the story. I know nothing more abruptly arresting than that sudden steepness, as of streets scaling the sky, where stands, now cased in tile and brick and stone, that small rock that rose and overshadowed the whole earth; the Capitol. Here in the grey dawn of our history sat the strong Republic that set her foot upon the necks of kings; and it was from here assuredly that the spirit of the Republic flew like an eagle to alight on that far-off pillar in the country of the Gauls. For it ought to be remembered (and it is too often forgotten) that if Paris inherited what may be called the authority of Rome, it is equally true that Rome anticipated all that is sometimes called the anarchy of Paris. The expansion of the Roman Empire was accompanied by a sort of permanent Roman Revolution, fully as furious as the French Revolution. So long as the Roman system was really strong, it was full of riots and mobs and democratic divisions; and any number of Bastilles fell as the temple of the victories rose. But though I had but a hurried glance at such things, there were among them some that further aided the solution of the problem. I saw the larger achievements of the later Romans; and the lesson that was still lacking was plainly there. I saw the Coliseum, a monument of that love of looking on at athletic sports, which is noted as a sign of decadence in the Roman Empire and of energy in the British Empire. I saw the Baths of Caracalla, witnessing to a cult of cleanliness, adduced also to prove the luxury of Ancient Romans and the simplicity of Anglo-Saxons. All it really proves either way is a love of washing on a large scale; which might merely indicate that Caracalla, like other Emperors, was a lunatic. But indeed what such things do indicate, if only indirectly, is something which is here much more important. They indicate not only a sincerity in the public spirit, but a certain smoothness in the public services. In a word, while there were many revolutions, there were no strikes. The citizens were often rebels; but there were men who were not rebels, because they were not citizens. The ancient world forced a number of people to do the work of the world first, before it allowed more privileged people to fight about the government of the world. The truth is trite

G. K. CHESTERTON

enough, of course; it is in the single word Slavery, which is not the name of a crime like Simony, but rather of a scheme like Socialism. Sometimes very like Socialism.

Only standing idly on one of those grassy mounds under one of those broken arches, I suddenly saw the Labour problem of London, as I could not see it in London. I do not mean that I saw which side was right, or what solution was reliable, or any partisan points or repartees, or any practical details about practical difficulties. I mean that I saw what it was; the thing itself and the whole thing. The Labour problem of to-day stood up quite simply, like a peak at which a man looks back and sees single and solid, though when he was walking over it it was a wilderness of rocks. The Labour problem is the attempt to have the democracy of Paris without the slavery of Rome. Between the Roman Republic and the French Republic something had happened. Whatever else it was, it was the abandonment of the ancient and fundamental human habit of slavery; the numbering of men for necessary labour as the normal foundation of society, even a society in which citizens were free and equal. When the idea of equal citizenship returned to the world, it found that world changed by a much more mysterious version of equality. So that London, handing on the lamp from Paris as well as Rome, is faced with a new problem touching the old practice of getting the work of the world done somehow. We have now to assume not only that all citizens are equal, but that all men are citizens. Capitalism attempted it by combining political equality with economic inequality; it assumed the rich could always hire the poor. But Capitalism seems to me to have collapsed; to be not only a discredited ethic but a bankrupt business. Whether we shall return to pagan slavery, or to small property, or by guilds or otherwise get to work in a new way, is not the question here. The question here was the one I asked myself standing on that green mound beside the yellow river; and the answer to it lay ahead of me, along the road that ran towards the rising sun.

What made the difference? What was it that had happened between the rise of the Roman Republic and the rise of the French Republic? Why did the equal citizens of the first take it for granted that there would be slaves? Why did the equal citizens of the second take it for granted that there would not be slaves? How had this immemorial institution disappeared in the interval, so that nobody even dreamed of it or suggested it? How was it that when equality returned, it was no longer the equality of citizens, and had to be the equality of men? The answer is that this equality of men is in more senses than one a mystery. It is a mystery which I pondered as I stood in the corridor of the train going south from Rome. It was at daybreak, and (as it happened) before any one else had risen, that I looked out of the long row of windows across a great landscape grey with olives and still dark against the dawn. The dawn itself looked rather like a row of wonderful windows; a line of low casements unshuttered and shining under the eaves of cloud. There was a curious clarity about the sunrise; as if its sun might be made of glass rather than gold. It was the first time I had seen so closely and covering such a landscape the grey convolutions and hoary foliage of the olive; and all those twisted trees went by like a dance of dragons in a dream. The rocking railway-train and the vanishing railway-line seemed to be going due east, as if disappearing into the sun; and save for the noise of the train there was no sound in all that grey and silver solitude; not even the sound of a bird. Yet the plantations were mostly marked out in private plots and bore every trace of the care of private owners. It is seldom, I confess, that I so catch the world asleep, nor do I know why my answer should have come to me thus when I was myself only half-awake. It is common in such a case to see some new signal or landmark; but in my experience it is rather the things already grown familiar that suddenly grow strange and significant. A million olives must have flashed by before I saw the first olive; the first, so to speak, which really waved the olive branch. For I remembered at last to what land I was going; and I knew the name of the magic which had made all those peasants out of pagan slaves, and has presented to the modern world a new problem of labour and liberty. It was as if I already saw against the clouds of daybreak that mountain which takes its title from the olive: and standing half visible upon it, a figure at which I did not look. *Ex oriente lux*; and I knew what dawn had broken over the ruins of Rome.

I have taken but this one text or label, out of a hundred such, the matter of labour and liberty; and thought it worth while to trace it from one blatant and bewildering yellow poster in the London streets to its high places in history. But it is only one example of the way in which a thousand things grouped themselves and fell into perspective as I passed farther and farther from them, and drew near the central origins of civilisation. I do not say that I saw the solution; but I saw the problem. In the litter of journalism and the chatter of politics, it is too much of a puzzle even to be a problem. For instance, a friend of mine described his book, *The Path to Rome*, as a journey through all Europe that the Faith had saved; and I might very well describe my own journey as one through all Europe that the War has saved. The trail of the actual fighting, of course, was awfully apparent everywhere; the plantations of pale crosses seemed to crop up on every side like growing things; and the first French villages through which I passed had heard in the distance, day and night, the guns of the long battle-line, like the breaking of an endless exterior sea of night upon the very borderland of the world. I felt it most as we passed the noble towers of Amiens, so near the high-water mark of the high tide of barbarism, in that night of terror just before the turning of the tide. For the truth which thus grew clearer with travel is rightly represented by the metaphor of the artillery, as the thunder and surf of a sea beyond the world. Whatever else the war was, it was like the resistance of something as solid as land, and sometimes as patient and inert as land, against something as unstable as water, as weak as water; but also as *strong* as water, as strong as water is in a cataract or a flood. It was the resistance of form to formlessness; that version or vision of it seemed to clarify itself more and more as I went on. It was the defence of that same ancient enclosure in which stood the broken columns of the Roman forum and the column in the Paris square, and of all other such enclosures down to the domestic enclosures of my own dog and donkey. All had the same design, the marking out of a square for the experiment of liberty; of the old civic liberty or the later universal liberty. I knew, to take the domestic metaphor, that the watchdog of the West had again proved too strong for the wild dogs of the Orient. For the foes of such creative limits are chaos and old night, whether they are the Northern barbarism that pitted tribal pride and brutal drill against the civic ideal of Paris, or the Eastern barbarism that brought brigands out of the wilds of Asia to sit on the throne of Byzantium. And as in the other case, what I saw was something simpler and larger than all the disputed details about the war and the peace. A man may think it extraordinary, as I do, that the natural dissolution of the artificial German Empire into smaller states should have actually been prevented by its enemies, when it was already accepted in despair by its friends. For we are now trying hard to hold the Prussian system together, having hammered hard for four mortal years to burst it asunder. Or he may think exactly the opposite; it makes no difference to the larger fact I have in mind. A man may think it simply topsy-turvy, as I do, that we should clear the Turks out of Turkey, but leave them in Constantinople. For that is driving the barbarians from their own rude tillage and pasturage, and giving up to them our own European and Christian city; it is as if the Romans annexed Parthia but surrendered Rome. But he may think exactly the opposite; and the larger and simpler truth will still be there. It was that the weeds and wild things had been everywhere breaking into our boundaries, climbing over the northern wall or crawling through the eastern gate, so that the city would soon have been swallowed in the jungle. And whether the lines had been redrawn logically or loosely, or particular things cleared with consistency or caprice, a line has been drawn somewhere and a clearance has been made somehow. The ancient plan of our city has been saved; a city at least capable of containing citizens. I felt this in the chance relics of the war itself; I felt it twenty times more in those older relics which even the war had never touched at all; I felt the change as much in the changeless East as in the ever-changing West. I felt it when I crossed another great square in Paris to look at a certain statue, which I had last seen hung with crape and such garlands as we give the dead; but on whose plain pedestal nothing now is left but the single word "Strasbourg." I felt it when I saw words merely scribbled with a pencil on a wall in a poor street in Brindisi; *Italia vittoriosa*. But I felt it as much or even more in things infinitely more ancient and remote; in those monuments like mountains that still seem to look down upon all modern things. For these things were more than a trophy that had been raised, they were a palladium that had been rescued. These were the things that had again been saved from chaos, as they were saved at Salamis and Lepanto; and I knew what had saved them or at least in what formation they had been saved. I knew that these scattered splendours of antiquity would hardly have descended to us at all, to be endangered or delivered, if all that pagan world had not crystallised into Christendom.

Crossing seas as smooth as pavements inlaid with turquoise and lapis lazuli, and relieved with marble mountains as clear and famous as marble statues, it was easy to feel all that had been pure and radiant even in the long evening of paganism; but that did not make me forget what strong stars had comforted the inevitable night. The historical moral was the same whether these marble outlines were merely "the isles" seen afar off like sunset clouds by the Hebrew prophets, or were felt indeed as Hellas, the great archipelago of arts and arms praised by the Greek poets; the historic heritage of both descended only to the Greek Fathers. In those wild times and places, the thing that preserved both was the only thing that would have permanently preserved either. It was but part of the same story when we passed the hoary hills that held the primeval culture of Crete, and remembered that it may well have been the first home of the Philistines. It mattered the less by now whether the pagans were best represented by Poseidon the deity or by Dagon the demon. It mattered the less what gods had blessed the Greeks in their youth and liberty; for I knew what god had blessed them in their despair. I knew by what sign they had survived the long slavery under Ottoman orientalism; and upon what name they had called in the darkness, when there was no light but the horned moon of Mahound. If the glory of Greece has survived in some sense, I knew why it had ever survived in any sense. Nor did this feeling of our fixed formation fail me when I came to the very gates of Asia and of Africa; when there rose out of the same blue seas the great harbour of Alexandria; where had shone the Pharos like the star of Hellas, and where men had heard from the lips of Hypatia the last words of Plato. I know the Christians tore Hypatia in pieces; but they did not tear Plato in pieces. The wild men that rode behind Omar the Arab would have thought nothing of tearing every page of Plato in pieces. For it is the nature of all this outer nomadic anarchy that it is capable sooner or later of tearing anything and everything in pieces; it has no instinct of preservation or of the permanent needs of men. Where it has passed the ruins remain ruins and are not renewed; where it has been resisted and rolled back, the links of our long history are never lost. As I went forward the vision of our own civilisation, in the form in which it finally found unity, grew clearer and clearer; nor did I ever know it more certainly than when I had left it behind.

For the vision was that of a shape appearing and reappearing among shapeless things; and it was a shape I knew.

The imagination was forced to rise into altitudes infinitely ancient and dizzy with distance, as if into the cold colours of primeval dawns, or into the upper strata and dead spaces of a daylight older than the sun and moon. But the character of that central clearance still became clearer and clearer. And my memory turned again homewards; and I thought it was like the vision of a man flying from Northolt, over that little market-place beside my own door; who can see nothing below him but a waste as of grey forests, and the pale pattern of a cross.

CHAPTER II

THE WAY OF THE DESERT

It may truly be said, touching the type of culture at least, that Egypt has an Egyptian lower class, a French middle class and an English governing class. Anyhow it is true that the civilisations are stratified in this formation, or superimposed in this order. It is the first impression produced by the darkness and density of the bazaars, the line of the lighted cafes and the blaze of the big hotels. But it contains a much deeper truth in all three cases, and especially in the case of the French influence. It is indeed one of the first examples of what I mean by the divisions of the West becoming clearer in the ancient centres of the East. It is often said that we can only appreciate the work of England in a place like India. In so far as this is true, it is quite equally true that we can only appreciate the work of France in a place like Egypt. But this work is of a peculiar and even paradoxical kind. It is too practical to be prominent, and so universal that it is unnoticed.

The French view of the Rights of Man is called visionary; but in practice it is very solid and even prosaic. The French have a unique and successful trick by which French things are not accepted as French. They are accepted as human. However many foreigners played football, they would still consider football an English thing. But they do not consider fencing a French thing, though all the terms of it are still French. If a Frenchman were to label his hostelry an inn or a public house (probably written publicouse) we

G. K. CHESTERTON

should think him a victim of rather advanced Anglomania. But when an Englishman calls it an hotel, we feel no special dread of him either as a dangerous foreigner or a dangerous lunatic. We need not recognise less readily the value of this because our own distinction is different; especially as our own distinction is being more distinguished. The spirit of the English is adventure; and it is the essence of adventure that the adventurer does remain different from the strange tribes or strange cities, which he studies because of their strangeness. He does not become like them, as did some of the Germans, or persuade them to become like him, as do most of the French. But whether we like or dislike this French capacity, or merely appreciate it properly in its place, there can be no doubt about the cause of that capacity. The cause is in the spirit that is so often regarded as wildly Utopian and unreal. The cause is in the abstract creed of equality and citizenship; in the possession of a political philosophy that appeals to all men. In truth men have never looked low enough for the success of the French Revolution. They have assumed that it claims to be a sort of divine and distant thing, and therefore have not noticed it in the nearest and most materialistic things. They have watched its wavering in the senate and never seen it walking in the streets; though it can be seen in the streets of Cairo as in the streets of Paris.

In Cairo a man thinks it English to go into a tea-shop; but he does not think it French to go into a cafe. And the people who go to the tea-shop, the English officers and officials, are stamped as English and also stamped as official. They are generally genial, they are generally generous, but they have the detachment of a governing group and even a garrison. They cannot be mistaken for human beings. The people going to a café are simply human beings going to it because it is a human place. They have forgotten how much is French and how much Egyptian in their civilisation; they simply think of it as civilisation. Now this character of the older French culture must be grasped because it is the clue to many things in the mystery of the modern East. I call it an old culture because as a matter of fact it runs back to the Roman culture. In this respect the Gauls really continue the work of the Romans, in making something official which comes at last to be regarded as ordinary. And the great fundamental fact which is incessantly forgotten and ought to be incessantly remembered, about these cities and provinces of the near East, is that they were once as Roman as Gaul.

There is a frivolous and fanciful debate I have often had with a friend, about whether it is better to find one's way or to lose it, to remember the road or to forget it. I am so constituted as to be capable of losing my way in my own village and almost in my own house. And I am prepared to maintain the privilege to be a poetic one. In truth I am prepared to maintain that both attitudes are valuable, and should exist side by side. And so my friend and I walk side by side along the ways of the world, he being full of a rich and humane sentiment, because he remembers passing that way a few hundred times since his childhood; while to me existence is a perpetual fairy-tale, because I have forgotten all about it. The lamp-post which moves him to a tear of reminiscence wrings from me a cry of astonishment; and the wall which to him is as historic as a pyramid is to me as arresting and revolutionary as a barricade. Now in this, I am glad to say, my temperament is very English; and the difference is very typical of the two functions of the English and the French. But in practical politics the French have a certain advantage in knowing where they are, and knowing it is where they have been before. It is in the Roman Empire.

The position of the English in Egypt or even in Palestine is something of a paradox. The real English claim is never heard in England and never uttered by Englishmen. We do indeed hear a number of false English claims, and other English claims that are rather irrelevant than false. We hear

G. K. CHESTERTON

pompous and hypocritical suggestions, full of that which so often accompanies the sin of pride, the weakness of provinciality. We hear suggestions that the English alone can establish anywhere a reign of law, justice, mercy, purity and all the rest of it. We also hear franker and fairer suggestions that the English have after all (as indeed they have) embarked on a spirited and stirring adventure; and that there has been a real romance in the extending of the British Empire in strange lands. But the real case for these semi-eastern occupations is not that of extending the British Empire in strange lands. Rather it is restoring the Roman Empire in familiar lands. It is not merely breaking out of Europe in the search for something non-European. It would be much truer to call it putting Europe together again after it had been broken. It may almost be said of the Britons, considered as the most western of Europeans, that they have so completely forgotten their own history that they have forgotten even their own rights. At any rate they have forgotten the claims that could reasonably be made for them, but which they never think of making for themselves. They have not the faintest notion, for instance, of why hundreds of years ago an English saint was taken from Egypt, or why an English king was fighting in Palestine. They merely have a vague idea that George of Cappadocia was naturalised much in the same way as George of Hanover. They almost certainly suppose that Coeur de Lion in his wanderings happened to meet the King of Egypt, as Captain Cook might happen to meet the King of the Cannibal Islands. To understand the past connection of England with the near East, it is necessary to understand something that lies behind Europe and even behind the Roman Empire; something that can only be conveyed by the name of the Mediterranean. When people talk, for instance, as if the Crusades were nothing more than an aggressive raid against Islam, they seem to forget in the strangest way that Islam itself was only an aggressive raid against the old and ordered civilisation in these parts. I do not say it in mere hostility to the religion of Mahomet; as will be apparent later, I am fully conscious of many values and virtues in it; but certainly it was Islam that was the invasion and Christendom that was the thing invaded. An Arabian gentleman found riding on the road to Paris or hammering on the gates of Vienna can hardly complain that we have sought him out in his simple tent in the desert. The conqueror of Sicily and Spain cannot reasonably express surprise at being an object of morbid curiosity to the people of Italy and France. In the city of Cairo the stranger feels many of the Moslem merits, but he certainly feels the militaristic character of the Moslem glories. The crown of the city is the citadel, built by the great Saladin but of the spoils of ancient Egyptian architecture; and that fact is in its turn very symbolical. The man was a great conqueror, but he certainly behaved like an invader; he spoiled the Egyptians. He broke the old temples and tombs and built his own out of fragments. Nor is this the only respect in which the citadel of Cairo is set high like a sign in heaven. The sign is also significant because from this superb height the traveller first beholds the desert, out of which the great conquest came.

Every one has heard the great story of the Greeks who cried aloud in triumph when they saw the sea afar off; but it is a stranger experience to see the earth afar off. And few of us, strictly speaking, have ever seen the earth at all. In cultivated countries it is always clad, as it were, in green garments. The first sight of the desert is like the sight of a naked giant in the distance. The image is all the more natural because of the particular formation which it takes, at least as it borders upon the fields of Egypt, and as it is seen from the high places of Cairo. Those who have seen the desert only in pictures generally think of it as entirely flat. But this edge of it at least stands up on the horizon, as a line of wrinkled and hollow hills like the scalps of bald men; or worse, of bald women. For it is impossible not to think of such repulsive images, in spite of real sublimity of the call to the imagination. There is something curiously hostile and inhuman about the first appearance of the motionless surges of that dry and dreadful sea. Afterwards, if the traveller has happened to linger here and there in the outposts of the desert, has seen the British camp at Kantara or the graceful French garden town of Ismalia, he comes to take the desert as a background, and sometimes a beautiful background; a mirror of mighty reflections and changing colours almost as strange as the colours of the sea. But when it is first seen abutting, and as it were, advancing, upon the fields and gardens of humanity, then it looks indeed like an enemy, or a long line of enemies; like a line of tawny wild beasts thus halted with their heads lifted. It is the feeling that such vain and sterile sand can yet make itself into something like a mountain range; and the traveller remembers all the tragedies of the desert, when he lifts up his eyes to those accursed hills, from whence no help can come.

But this is only a first glimpse from a city set among green fields; and is concerned rather with what the desert has been in its relation to men than with what the desert is in itself. When the mind has grown used to its monotony, a curious change takes place which I have never seen noted or explained by the students of mental science. It may sound strange to say that monotony of its nature becomes novelty. But if any one will try the common experiment of saying some ordinary word such as "moon" or "man" about fifty times, he will find that the expression has become extra-ordinary by sheer repetition. A man has become a strange animal with a name as queer as that of the gnu; and the moon something monstrous like the moon-calf. Something of this magic of monotony is effected by the monotony of deserts; and the traveller feels as if he had entered into a secret, and was looking at everything from another side. Something of this simplification appears, I think, in the religions of the desert, especially in the religion of Islam. It explains something of the super-human hopes that fill the desert prophets concerning the future; it explains something also about their barbarous indifference to the past.

We think of the desert and its stones as old; but in one sense they are unnaturally new. They are unused, and perhaps unusable. They might be the raw material of a world; only they are so raw as to be rejected. It is not easy to define this quality of something primitive, something not mature enough to be fruitful. Indeed there is a hard simplicity about many Eastern things that is as much crude as archaic. A palm-tree is very like a tree drawn by a child - or by a very futurist artist. Even a pyramid is like a mathematical figure drawn by a schoolmaster teaching children; and its very impressiveness is that of an ultimate Platonic abstraction. There is something curiously simple about the shape in which these colossal crystals of the ancient sands have been cast. It is only when we have felt something of this element, not only of simplicity, but of crudity, and even in a sense of novelty, that we can begin to understand both the immensity and the insufficiency of that power that came out of the desert, the great religion of Mahomet.

In the red circle of the desert, in the dark and secret place, the prophet discovers the obvious things. I do not say it merely as a sneer, for obvious things are very easily forgotten; and indeed every high civilisation decays by forgetting obvious things. But it is true that in such a solitude men tend to take very simple ideas as if they were entirely new ideas. There is a love of concentration which comes from the lack of comparison. The lonely man looking at the lonely palm-tree does see the elementary truths about the palm-tree; and the elementary truths are very essential. Thus he does see that though the palm-tree may be a very simple design, it was not he who designed it. It may look like a tree drawn by a child, but he is not the child who could draw it. He has not command of that magic slate on which the pictures can come to life, or of that magic green chalk of which the green lines can grow.

He sees at once that a power is at work in whose presence he and the palm-tree are alike little children. In other words, he is intelligent enough to believe in God; and the Moslem, the man of the desert, is intelligent enough to believe in God. But his belief is lacking in that humane complexity that comes from comparison. The man looking at the palm-tree does realise the simple fact that God made it; while the man looking at the lamp-post in a large modern city can be persuaded by a hundred sophistical circumlocutions that he made it himself. But the man in the desert cannot compare the palm-tree with the lamp-post, or even with all the other trees which may be better worth looking at than the lamp-post. Hence his religion, though true as far as it goes, has not the variety and vitality of the churches that were designed by men walking in the woods and orchards. I speak here of the Moslem type of religion and not of the oriental type of ornament, which is much older than the Moslem type of religion. But even the oriental type of ornament, admirable as it often is, is to the ornament of a gothic cathedral what a fossil forest is to a forest full of birds. In short, the man of the desert tends to simplify too much, and to take his first truth for the last truth. And as it is with religion so it is with morality. He who believes in the existence of God believes in the equality of man. And it has been one of the merits of the Moslem faith that it felt men as men, and was not incapable of welcoming men of many different races. But here again it was so hard and crude that its very equality was like a desert rather than a field. Its very humanity was inhuman.

But though this human sentiment is rather rudimentary it is very real. When a man in the desert meets another man, he is really a man; the proverbial two-legged fowl without feathers. He is an absolute and elementary shape, like the palm-tree or the pyramid. The discoverer does not pause to consider through what gradations he may have been evolved from a camel. When the man is a mere dot in the distance, the other man does not shout at him and ask whether he had a university education, or whether he is quite sure he is purely Teutonic and not Celtic or Iberian. A man is a man; and a man is a very important thing. One thing redeems the Moslem morality which can be set over against a mountain of crimes; a considerable deposit of common sense. And the first fact of common sense is the common bond of men. There is indeed in the Moslem character also a deep and most dangerous potentiality of fanaticism of the menace of which something may be said later. Fanaticism sounds like the flat contrary of common sense; yet curiously enough they are both sides of the same thing. The fanatic of the desert is dangerous precisely because he does take his faith as a fact, and not even as a truth in our more transcendental sense. When he does take up a mystical idea he takes it as he takes the man or the palm-tree; that is, quite literally. When he does distinguish somebody not as a man but as a Moslem, then he divides the Moslem from the non-Moslem exactly as he divides the man from the camel. But even then he recognises the equality of men in the sense of the equality of Moslems. He does not, for instance, complicate his conscience with any sham science about races. In this he has something like an intellectual advantage over the Jew, who is generally so much his intellectual superior; and even in some ways his spiritual superior. The Jew has far more moral imagination and sympathy with the subtler ideals of the soul. For instance, it is said that many Jews disbelieve in a future life; but if they did believe in a future life, it would be something more worthy of the genius of Isaiah and Spinoza. The Moslem Paradise is a very Earthly Paradise. But with all their fine apprehensions, the Jews suffer from one heavy calamity; that of being a Chosen Race. It is the vice of any patriotism or religion depending on race that the individual is himself the thing to be worshipped; the individual is his own ideal, and even his own idol. This fancy was fatal to the Germans; it is fatal to the Anglo-Saxons, whenever any of them forswear the glorious name of Englishmen and Americans to fall into that forlorn description. This is not so when the nation is felt as a noble abstraction, of which the individual is proud in the abstract. A Frenchman is proud of France, and therefore may think himself unworthy of France. But a German is proud of being a German; and he cannot be too unworthy to be a German when he is a German. In short, mere family pride flatters every member of the family; it produced the arrogance of the Germans, and it is capable of producing a much subtler kind of arrogance in the Jews. From this particular sort of self-deception the more savage man of the desert is free. If he is not considering somebody as a Moslem, he will consider him as a man. At the price of something like barbarism, he has at least been saved from ethnology.

But here again the obvious is a limit as well as a light to him. It does not permit, for instance, anything fine or subtle in the sentiment of sex. Islam asserts admirably the equality of men; but it is the equality of males. No one can deny that a noble dignity is possible even to the poorest, who has seen the Arabs coming in from the desert to the cities of Palestine or Egypt. No one can deny that men whose rags are dropping off their backs can bear themselves in a way befitting kings or prophets in the great stories of Scripture. No one can be surprised that so many fine artists have delighted to draw such models on the spot, and to make realistic studies for illustrations to the Old and New Testaments. On the road to Cairo one may see twenty groups exactly like that of the Holy Family in the pictures of the Flight into Egypt; with only one difference. The man is riding on the ass.

In the East it is the male who is dignified and even ceremonial. Possibly that is why he wears skirts. I pointed out long ago that petticoats, which some regard as a garb of humiliation for women are really regarded as the only garb of magnificence for men, when they wish to be something more than men. They are worn by kings, by priests, and by judges. The male Moslem, especially in his own family, is the king and the priest and the judge. I do not mean merely that he is the master, as many would say of the male in many Western societies, especially simple and self-governing societies. I mean something more; I mean that he has not only the kingdom and the power but the glory, and even as it were the glamour. I mean he has not only the rough leadership that we often give to the man, but the special sort of social beauty and stateliness that we generally expect only of the woman. What we mean when we say that an ambitious man wants to have a fine woman at the head of the dinner-table, that the Moslem world really means when it expects to see a fine man at the head of the house. Even in the street he is the peacock, coloured much more splendidly than the peahen. Even when clad in comparatively sober and partly European costume, as outside the cafes of Cairo and the great cities, he exhibits this indefinable character not merely of dignity but of pomp. It can be traced even in the tarbouch, the minimum of Turkish attire worn by all the commercial classes; the thing more commonly called in England a fez. The fez is not a sort of smoking cap. It is a tower of scarlet often tall enough to be the head-dress of a priest. And it is a hat one cannot take off to a lady.

This fact is familiar enough in talk about Moslem and oriental life generally; but I only repeat it in order to refer it back to the same simplification which is the advantage and disadvantage of the philosophy of the desert. Chivalry is not an obvious idea. It is not as plain as a pike-staff or as a palm-tree. It is a delicate balance between the sexes which gives the rarest and most poetic kind of pleasure to those who can strike it. But it is not self-evident to a savage merely because he is also a sane man. It often seems to him as much a part of his own coarse common sense that all the fame and fun should go to the sex that is stronger and less tied, as that all the authority should go to the parents rather than the children. Pity for weakness he can understand; and the Moslem is quite capable of giving royal alms to a cripple or an orphan. But reverence for weakness is to him simply meaningless. It is a mystical idea that is to him no more than a mystery. But the same is true touching what may be called the lighter side of the more civilised sentiment. This hard and literal view of life gives no place for that slight element of a magnanimous sort of play-acting, which has run through all our tales of true lovers in the West. Wherever there is chivalry there is courtesy; and wherever there is courtesy there is comedy. There is no comedy in the desert.

Another quite logical and consistent element, in the very logical and consistent creed we call Mahometanism, is the element that we call Vandalism. Since such few and obvious things alone are vital, and since a half-artistic half-antiquarian affection is not one of these things, and cannot be called obvious, it is largely left out. It is very difficult to say in a few well-chosen words exactly what is now the use of the Pyramids. Therefore Saladin, the great Saracen warrior, simply stripped the Pyramids to build a military fortress on the heights of Cairo. It is a little difficult to define exactly what is a man's duty to the Sphinx; and therefore the Mamelukes used it entirely as a target. There was little in them of that double feeling, full of pathos and irony, which divided the hearts of the primitive Christians in presence of the great pagan literature and art. This is not concerned with brutal outbreaks of revenge which may be found on both sides, or with chivalrous caprices of toleration, which may also be found on both sides; it is concerned with the inmost mentality of the two religions, which must be understood in order to do justice to either. The Moslem mind never tended to that mystical mode of "loving yet leaving" with which Augustine cried aloud upon the ancient beauty, or Dante said farewell to Virgil when he left him in the limbo of the pagans. The Moslem traditions, unlike the medieval legends, do not suggest the image of a knight who kissed Venus before he killed her. We see in all the Christian ages this combination which is not a compromise, but rather a complexity made by two contrary enthusiasms; as when the Dark Ages copied out the pagan poems while denying the pagan legends; or when the popes of the Renascence imitated the Greek temples while denying the Greek gods. This high inconsistency is inconsistent with Islam. Islam, as I have said, takes everything literally, and does not know how to play with anything. And the cause of the contrast is the historical cause of which we must be conscious in all studies of this kind. The Christian Church had from a very early date the idea of reconstructing a whole civilisation, and even a complex civilisation. It was the attempt to make a new balance, which differed from the old balance of the stoics of Rome; but which could not afford to lose its balance any more than they. It differed because the old system was one of many religions under one government, while the new was one of many governments under one religion. But the idea of variety in unity remained though it was in a sense reversed. A historical instinct made the men of the new Europe try hard to find a place for everything in the system, however much might be denied to the individual. Christians might lose everything, but Christendom, if possible, must not lose anything. The very nature of Islam, even at its best, was quite different from this. Nobody supposed, even subconsciously, that Mahomet meant to restore ancient Babylon as medievalism vaguely sought to restore ancient Rome. Nobody thought that the builders of the Mosque of Omar had looked at the Pyramids as the builders of St. Peter's might have looked at the Parthenon. Islam began at the beginning; it was content with the idea that it had a great truth; as indeed it had a colossal truth. It was so huge a truth that it was hard to see it was a half-truth.

Islam was a movement; that is why it has ceased to move. For a movement can only be a mood. It may be a very necessary movement arising from a very noble mood, but sooner or later it must find its level in a larger philosophy, and be balanced against other things. Islam was a reaction towards simplicity; it was a violent simplification, which turned out to be an over-simplification. Stevenson has somewhere one of his perfectly picked phrases for an empty-minded man; that he has not one thought to rub against another while he waits for a train. The Moslem had one thought, and that a most vital one; the greatness of God which levels all men. But the Moslem had not one thought to rub against another, because he really had not another. It is the friction of two spiritual things, of tradition and invention, or of substance and symbol, from which the mind takes fire. The creeds condemned as complex have something like the secret of sex; they can breed thoughts.

An idealistic intellectual remarked recently that there were a great many things in the creed for which he had no use. He might just as well have said that there were a great many things in the *Encyclopedia Britannica* for which he had no use. It would probably have occurred to him that the work in question was meant for humanity and not for him. But even in the case of the *Encyclopedia*, it will often be found a stimulating exercise to read two articles on two widely different subjects and note where they touch. In fact there is really a great deal to be said for the man in *Pickwick* who read first about China and then about metaphysics and combined his information. But however this may be in the famous case of Chinese metaphysics, it is this which is chiefly lacking in Arabian metaphysics. They suffer, as I have said of the palm-tree in the desert, from a lack of the vitality that comes from complexity, and of the complexity that comes from comparison. They suffer from having been in a single movement in a single direction; from having begun as a mood and ended rather as a mode, that is a mere custom or fashion. But any modern Christian thus criticising the Moslem movement will do well to criticise himself and his world at the same time. For in truth most modern things are mere movements in the same sense as the Moslem movement. They are at best fashions, in which one thing is exaggerated because it has been neglected. They are at worst mere monomanias, in which everything is neglected that one thing may be exaggerated. Good or bad, they are alike movements which in their nature can only move for a certain distance and then stop. Feminism, for instance, is in its nature a movement, and one that must stop somewhere. But the Suffragettes no more established a philosophy of the sexes by their feminism than the Arabs did by their anti-feminism. A woman can find her home on the hustings even less than in the harem; but such movements do not really attempt to find a final home for anybody or anything. Bolshevism is a movement; and in my opinion a very natural and just movement considered as a revolt against the crude cruelty of Capitalism. But when we find the Bolshevists making a rule that the drama "must encourage the proletarian spirit," it is obvious that those who say so are not only maniacs but, what is more to the point here, are monomaniacs. Imagine having to apply that principle, let us say, to "Charley's Aunt." None of these things seek to establish a complete philosophy such as Aquinas founded on Aristotle. The only two modern men who attempted it were Comte and Herbert Spencer. Spencer, I think, was too small a man to do it at all; and Comte was a great enough man to show how difficult it is to do it in modern times. None of these movements can do anything but move; they have not discovered where to rest.

And this fact brings us back to the man of the desert, who moves and does not rest; but who has many superiorities to the restless races of the industrial city. Men who have been in the Manchester movement in 1860 and the Fabian movement in 1880 cannot sneer at a religious mood that lasted for eight hundred years. And those who tolerate the degraded homelessness of the slums cannot despise the much more dignified homelessness of the desert. Nevertheless, the thing is a homelessness and not a home; and there runs through it all the note of the nomad. The Moslem takes literally, as he takes everything, the truth that here we have no abiding city. He can see no meaning in the mysticism of materialism, the sacramental idea that a French poet expressed so nobly, when he said that our earthly city is the body of the city of God. He has no true notion of building a house, or in our Western sense of recognising the kindred points of heaven and home. Even the exception to this rule is an exception at once terrible and touching. There is one house that the Moslem does build like a house and even a home, often with walls and roof and door; as square as a cottage, as solid as a fort. And that is his grave. A Moslem cemetery is literally like a little village. It is a village, as the saying goes, that one would not care to walk through at night. There is something singularly creepy about so strange a street of houses, each with a door that might be opened by a dead man. But in a less fanciful sense, there is about it something profoundly pathetic and human. Here indeed is the sailor home from sea, in the only port he will consent to call his home; here at last the nomad confesses the common need of men. But even about this there broods the presence of the desert and its dry bones of reason. He will accept nothing between a tent and a tomb.

The philosophy of the desert can only begin over again. It cannot grow; it cannot have what Protestants call progress and Catholics call development. There is death and hell in the desert when it does begin over again. There is always the possibility that a new prophet will rediscover the old truth; will find again written on the red sands the secret of the obvious. But it will always be the same secret, for which thousands of these simple and serious and splendidly valiant men will die. The highest message of Mahomet is a piece of divine tautology. The very cry that God is God is a repetition of words, like the repetitions of wide sands and rolling skies. The very phrase is like an everlasting echo, that can never cease to say the same sacred word; and when I saw afterwards the mightiest and most magnificent of all the mosques of that land, I found that its inscriptions had the same character of a deliberate and defiant sameness. The ancient Arabic alphabet and script is itself at once so elegant and so exact that it can be used as a fixed ornament, like the egg and dart pattern or the Greek key. It is as if we could make a heraldry of handwriting, or cover a wall-paper with signatures. But the literary style is as recurrent as the decorative style; perhaps that is why it can be used as a decorative style. Phrases are repeated again and again like ornamental stars or flowers. Many modern people, for example, imagine that the Athanasian Creed is full of vain repetitions; but that is because people are too lazy to listen to it, or not lucid enough to understand it. The same terms are used throughout, as they are in a proposition of Euclid. But the steps are all as differentiated and progressive as in a proposition of Euclid. But in the inscriptions of the Mosque whole sentences seem to occur, not like the steps of an argument, but rather like the chorus of a song. This is the impression everywhere produced by this spirit of the sandy wastes; this is the voice of the desert, though the muezzin cries from the high turrets of the city. Indeed one is driven to repeating oneself about the repetition, so overpowering is the impression of the tall horizons of those tremendous plains, brooding upon the soul with all the solemn weight of the self-evident.

There is indeed another aspect of the desert, yet more ancient and momentous, of which I may speak; but here I only deal with its effect on this great religion of simplicity. For it is through the atmosphere of that religion that a man makes his way, as so many pilgrims have done, to the goal of this pilgrimage. Also this particular aspect remained the more sharply in my memory because of the suddenness with which I escaped from it. I had not expected the contrast; and it may have coloured all my after experiences. I descended from the desert train at Ludd, which had all the look of a large camp in the desert; appropriately enough perhaps, for it is the traditional birthplace of the soldier St.

G. K. CHESTERTON

George. At the moment, however, there was nothing rousing or romantic about its appearance. It was perhaps unusually dreary; for heavy rain had fallen; and the water stood about in what it is easier to call large puddles than anything so poetic as small pools. A motor car sent by friends had halted beside the platform; I got into it with a not unusual vagueness about where I was going; and it wound its way up miry paths to a more rolling stretch of country with patches of cactus here and there. And then with a curious abruptness I became conscious that the whole huge desert had vanished, and I was in a new land. The dark red plains had rolled away like an enormous nightmare; and I found myself in a fresh and exceedingly pleasant dream.

I know it will seem fanciful; but for a moment I really felt as if I had come home; or rather to that home behind home for which we are all homesick. The lost memory of it is the life at once of faith and of fairy-tale. Groves glowing with oranges rose behind hedges of grotesque cactus or prickly pear; which really looked like green dragons guarding the golden apples of the Hesperides. On each side of the road were such flowers as I had never seen before under the sun; for indeed they seemed to have the sun in them rather than the sun on them. Clusters and crowds of crimson anemones were of a red not to be symbolised in blood or wine; but rather in the red glass that glows in the window dedicated to a martyr. Only in a wild Eastern tale could one picture a pilgrim or traveller finding such a garden in the desert; and I thought of the oldest tale of all and the garden from which we came. But there was something in it yet more subtle; which there must be in the impression of any earthly paradise. It is vital to such a dream that things familiar should be mixed with things fantastic; as when an actual dream is filled with the faces of old friends. Sparrows, which seem to be the same all over the world, were darting hither and thither among the flowers; and I had the fancy that they were the souls of the town-sparrows of London and the smoky cities, and now gone wherever the good sparrows go. And a little way up the road before me, on the hill between the cactus hedges, I saw a grey donkey trotting; and I could almost have sworn that it was the donkey I had left at home.

He was trotting on ahead of me, and the outline of his erect and elfish ears was dark against the sky. He was evidently going somewhere with great determination; and I thought I knew to what appropriate place he was going, and that it was my fate to follow him like a moving omen. I lost sight of him later, for I had to complete the journey by train; but the train followed the same direction, which was up steeper and steeper hills. I began to realise more clearly where I was; and to know that the garden in the desert that had bloomed so suddenly about me had borne for many desert wanderers the name of the promised land. As the rocks rose higher and higher on every side, and hung over us like terrible and tangible clouds, I saw in the dim grass of the slopes below them something I had never seen before. It was a rainbow fallen upon the earth, with no part of it against the sky, but only the grasses and the flowers shining through its fine shades of fiery colour. I thought this also was like an omen; and in such a mood of idle mysticism there fell on me another accident which I was content to count for a third. For when the train stopped at last in the rain, and there was no other vehicle for the last lap of the journey, a very courteous officer, an army surgeon, gave me a seat in an ambulance wagon; and it was under the shield of the red cross that I entered Jerusalem.

For suddenly, between a post of the wagon and a wrack of rainy cloud I saw it, uplifted and withdrawn under all the arching heavens of its history, alone with its benediction and its blasphemy, the city that is set upon a hill, and cannot be hid.

G. K. CHESTERTON

CHAPTER III

THE GATES OF THE CITY

The men I met coming from Jerusalem reported all sorts of contradictory impressions; and yet my own impression contradicted them all. Their impressions were doubtless as true as mine; but I describe my own because it is true, and because I think it points to a neglected truth about the real Jerusalem. I need not say I did not expect the real Jerusalem to be the New Jerusalem; a city of charity and peace, any more than a city of chrysolite and pearl. I might more reasonably have expected an austere and ascetic place, oppressed with the weight of its destiny, with no inns except monasteries, and these sealed with the terrible silence of the Trappists; an awful city where men speak by signs in the street. I did not need the numberless jokes about Jerusalem to-day, to warn me against expecting this; anyhow I did not expect it, and certainly I did not find it. But neither did I find what I was much more inclined to expect; something at the other extreme. Many reports had led me to look for a truly cosmopolitan town, that is a truly conquered town. I looked for a place like Cairo, containing indeed old and interesting things, but open on every side to new and vulgar things; full of the touts who seem only created for the tourists and the tourists who seem only created for the touts. There may be more of this in the place than pleases those who would idealise it. But I fancy there is much less of it than is commonly supposed in the reaction from such an ideal. It does not, like Cairo, offer the exciting experience of twenty guides fighting for one traveller; of young Turks drinking American cocktails as a protest against Christian wine. The town is quite inconvenient enough to make it a decent place for pilgrims. Or a stranger might have imagined a place even less Western than Cairo, one of those villages of Palestine described in dusty old books of Biblical research. He might remember drawings like diagrams representing a well or a wine-press, rather a dry well, so to speak, and a wine-press very difficult to associate with wine. These hard colourless outlines never did justice to the colour of the East, but even to give it the colour of the East would not do justice to Jerusalem. If I had anticipated the Bagdad of all our dreams, a maze of bazaars glowing with gorgeous wares, I should have been wrong again. There is quite enough of this vivid and varied colour in Jerusalem, but it is not the first fact that arrests the attention, and certainly not the first that arrested mine. I give my own first impression as a fact, for what it is worth and exactly as it came. I did not expect it, and it was some time before I even understood it. As soon as I was walking inside the walls of Jerusalem, I had an overwhelming impression that I was walking in the town of Rye, where it looks across the flat sea-meadows towards Winchelsea.

As I tried to explain this eccentric sentiment to myself, I was conscious of another which at once completed and contradicted it. It was not only like a memory of Rye, it was mixed with a memory of the Mount St. Michael, which stands among the sands of Normandy on the other side of the narrow seas. The first part of the sensation is that the traveller, as he walks the stony streets between the walls, feels that he is inside a fortress. But it is the paradox of such a place that, while he feels in a sense that he is in a prison, he also feels that he is on a precipice. The sense of being uplifted, and set on a high place, comes to him through the smallest cranny, or most accidental crack in rock or stone; it comes to him especially through those long narrow windows in the walls of the old fortifications; those slits in the stone through which the medieval archers used their bows and the medieval artists used their eyes, with even greater success. Those green glimpses of fields far below or of flats far away, which delight us and yet make us dizzy (by being both near and far) when seen through the windows of Memling, can often be seen from the walls of Jerusalem. Then I remembered that in the same strips of medieval landscape could be seen always, here and there, a steep hill crowned with a city of towers. And I knew I had the mystical and double pleasure of seeing such a hill and standing on it. A city that is set upon a hill cannot be hid; but it is more strange when the hill cannot anywhere be hid, even from the citizen in the city.

Then indeed I knew that what I saw was Jerusalem of the Crusaders; or at least Jerusalem of the Crusades. It was a medieval town, with walls and gates and a citadel, and built upon a hill to be defended by bowmen. The greater part of the actual walls now standing were built by Moslems late in the Middle Ages; but they are almost exactly like the walls that were being built by the Christians at or before that time. The Crusader Edward, afterwards Edward the First, reared such battlements far away among the rainy hills of Wales. I do not know what elements were originally Gothic or what originally Saracenic. The Crusaders and the Saracens constantly copied each other while they combated each other; indeed it is a fact always to be found in such combats. It is one of the arguments against war that are really human, and therefore are never used by humanitarians. The curse of war is that it does lead to more international imitation; while in peace and freedom men can afford to have national variety. But some things in this country were certainly copied from the Christian invaders, and even if they are not Christian they are in many ways strangely European. The wall and gates which now stand, whatever stood before them and whatever comes after them, carry a memory of those men from the West who came here upon that wild adventure, who climbed this rock and clung to it so perilously from the victory of Godfrey to the victory of Saladin; and that is why this momentary Eastern exile reminded me so strangely of the hill of Rye and of home.

I do not forget, of course, that all these visible walls and towers are but the battlements and pinnacles of a buried city, or of many buried cities. I do not forget that such buildings have foundations that are to us almost like fossils; the gigantic fossils of some other geological epoch. Something may be said later of those lost empires whose very masterpieces are to us like petrified monsters. From this height, after long histories unrecorded, fell the forgotten idol of the Jebusites, on that day when David's javelin-men scaled the citadel and carried through it, in darkness behind his coloured curtains, the god whose image had never been made by man. Here was waged that endless war between the graven gods of the plain and the invisible god of the mountain; from here the hosts carrying the sacred fish of the Philistines were driven back to the sea from which their worship came. Those who worshipped on this hill had come out of bondage in Egypt and went into bondage in Babylon; small as was their country, there passed before them almost the whole pageant of the old pagan world. All its strange shapes and strong almost cruel colours remain in the records of their prophets; whose lightest phrase seems heavier than the pyramids of Egypt; and whose very words are like winged bulls walking. All this historic or pre-historic interest may be touched on in its turn; but I am not dealing here with the historic secrets unearthed by the study of the place, but with the historic associations aroused by the sight of it. The traveller is in the position of that famous fantastic who tied his horse to a wayside cross in the snow, and afterward saw it dangling from the church-spire of what had been a buried city. But here the cross does not stand as it does on the top of a spire; but as it does on the top of an Egyptian obelisk in Rome, - where the priests have put a cross on the top of the heathen monument; for fear it should walk. I entirely sympathise with their sentiment; and I shall try to suggest later why I think that symbol the logical culmination of heathen as well as Christian things. The traveller in the traveller's tale looked up at last and saw, from the streets far below, the spire and cross dominating a Gothic city. If I looked up in a vision and saw it dominating a Babylonian city, that blocked the heavens with monstrous palaces and temples, I should still think it natural that it should dominate. But the point here is that what I saw above ground was rather the Gothic town than the Babylonian; and that it reminded me, if not specially of the cross, at least of the soldiers who took the cross.

Nor do I forget the long centuries that have passed over the place since these medieval walls were built, any more than the far more interesting centuries that passed before they were built. But any one taking exception to the description on that ground may well realise, on consideration, that it is an exception that proves the rule. There is something very negative about Turkish rule; and the best and worst of it is in the word neglect. Everything that lived under the vague empire of Constantinople remained in a state of suspended animation like something frozen rather than decayed, like something sleeping rather than dead. It was a sort of Arabian spell, like that which turned princes and princesses into marble statues in the *Arabian Nights*. All that part of the history of the place is a kind of sleep; and that of a sleeper who hardly knows if he has slept an hour or a hundred years. When I first found myself in the Jaffa Gate of Jerusalem, my eye happened to fall on something that might be seen anywhere, but which seemed somehow to have a curious significance there. Most people are conscious of some common object which still strikes them as uncommon; as if it were the first fantastic sketch in the sketch-book of nature. I myself can never overcome the sense of something almost unearthly about grass growing upon human buildings. There is in it a wild and even horrible fancy, as if houses could grow hair. When I saw that green hair on the huge stone blocks of the citadel, though I had seen the same thing on any number of ruins, it came to me like an omen or a vision, a curious vision at once of chaos and of sleep. It is said that the grass will not grow where the Turk sets his foot; but it is the other side of the same truth to say that it would grow anywhere but where it ought to grow. And though in this case it was but an accident and a symbol, it was a very true symbol. We talk of the green banner of the Turk having been planted on this or that citadel; and certainly it was so planted with splendid valour and sensational victory. But this is the green banner that he plants on all his high cities in the end.

Therefore my immediate impression of the walls and gates was not contradicted by my consciousness of what came before and what came after that medieval period. It remained primarily a thing of walls and gates; a thing which the modern world does not perhaps understand so well as the medieval world. There is involved in it all that idea of definition which those who do not like it are fond of describing as dogma. A wall is like rule; and the gates are like the exceptions that prove the rule. The man making it has to decide where his rule will run and where his exception shall stand. He cannot have a city that is all gates any more than a house that is all windows; nor is it possible to have a law that consists entirely of liberties. The ancient races and religions that contended for this city agreed with each other in this, when they differed about everything else. It was true of practically all of them that when they built a city they built a citadel. That is, whatever strange thing they may have made, they regarded it as something to be defined and to be defended.

And from this standpoint the holy city was a happy city; it had no suburbs. That is to say, there are all sorts of buildings outside the wall; but they are outside the wall. Everybody is conscious of being inside or outside a boundary; but it is the whole character of the true suburbs which grow round our great industrial towns that they grow, as it were, unconsciously and blindly, like grass that covers up a boundary line traced on the earth. This indefinite expansion is controlled neither by the soul of the city from within, nor by the resistance of the lands round about. It destroys at once the dignity of a town and the freedom of a countryside. The citizens are too new and numerous for citizenship; yet they never learn what there is to be learned of the ancient traditions of agriculture. The first sight of the sharp outline of Jerusalem is like a memory of the older types of limitation and liberty. Happy is the city that has a wall; and happier still if it is a precipice.

Again, Jerusalem might be called a city of staircases. Many streets are steep and most actually cut into steps. It is, I believe, an element in the controversy about the cave at Bethlehem traditionally connected with the Nativity that the sceptics doubt whether any beasts of burden could have entered a stable that has to be reached by such steps. And indeed to any one in a modern city like London or Liverpool it may well appear odd, like a cab-horse climbing a ladder. But as a matter of fact, if the asses and goats of Jerusalem could not go up and downstairs, they could not go anywhere. However this may be, I mention the matter here merely as adding another touch to that angular profile which is the impression involved here. Strangely enough, there is something that leads up to this impression even in the labyrinth of mountains through which the road winds its way to the city. The hills round Jerusalem are themselves often hewn out in terraces, like a huge stairway. This is mostly for the practical and indeed profitable purpose of vineyards; and serves for a reminder that this ancient seat of civilisation has not lost the tradition of the mercy and the glory of the vine. But in outline such a mountain looks much like the mountain of Purgatory that Dante saw in his vision, lifted in terraces, like titanic steps up to God. And indeed this shape also is symbolic; as symbolic as the pointed profile of the Holy City. For a creed is like a ladder, while an evolution is only like a slope. A spiritual and social evolution is generally a pretty slippery slope; a miry slope where it is very easy to slide down again.

Such is something like the sharp and even abrupt impression produced by this mountain city; and especially by its wall with gates like a house with windows. A gate, like a window, is primarily a picture-frame. The pictures that are found within the frame are indeed very various and sometimes very alien. Within this frame-work are indeed to be found things entirely Asiatic, or entirely Moslem, or even entirely nomadic. But Jerusalem itself is not nomadic. Nothing could be less like a mere camp of tents pitched by Arabs. Nothing could be less like the mere chaos of colour in a temporary and tawdry bazaar. The Arabs are there and the colours are there, and they make a glorious picture; but the picture is in a Gothic frame, and is seen so to speak through a Gothic window. And the meaning of all this is the meaning of all windows, and especially of Gothic windows. It is that even light itself is most divine within limits; and that even the shining one is most shining, when he takes upon himself a shape.

Such a system of walls and gates, like many other things thought rude and primitive, is really very rationalistic. It turns the town, as it were, into a plan of itself, and even into a guide to itself. This is especially true, as may be suggested in a moment, regarding the direction of the roads leading out of it. But anyhow, a man must decide which way he will leave the city; he cannot merely drift out of the city as he drifts out of the modern cities through a litter of slums. And there is no better way to get a preliminary plan of the city than to follow the wall and fix the gates in the memory. Suppose, for instance, that a man begins in the south with the Zion Gate, which bears the ancient name of Jerusalem. This, to begin with, will sharpen the medieval and even the Western impression first because it is here that he has the strongest sentiment of threading the narrow passages of a great castle; but also because the very name of the gate was given to this south-western hill by Godfrey and Tancred during the period of the Latin kingdom. I believe it is one of the problems of the scholars why the Latin conquerors called this hill the Zion Hill, when the other is obviously the sacred hill. Jerusalem is traditionally divided into four hills, but for practical purposes into two; the lower eastern hill where stood the Temple, and now stands the great Mosque, and the western where is the citadel and the Zion Gate to the south of it. I know nothing of such questions; and I attach no importance to the notion that has crossed my own mind, and which I only mention in passing, for I have no doubt there are a hundred objections to it. But it is known that Zion or Sion was the old name of the place before it was stormed by David; and even afterwards the Jebusites remained on this western hill, and some compromise seems to have been made with them. Is it conceivable, I wonder, that even in the twelfth century there lingered some local memory of what had once been a way of distinguishing Sion of the Jebusites from Salem of the Jews? The Zion Gate, however, is only a starting-point here; if we go south-eastward from it we descend a steep and rocky path, from which can be caught the first and finest vision of what stands on the other hill to the east. The great Mosque of Omar stands up like a peacock, lustrous with mosaics that are like plumes of blue and green.

Scholars, I may say here, object to calling it the Mosque of Omar; on the petty and pedantic ground that it is not a mosque and was not built by Omar. But it is my fixed intention to call it the Mosque of Omar, and with ever renewed pertinacity to continue calling it the Mosque of Omar. I possess a special permit from the Grand Mufti to call it the Mosque of Omar. He is the head of the whole Moslem religion, and if he does not know, who does? He told me, in the beautiful French which matches his beautiful manners, that it really is not so ridiculous after all to call the place the Mosque of Omar, since the great Caliph desired and even designed such a building, though he did not build it. I suppose it is rather as if Solomon's Temple had been called David's Temple. Omar was a great man and the Mosque was a great work, and the two were telescoped together by the excellent common sense of vulgar tradition. There could not be a better example of that great truth for all travellers; that popular tradition is never so right as when it is wrong; and that pedantry is never so wrong as when it is right. And as for the other objection, that the Dome of the Rock (to give it its other name) is not actually used as a Mosque, I answer that Westminster Abbey is not used as an Abbey. But modern Englishmen would be much surprised if I were to refer to it as Westminster Church; to say nothing of the many modern Englishmen for whom it would be more suitable to call it Westminster Museum. And for whatever purposes the Moslems may actually use their great and glorious sanctuary, at least they have not allowed it to become the private house of a particular rich man. And that is what we have suffered to happen, if not to Westminster Abbey, at least to Welbeck Abbey.

The Mosque of Omar (I repeat firmly) stands on the great eastern plateau in place of the Temple; and the wall that runs round to it on the south side of the city contains only the Dung Gate, on which the fancy need not linger. All along outside this wall the ground falls away into the southern valley; and upon the dreary and stony steep opposite is the place called Acaldama. Wall and valley turn together round the corner of the great temple platform, and confronting the eastern wall, across the ravine, is the mighty wall of the Mount of Olives. On this side there are several gates now blocked up, of which the most famous, the Golden Gate, carries in its very uselessness a testimony to the fallen warriors of the cross. For there is a strange Moslem legend that through this gate, so solemnly sealed up, shall ride the Christian King who shall again rule in

Jerusalem. In the middle of the square enclosure rises the great dark Dome of the Rock; and standing near it, a man may see for the first time in the distance, another dome. It lies away to the west, but a little to the north; and it is surmounted, not by a crescent but a cross. Many heroes and holy kings have desired to see this thing, and have not seen it.

It is very characteristic of the city, with its medieval medley and huddle of houses, that a man may first see the Church of the Holy Sepulchre which is in the west, by going as far as possible to the east. All the sights are glimpses; and things far can be visible and things near invisible. The traveller comes on the Moslem dome round a corner; and he finds the Christian dome, as it were, behind his own back. But if he goes on round the wall to the north-east corner of the Court of the Temple, he will find the next entrance; the Gate of St. Stephen. On the slope outside, by a strange and suitable coincidence, the loose stones which lie on every side of the mountain city seemed to be heaped higher; and across the valley on the skirts of the Mount of Olives is the great grey olive of Gethsemane.

On the northern side the valley turns to an artificial trench, for the ground here is higher; and the next or northern gate bears the name of Herod; though it might well bear the name either of Godfrey or Saladin. For just outside it stands a pine-tree, and beside it a rude bulk of stone; where stood these great captains in turn, before they took Jerusalem. Then the wall runs on till it comes to the great Damascus Gate, graven I know not why with great roses in a style wholly heraldic and occidental, and in no way likely to remind us of the rich roses of Damascus; though their name has passed into our own English tongue and tradition, along with another word for the delicate decoration of the sword. But at the first glance, at any rate, it is hard to believe that the roses on the walls are not the Western roses of York or Lancaster, or that the swords which guarded them were not the straight swords of England or of France. Doubtless a deeper and more solemn memory ought to return immediately to the mind where that gate looks down the great highway; as if one could see, hung over it in the sky for ever, the cloud concealing the sunburst that broods upon the road to Damascus. But I am here only confessing the facts or fancies of my first impression; and again the fancy that came to me first was not of any such alien or awful things. I did not think of damask or damascene or the great Arabian city or even the conversion of St. Paul. I thought of my own little house in Buckinghamshire, and how the edge of the country town where it stands is called Aylesbury End, merely because it is the corner nearest to Aylesbury. That is what I mean by saying that these ancient customs are more rational and even utilitarian than the fashions of modernity. When a street in a new suburb is called Pretoria Avenue, the clerk living there does not set out from his villa with the cheerful hope of finding the road lead him to Pretoria. But the man leaving Aylesbury End does know it would lead him to Aylesbury; and the man going out at the Damascus Gate did know it would lead him to Damascus. And the same is true of the next and last of the old entrances, the Jaffa Gate in the east; but when I saw that I saw something else as well.

I have heard that there is a low doorway at the entrance to a famous shrine which is called the Gate of Humility; but indeed in this sense all gates are gates of humility, and especially gates of this kind. Any one who has ever looked at a landscape under an archway will know what I mean, when I say that it sharpens a pleasure with a strange sentiment of privilege. It adds to the grace of distance something that makes it not only a grace but a gift. Such are the visions of remote places that appear in the low gateways of a Gothic town; as if each gateway led into a separate world; and almost as if each dome of sky were a different chamber. But he who walks round the walls of this city in this spirit will come suddenly upon an exception which will surprise him like an earthquake. It looks indeed rather like something done by an earthquake; an earthquake with a half-witted sense of humour. Immediately at the side of one of these humble and human gateways there is a great gap in the wall, with a wide road running through it. There is something of unreason in the sight which affects the eye as well as the reason. It recalls some crazy tale about the great works of the Wise Men of Gotham. It suggests the old joke about the man who made a small hole for the kitten as well as a large hole for the cat. Everybody has read about it by this time; but the immediate impression of it is not merely an effect of reading or even of reasoning. It looks lop-sided; like something done by a one-eyed giant. But it was done by the last prince of the great Prussian imperial system, in what was probably the proudest moment in all his life of pride.

What is true has a way of sounding trite; and what is trite has a way of sounding false. We shall now probably weary the world with calling the Germans barbaric, just as we very recently wearied the world with calling them cultured and progressive and scientific. But the thing is true though we say it a thousand times. And any one who wishes to understand the sense in which it is true has only to contemplate that fantasy and fallacy in stone; a gate with an open road beside it. The quality I mean, however, is not merely in that particular contrast; as of a front door standing by itself in an open field. It is also in the origin, the occasion and the whole story of the thing. There is above all this supreme stamp of the barbarian; the sacrifice of the permanent to the temporary. When the walls of the Holy City were overthrown for the glory of the German Emperor, it was hardly even for that everlasting glory which has been the vision and the temptation of great men. It was for the glory of a single day. It was something rather in the nature of a holiday than anything that could be even in the most vainglorious sense a heritage. It did not in the ordinary sense make a monument, or even a trophy. It destroyed a monument to make a procession. We might almost say that it destroyed a trophy to make a triumph. There is the true barbaric touch in this oblivion of what Jerusalem would look like a century after, or a year after, or even the day after. It is this which distinguishes the savage tribe on the march after a victory from the civilised army establishing a government, even if it be a tyranny. Hence the very effect of it, like the effect of the whole Prussian adventure in history, remains something negative and even nihilistic. The Christians made the Church of the Holy Sepulchre and the Moslems made the Mosque of Omar; but this is what the most scientific culture made at the end of the great century of science. It made an enormous hole. The only positive contribution of the nineteenth century to the spot is an unnaturally ugly clock, at the top of an ornamental tower, or a tower that was meant to be ornamental. It was erected, I believe, to commemorate the reign of Abdul Hamid; and it seems perfectly adapted to its purpose, like one of Sir William Watson's sonnets on the same subject. But this object only adds a touch of triviality to the much more tremendous negative effect of the gap by the gate. That remains a parable as well as a puzzle, under all the changing skies of day and night; with the shadows that gather tinder the narrow Gate of Humility; and beside it, blank as daybreak and abrupt as an abyss, the broad road that has led already to destruction.

The gap remains like a gash, a sort of wound in the walls; but it only strengthens by contrast the general sense of their continuity. Save this one angle where the nineteenth century has entered, the vague impression of the thirteenth or fourteenth century rather deepens than dies away. It is supported more than many would suppose even by the figures that appear in the gateways or pass in procession under the walls. The brown Franciscans and the white Dominicans would alone give some colour to a memory of the Latin kingdom of Jerusalem; and there are other examples and effects which are less easily imagined in the West. Thus as I look down the street, I see coming out from under an archway a woman wearing a high white head-dress very like those we have all seen in a hundred pictures of tournaments or hunting parties, or the Canterbury Pilgrimage or the Court of Louis XI. She is as white as a woman of the North; and it is not, I think, entirely fanciful to trace a certain freedom and dignity in her movement, which is quite different at least from the shuffling walk of the shrouded Moslem women. She is a woman of Bethlehem, where a tradition, it is said, still claims as a heroic heritage the blood of the Latin knights of the cross. This is, of course, but one aspect of the city; but it is one which may be early noted, yet one which is generally neglected. As I have said, I had expected many things of Jerusalem, but I had not expected this. I had expected to be disappointed with it as a place utterly profaned and fallen below its mission. I had expected to be awed by it; indeed I had expected to be frightened of it, as a place dedicated and even doomed by its mission. But I had never fancied that it would be possible to be fond of it; as one might be fond of a little walled town among the orchards of Normandy or the hop-fields of Kent.

And just then there happened a coincidence that was also something like a catastrophe. I was idly watching, as it moved down the narrow street to one of the dark doorways, the head-dress, like a tower of white drapery, belonging to the Christian woman from the place where Christ was born. After she had disappeared into the darkness of the porch I continued to look vaguely at the porch, and thought how easily it might have been a small Gothic gate in some old corner of Rouen, or even Canterbury. In twenty such places in the town one may see the details that appeal to the same associations, so different and so distant. One may see that angular dogtooth ornament that makes the round Norman gateways look like the gaping mouths of sharks. One may see the pointed niches in the walls, shaped like windows and serving somewhat the purpose of brackets, on which were to stand sacred images possibly removed by the Moslems. One may come upon a small court planted with ornamental trees with some monument in the centre, which makes the precise impression of something in a small French town. There are no Gothic spires, but there are numberless Gothic doors and windows; and he who first strikes the place at this angle, as it were, may well feel the Northern element as native and the Eastern element as intrusive. While I was thinking all these things, something happened which in that place was almost a portent.

It was very cold; and there were curious colours in the sky. There had been chilly rains from time to time; and the whole air seemed to have taken on something sharper than a chill. It was as if a door had been opened in the northern corner of the heavens; letting in something that changed all the face of the earth. Great grey clouds with haloes of lurid pearl and pale-green were coming up from the plains or the sea and spreading over the towers of the city. In the middle of the moving mass of grey vapours was a splash of paler vapour; a wan white cloud whose white seemed somehow more ominous than gloom. It went over the high citadel like a white wild goose flying; and a few white feathers fell.

It was the snow; and it snowed day and night until that Eastern city was sealed up like a village in Norway or Northern Scotland. It rose in the streets till men might almost have been drowned in it like a sea of solid foam. And the people of the place told me there had been no such thing seen in it in all recent records, or perhaps in the records of all its four thousand years.

All this came later; but for me at the moment, looking at the scene in so dreamy a fashion, it seemed merely like a dramatic conclusion to my dream. It was but an accident confirming what was but an aspect. But it confirmed it with a strange and almost supernatural completeness. The white light out of the window in the north lay on all the roofs and turrets of the mountain town; for there is an aspect in which snow looks less like frozen water than like solidified light. As the snow accumulated there accumulated also everywhere those fantastic effects of frost which seem to fit in with the fantastic qualities of medieval architecture; and which make an icicle seem like the mere extension of a gargoyle. It was the atmosphere that has led so many romancers to make medieval Paris a mere black and white study of night and snow. Something had redrawn in silver all things from the rude ornament on the old gateways to the wrinkles on the ancient hills of Moab. Fields of white still spotted with green swept down into the valleys between us and the hills; and high above them the Holy City lifted her head into the thunder-clouded heavens, wearing a white head-dress like a daughter of the Crusaders.

CHAPTER IV

THE PHILOSOPHY OF SIGHT-SEEING

Various cultivated critics told me that I should find Jerusalem disappointing; and I fear it will disappoint them that I am not disappointed. Of the city as a city I shall try to say something elsewhere; but the things which these critics have especially in mind are at once more general and more internal. They concern something tawdry, squalid or superstitious about the shrines and those who use them. Now the mistake of critics is not that they criticise the world; it is that they never criticise themselves. They compare the alien with the ideal; but they do not at the same time compare themselves with the ideal; rather they identify themselves with the ideal. I have met a tourist who had seen the great Pyramid, and who told me that the Pyramid looked small. Believe me, the tourist looked much smaller. There is indeed another type of traveller, who is not at all small in the moral mental sense, who will confess such disappointments quite honestly, as a piece of realism about his own sensations. In that case he generally suffers from the defect of most realists; that of not being realistic enough. He does not really think out his own impressions thoroughly; or he would generally find they are not so disappointing after all. A humorous soldier told me that he came from Derbyshire, and that he did not think much of the Pyramid because it was not so tall as the Peak. I pointed out to him that he was really offering the tallest possible tribute to a work of man in comparing it to a mountain; even if he thought it was a rather small mountain. I

G. K. CHESTERTON

suggested that it was a rather large tombstone. I appealed to those with whom I debated in that district, as to whether they would not be faintly surprised to find such a monument during their quiet rambles in a country churchyard. I asked whether each one of them, if he had such a tombstone in the family, would not feel it natural, if hardly necessary, to point it out; and that with a certain pride. The same principle of the higher realism applies to those who are disappointed with the sight of the Sphinx. The Sphinx really exceeds expectations because it escapes expectations. Monuments commonly look impressive when they are high and often when they are distant. The Sphinx is really unexpected, because it is found suddenly in a hollow, and unnaturally near. Its face is turned away; and the effect is as creepy as coming into a room apparently empty, and finding somebody as still as the furniture. Or it is as if one found a lion couchant in that hole in the sand; as indeed the buried part of the monster is in the form of a couchant lion. If it was a real lion it would hardly be less arresting merely because it was near; nor could the first emotion of the traveller be adequately described as disappointment. In such cases there is generally some profit in looking at the monument a second time, or even at our own sensations a second time. So I reasoned, striving with wild critics in the wilderness; but the only part of the debate which is relevant here can be expressed in the statement that I do think the Pyramid big, for the deep and simple reason that it is bigger than I am. I delicately suggested to those who were disappointed in the Sphinx that it was just possible that the Sphinx was disappointed in them. The Sphinx has seen Julius Caesar; it has very probably seen St. Francis, when he brought his flaming charity to Egypt; it has certainly looked, in the first high days of the revolutionary victories, on the face of the young Napoleon. Is it not barely possible, I hinted to my friends and fellow-tourists, that after these experiences, it might be a little depressed at the sight of you and me? But as I say, I only reintroduce my remarks in connection with a greater matter than these dead things of the desert; in connection with a tomb to which even the Pyramids are but titanic lumber, and a presence greater than the Sphinx, since it is not only a riddle but an answer.

Before I go on to deeper defences of any such cult or culture, I wish first to note a sort of test for the first impressions of an ordinary tourist like myself, to whom much that is really full of an archaic strength may seem merely stiff, or much that really deals with a deep devotional psychology may seem merely distorted. In short I would put myself in the position of the educated Englishman who does quite honestly receive a mere impression of idolatry. Incidentally, I may remark, it is the educated Englishman who is the idolater. It is he who only reverences the place, and does not reverence the reverence for the place. It is he who is supremely concerned about whether a mere object is old or new, or whether a mere ornament is gold or gilt. In other words, it is he who values the visible things rather than the invisible; for no sane man can doubt that invisible things are vivid to the priests and pilgrims of these shrines.

In the midst of emotions that have moved the whole world out of its course, girt about with crowds who will die or do murder for a definition, the educated English gentleman in his blindness bows down to wood and stone. For the only thing wrong about that admirable man is that he is blind about himself.

No man will really attempt to describe his feelings, when he first stood at the gateway of the grave of Christ. The only record relevant here is that I did not feel the reaction, not to say repulsion, that many seem to have felt about its formal surroundings.

Either I was particularly fortunate or others are particularly fastidious. The guide who showed me the Sepulchre was not particularly noisy or profane or palpably mercenary; he was rather more than less sympathetic than the same sort of man who might have shown me Westminster Abbey or Stratford-on-Avon. He was a small, solemn, owlish old man, a Roman Catholic in religion; but so far from deserving the charge of not knowing the Bible, he deserved rather a gentle remonstrance against his assumption that nobody else knew it. If there was anything to smile at, in associations so sacred, it was the elaborate simplicity with which he told the first facts of the Gospel story, as if he were evangelising a savage. Anyhow, he did not talk like a cheap-jack at a stall; but rather like a teacher in an infant school. He made it very clear that Jesus Christ was crucified in case any one should suppose he was beheaded; and often stopped in his narrative to repeat that the hero of these events was Jesus Christ, lest we should fancy it was Nebuchadnezzar or the Duke of Wellington. I do not in the least mind being amused at this; but I have no reason whatever for doubting that he may have been a better man than I. I gave him what I should have given a similar guide in my own country; I parted from him as politely as from one of my own countrymen. I also, of course, gave money, as is the custom, to the various monastic custodians of the shrines; but I see nothing surprising about that. I am not quite so ignorant as not to know that without the monastic brotherhoods, supported by such charity, there would not by this time be anything to see in Jerusalem at all. There was only one class of men whose consistent concern was to watch these things, from the age of heathens and heresies to the age of Turks and tourists; and I am certainly not going to sneer at them for doing no practical work, and then refuse to pay them for the practical work they do. For the rest, even the architectural defacement is overstated, the church was burned down and rebuilt in a bad and modern period; but the older parts, especially the Crusaders' porch, are as grand as the men who made them. The incongruities there are, are those of local colour. In connection, by the way, with what I said about beasts of burden, I mounted a series of steep staircases to the roof of the convent beside the Holy Sepulchre. When I got to the top I found myself in the placid presence of two camels. It would be curious to meet two cows on the roof of a village church. Nevertheless it is the only moral of the chapter interpolated here, that we can meet things quite as curious in our own country.

When the critic says that Jerusalem is disappointing he generally means that the popular worship there is weak and degraded, and especially that the religious art is gaudy and grotesque. In so far as there is any kind of truth in this, it is still true that the critic seldom sees the whole truth. What is wrong with the critic is that he does not criticise himself. He does not honestly compare what is weak, in this particular world of ideas, with what is weak in his own world of ideas. I will take an example from my own experience, and in a manner at my own expense. If I have a native heath it is certainly Kensington High Street, off which stands the house of my childhood. I grew up in that thorough-fare which Mr. Max Beerbohm, with his usual easy exactitude of phrase, has described as "dapper, with a leaning to the fine arts." Dapper was never perhaps a descriptive term for myself; but it is quite true that I owe a certain taste for the arts to the sort of people among whom I was brought up. It is also true that such a taste, in various forms and degrees, was fairly common in the world which may be symbolised as Kensington High Street. And whether or no it is a tribute, it is certainly a truth that most people with an artistic turn in Kensington High Street would have been very much shocked, in their sense of propriety, if they had seen the popular shrines of Jerusalem; the sham gold, the garish colours, the fantastic tales and the feverish tumult. But what I want such people to do, and what they never do, is to turn this truth round. I want them to imagine, not a Kensington aesthete walking down David Street to the Holy Sepulchre, but a Greek monk or a Russian pilgrim walking down Kensington High Street to Kensington Gardens. I will not insist here on all the hundred plagues of plutocracy that would really surprise such a Christian peasant; especially that curse of an irreligious society (unknown in religious societies, Moslem as well as Christian) the detestable denial of all dignity to the poor. I am not speaking now of moral but of artistic things; of the concrete arts and crafts used in popular worship. Well, my imaginary pilgrim would walk past Kensington Gardens till his sight was blasted by a prodigy. He would either fall on his knees as before a shrine, or cover his face as from a sacrilege. He would have seen the Albert Memorial. There is nothing so conspicuous in Jerusalem. There is nothing so gilded and gaudy in Jerusalem. Above all, there is nothing in Jerusalem that is on so large a scale and at the same time in so gay and glittering a style. My simple Eastern Christian would almost certainly be driven to cry aloud, "To what superhuman God was this enormous temple erected? I hope it is Christ; but I fear it is Antichrist." Such, he would think, might well be the great and golden image of the Prince of the World, set up in this great open space to receive the heathen prayers and heathen sacrifices of a lost humanity. I fancy he would feel a desire to be at home again amid the humble shrines of Zion. I really cannot imagine *what* he would feel, if he were told that the gilded idol was neither a god nor a demon, but a petty German prince who had some slight influence in turning us into the tools of Prussia.

Now I myself, I cheerfully admit, feel that enormity in Kensington Gardens as something quite natural. I feel it so because I have been brought up, so to speak, under its shadow; and stared at the graven images of Raphael and Shakespeare almost before I knew their names; and long before I saw anything funny in their figures being carved, on a smaller scale, under the feet of Prince Albert. I even took a certain childish pleasure in the gilding of the canopy and spire, as if in the golden palace of what was, to Peter Pan and all children, something of a fairy garden. So do the Christians of Jerusalem take pleasure, and possibly a childish pleasure, in the gilding of a better palace, besides a nobler garden, ornamented with a somewhat worthier aim. But the point is that the people of Kensington, whatever they might think about the Holy Sepulchre, do not think anything at all about the Albert Memorial. They are quite unconscious of how strange a thing it is; and that simply because they are used to it. The religious groups in Jerusalem are also accustomed to their coloured background; and they are surely none the worse if they still feel rather more of the meaning of the colours. It may be said that they retain their childish illusion about *their* Albert Memorial. I confess I cannot manage to regard Palestine as a place where a special curse was laid on those who can become like little children. And I never could understand why such critics who agree that the kingdom of heaven is for children, should forbid it to be the only sort of kingdom that children would really like; a kingdom with real crowns of gold or even of tinsel. But that is another question, which I shall discuss in another place; the point is for the moment that such people would be quite as much surprised at the place of tinsel in our lives as we are at its place in theirs. If we are critical of the petty things they do to glorify great things, they would find quite as much to criticise (as in Kensington Gardens) in the great things we do to glorify petty things. And if we wonder at the way in which they seem to gild the lily, they would wonder quite as much at the way we gild the weed.

There are countless other examples of course of this principle of self-criticism, as the necessary condition of all criticism. It applies quite as much, for instance, to the other great complaint which my Kensington friend would make after the complaint about paltry ornament; the complaint about what is commonly called backsheesh. Here again there is really something to complain of; though much of the fault is not due to Jerusalem, but rather to London and New York. The worst superstition of Jerusalem, like the worst profligacy of Paris, is a thing so much invented for

Anglo-Saxons that it might be called an Anglo-Saxon institution. But here again the critic could only really judge fairly if he realised with what abuses at home he ought really to compare this particular abuse abroad. He ought to imagine, for example, the feelings of a religious Russian peasant if he really understood all the highly-coloured advertisements covering High Street Kensington Station. It is really not so repulsive to see the poor asking for money as to see the rich asking for more money. And advertisement is the rich asking for more money. A man would be annoyed if he found himself in a mob of millionaires, all holding out their silk hats for a penny; or all shouting with one voice, "Give me money." Yet advertisement does really assault the eye very much as such a shout would assault the ear. "Budge's Boots are the Best" simply means "Give me money"; "Use Seraphic Soap" simply means "Give me money." It is a complete mistake to suppose that common people make our towns commonplace, with unsightly things like advertisements. Most of those whose wares are thus placarded everywhere are very wealthy gentlemen with coronets and country seats, men who are probably very particular about the artistic adornment of their own homes. They disfigure their towns in order to decorate their houses. To see such men crowding and clamouring for more wealth would really be a more unworthy sight than a scramble of poor guides; yet this is what would be conveyed by all the glare of gaudy advertisement to anybody who saw and understood it for the first time. Yet for us who are familiar with it all that gaudy advertisement fades into a background, just as the gaudy oriental patterns fade into a background for those oriental priests and pilgrims. Just as the innocent Kensington gentleman is wholly unaware that his black top hat is relieved against a background, or encircled as by a halo, of a yellow hoarding about mustard, so is the poor guide sometimes unaware that his small doings are dark against the fainter and more fading gold in which are traced only the humbler haloes of the Twelve Apostles.

But all these misunderstandings are merely convenient illustrations and introductions, leading up to the great fact of the main misunderstanding. It is a misunderstanding of the whole history and philosophy of the position; that is the whole of the story and the whole moral of the story. The critic of the Christianity of Jerusalem emphatically manages to miss the point. The lesson he ought to learn from it is one which the Western and modern man needs most, and does not even know that he needs. It is the lesson of constancy. These people may decorate their temples with gold or with tinsel; but their tinsel has lasted longer than our gold. They may build things as costly and ugly as the Albert Memorial; but the thing remains a memorial, a thing of immortal memory. They do not build it for a passing fashion and then forget it, or try hard to forget it. They may paint a picture of a saint as gaudy as any advertisement of a soap; but one saint does not drive out another saint as one soap drives out another soap. They do not forget their recent idolatries, as the educated English are now trying to forget their very recent idolatry of everything German. These Christian bodies have been in Jerusalem for at least fifteen hundred years. Save for a few years after the time of Constantine and a few years after the First Crusade, they have been practically persecuted all the time. At least they have been under heathen masters whose attitude towards Christendom was hatred and whose type of government was despotism. No man living in the West can form the faintest conception of what it must have been to live in the very heart of the East through the long and seemingly everlasting epoch of Moslem power. A man in Jerusalem was in the centre of the Turkish Empire as a man in Rome was in the centre of the Roman Empire. The imperial power of Islam stretched away to the sunrise and the sunset; westward to the mountains of Spain and eastward towards the wall of China. It must have seemed as if the whole earth belonged to Mahomet to those who in this rocky city renewed their hopeless witness to Christ. What we have to ask ourselves is not whether we happen in all respects to agree with them, but whether we in the same condition should even have the courage to agree with ourselves. It is not a question of how much of their religion is superstition, but of how much of our religion is convention; how much is custom and how much a compromise even with custom; how much a thing made facile by the security of our own society or the success of our own state. These are powerful supports; and the enlightened Englishman, from a cathedral town or a suburban chapel, walks these wild Eastern places with a certain sense of assurance and stability. Even after centuries of Turkish supremacy, such a man feels, he would not have descended to such a credulity. He would not be fighting for the Holy Fire or wrangling with beggars in the Holy Sepulchre. He would not be hanging fantastic lamps on a pillar peculiar to the Armenians, or peering into the gilded cage that contains the brown Madonna of the Copts. He would not be the dupe of such degenerate fables; God forbid. He would not be grovelling at such grotesque shrines; no indeed. He would be many hundred yards away, decorously bowing towards a more distant city; where, above the only formal and official open place in Jerusalem, the mighty mosaics of the Mosque of Omar proclaim across the valleys the victory and the glory of Mahomet.

That is the real lesson that the enlightened traveller should learn; the lesson about himself. That is the test that should really be put to those who say that the Christianity of Jerusalem is degraded. After a thousand years of Turkish tyranny, the religion of a London fashionable preacher would not be degraded. It would be destroyed. It would not be there at all, to be jeered at by every prosperous tourist out of a *train de luxe*. It is worth while to pause upon the point; for nothing has been so wholly missed in our modern religious ideals as the ideal of tenacity. Fashion is called progress. Every new fashion is called a new faith. Every faith is a faith which offers everything except faith-fulness. It was never so necessary to insist that most of the really vital and valuable ideas in the world, including

Christianity, would never have survived at all if they had not survived their own death, even in the sense of dying daily. The ideal was out of date almost from the first day; that is why it is eternal; for whatever is dated is doomed. As for our own society, if it proceeds at its present rate of progress and improvement, no trace or memory of it will be left at all. Some think that this would be an improvement in itself. We have come to live morally, as the Japs live literally, in houses of paper. But they are pavilions made of the morning papers, which have to be burned on the appearance of the evening editions. Well, a thousand years hence the Japs may be ruling in Jerusalem; the modern Japs who no longer live in paper houses, but in sweated factories and slums. They and the Chinese (that much more dignified and democratic people) seem to be about the only people of importance who have not yet ruled Jerusalem. But though we may think the Christian chapels as thin as Japanese tea-houses, they will still be Christian; though we may think the sacred lamps as cheap as Chinese lanterns, they will still be burning before a crucified creator of the world.

But besides this need of making strange cults the test not of themselves but ourselves, the sights of Jerusalem also illustrate the other suggestion about the philosophy of sight-seeing. It is true, as I have suggested, that after all the Sphinx is larger than I am; and on the same principle the painted saints are saintlier than I am, and the patient pilgrims more constant than I am. But it is also true, as in the lesser matter before mentioned, that even those who think the Sphinx small generally do not notice the small things about it. They do not even discover what is interesting about their own disappointment. And similarly even those who are truly irritated by the unfamiliar fashions of worship in a place like Jerusalem, do not know how to discover what is interesting in the very existence of what is irritating. For instance, they talk of Byzantine decay or barbaric delusion, and they generally go away with an impression that the ritual and symbolism is something dating from the Dark Ages. But if they would really note the details of their surroundings, or even of their sensations, they would observe a rather curious fact about such ornament of such places as the Church of the Holy Sepulchre as may really be counted unworthy of them. They would realise that what they would most instinctively reject as superstitious does not date from what they would regard as the ages of superstition. There really are bad pictures but they are not barbaric pictures; they are florid pictures in the last faded realism of the Renascence. There really is stiff and ungainly decoration, but it is not the harsh or ascetic decoration of a Spanish cloister; it is much more like the pompous yet frivolous decorations of a Parisian hotel. In short, in so far as the shrine has really been defaced it has not been defaced by the Dark Ages, but rather if anything by the Age of Reason. It is the enlightened eighteenth century, which regarded itself as the very noonday of natural culture and common sense, that has really though indirectly laid its disfiguring finger on the dark but dignified Byzantine temple. I do not particularly mind it myself; for in such great matters I do not think taste is the test. But if taste is to be made the test, there is matter for momentary reflection in this fact; for it is another example of the weakness of what may be called fashion. Voltaire, I believe, erected a sort of temple to God in his own garden; and we may be sure that it was in the most exquisite taste of the time. Nothing would have surprised him more than to learn that, fifty years after the success of the French Revolution, almost every freethinker of any artistic taste would think his temple far less artistically admirable than the nearest gargoyle on Notre Dame. Thus it is progress that must be blamed for most of these things: and we ought not to turn away in contempt from something antiquated, but rather recognise with respect and even alarm a sort of permanent man-trap in the idea of being modern. So that the moral of this matter is the same as that of the other; that these things should raise in us, not merely the question of whether we like them, but of whether there is anything very infallible or imperishable about what we like. At least the essentials of these things endure; and if they seem to have remained fixed as effigies, at least they have not faded like fashion-plates.

It has seemed worth while to insert here this note on the philosophy of sight-seeing, however dilatory or disproportionate it may seem. For I am particularly and positively convinced that unless these things can somehow or other be seen in the right historical perspective and philosophical proportion, they are not worth seeing at all. And let me say in conclusion that I can not only respect the sincerity, but understand the sentiments, of a man who says they are not worth seeing at all. Sight-seeing is a far more difficult and disputable matter than many seem to suppose; and a man refusing it altogether might be a man of sense and even a man of imagination. It was the great Wordsworth who refused to revisit Yarrow; it was only the small Wordsworth who revisited it after all. I remember the first great sight in my own entrance to the Near East, when I looked by accident out of the train going to Cairo, and saw far away across the luminous flats a faint triangular shape; the Pyramids. I could understand a man who had seen it turning his back and retracing his whole journey to his own country and his own home, saying, "I will go no further; for I have seen afar off the last houses of the kings." I can understand a man who had only seen in the distance Jerusalem sitting on the hill going no further and keeping that vision for ever. It would, of course, be said that it was absurd to come at all, and to see so little. To which I answer that in that sense it is absurd to come at all. It is no more fantastic to turn back for such a fancy than it was to come for a similar fancy. A man cannot eat the Pyramids; he cannot buy or sell the Holy City; there can be no practical aspect either of his coming or going. If he has not come for a poetic mood he has come for nothing; if he has come for such a mood, he is not a fool to obey that mood.

The way to be really a fool is to try to be practical about unpractical things. It is to try to collect clouds or preserve moonshine like money. Now there is much to be said for the view that to search for a mood is in its nature moonshine. It may be said that this is especially true in the crowded and commonplace conditions in which most sight-seeing has to be done. It may be said that thirty tourists going together to see a tombstone is really as ridiculous as thirty poets going together to write poems about the nightingale. There would be something rather depressing about a crowd of travellers, walking over hill and dale after the celebrated cloud of Wordsworth; especially if the crowd is like the cloud, and moveth all together if it move at all. A vast mob assembled on Salisbury Plain to listen to Shelley's skylark would probably (after an hour or two) consider it a rather subdued sort of skylarking. It may be argued that it is just as illogical to hope to fix beforehand the elusive effects of the works of man as of the works of nature. It may be called a contradiction in terms to expect the unexpected. It may be counted mere madness to anticipate astonishment, or go in search of a surprise. To all of which there is only one answer; that such anticipation is absurd, and such realisation will be disappointing, that images will seem to be idols and idols will seem to be dolls, unless there be some rudiment of such a habit of mind as I have tried to suggest in this chapter. No great works will seem great, and no wonders of the world will seem wonderful, unless the angle from which they are seen is that of historical humility.

One more word may be added of a more practical sort. The place where the most passionate convictions on this planet are concentrated is not one where it will always be wise, even from a political standpoint, to air our plutocratic patronage and our sceptical superiority. Strange scenes have already been enacted round that fane where the Holy Fire bursts forth to declare that Christ is risen; and whether or no we think the thing holy there is no doubt about it being fiery. Whether or no the superior person is right to expect the unexpected, it is possible that something may be revealed to him that he really does not expect. And whatever he may think about the philosophy of sight-seeing, it is not unlikely that he may see some sights.

G. K. CHESTERTON

CHAPTER V

THE STREETS OF THE CITY

When Jerusalem had been half buried in snow for two or three days, I remarked to a friend that I was prepared henceforward to justify all the Christmas cards. The cards that spangle Bethlehem with frost are generally regarded by the learned merely as vulgar lies. At best they are regarded as popular fictions, like that which made the shepherds in the Nativity Play talk a broad dialect of Somerset. In the deepest sense of course this democratic tradition is truer than most history. But even in the cruder and more concrete sense the tradition about the December snow is not quite so false as is suggested. It is not a mere local illusion for Englishmen to picture the Holy Child in a snowstorm, as it would be for the Londoners to picture him in a London fog. There can be snow in Jerusalem, and there might be snow in Bethlehem; and when we penetrate to the idea behind the image, we find it is not only possible but probable. In Palestine, at least in these mountainous parts of Palestine, men have the same general sentiment about the seasons as in the West or the North. Snow is a rarity, but winter is a reality. Whether we regard it as the divine purpose of a mystery or the human purpose of a myth, the purpose of putting such a feast in winter would be just the same in Bethlehem as it would be in Balham. Any one thinking of the Holy Child as born in December would mean by it exactly what we mean by it; that Christ is not merely a summer sun of the prosperous but a winter fire for the unfortunate.

In other words, the semi-tropical nature of the place, like its vulgarity and desecration, can be, and are, enormously exaggerated. But it is always hard to correct the exaggeration without exaggerating the correction. It would be absurd seriously to deny that Jerusalem is an Eastern town; but we may say it was Westernised without being modernised. Anyhow, it was medievalised before it was modernised. And in the same way it would be absurd to deny that Jerusalem is a Southern town, in the sense of being normally out of the way of snowstorms, but the truth can be suggested by saying that it has always known the quality of snow, but not the quantity. And the quantity of snow that fell on this occasion would have been something striking and even sensational in Sussex or Kent. And yet another way of putting the proportions of the thing would be to say that Jerusalem has been besieged more often and by more different kinds of people than any town upon the globe; that it has been besieged by Jews and Assyrians, Egyptians and Babylonians, Greeks and Romans, Persians and Saracens, Frenchmen and Englishmen; but perhaps never before in all its agony of ages has it ever really been besieged by winter. In this case it was not only snowed on, it was snowed up.

For some days the city was really in a state of siege. If the snow had held for a sufficient number of days it might have been in a state of famine. The railway failed between Jerusalem and the nearest station. The roads were impassable between Jerusalem and the nearest village, or even the nearest suburb. In some places the snow drifted deep enough to bury a man, and in some places, alas, it did actually bury little children; poor little Arabs whose bodies were stiff where they had fallen. Many mules were overwhelmed as if by floods, and countless trees struck down as if by lightning. Even when the snow began at last to melt it only threatened to turn the besieged fortress into a sort of island. A river that men could not ford flowed between Jerusalem and the Mount of Olives. Even a man walking about the ordinary streets could easily step up to his knees or up to his waist. Snow stood about like a new system of natural barricades reared in some new type of revolution. I have already remarked that what struck me most about the city was the city wall; but now a new white wall stood all round the city; and one that neither friend nor foe could pass.

But a state of siege, whatever its inconveniences, is exceedingly convenient for a critic and observer of the town. It concentrated all that impression of being something compact and what, with less tragic attendant circumstances, one might call cosy. It fixed the whole picture in a frame even more absolute than the city wall; and it turned the eyes of all spectators inwards. Above all, by its very abnormality it accentuated the normal divisions and differences of the place; and made it more possible to distinguish and describe them like *dramatis personae*. The parts they played in the crisis of the snow were very like the parts they played in the general crisis of the state. And the very cut and colour of the figures, turban and tarbouch, khaki and burnous and gabardine, seemed to stand out more sharply against that blank background of white.

The first fact of course was a fact of contrast. When I said that the city struck me in its historic aspect as being at least as much a memory of the Crusaders as of the Saracens, I did not of course mean to deny the incidental contrasts between this Southern civilisation and the civilisation of Europe, especially northern Europe. The immediate difference was obvious enough when the gold and the gaudy vegetation of so comparatively Asiatic a city were struck by this strange blast out of the North. It was a queer spectacle to see a great green palm bowed down under a white load of snow; and it was a stranger and sadder spectacle to see the people accustomed to live under such palm-trees bowed down under such unearthly storms. Yet the very manner in which they bore it is perhaps the first fact to be noted among all the facts that make up the puzzling problem of Jerusalem. Odd as it may sound you can see that the true Orientals are not familiar with snow by the very fact that they accept it. They accept it as we should accept being swallowed by an earthquake; because we do not know the answer to an earthquake. The men from the desert do not know the answer to the snow, it seems to them unanswerable. But Christians fight with snow in a double sense; they fight with snow as they fight with snowballs. A Moslem left to himself would no more play with a snowball than make a toy of a thunderbolt. And this is really a type of the true problem that was raised by the very presence of the English soldier in the street, even if he was only shovelling away the snow.

It would be far from a bad thing, I fancy, if the rights and wrongs of these Bible countries could occasionally be translated into Bible language. And I suggest this here, not in the least because it is a religious language, but merely because it is a simple language. It may be a good thing, and in many ways it certainly is a good thing, that the races native to the Near East, to Egypt or Arabia, should come in contact with Western culture; but it will be unfortunate if this only means coming in contact with Western pedantry and even Western hypocrisy. As it is there is only too much danger that the local complaints against the government may be exactly like the official explanations of the government; that is, mere strings of long words with very little meaning involved. In short, if people are to learn to talk English it will be a refreshing finishing touch to their culture if they learn to talk plain English. Of this it would be hard to find a better working model than what may be called scriptural English. It would be a very good thing for everybody concerned if any really unjust or unpopular official were described only in terms taken from the denunciations of Jezebel and Herod. It would especially be a good thing for the official. If it were true it would be appropriate, and if it were untrue it would be absurd.

When people are really oppressed, their condition can generally be described in very plain terms connected with very plain things; with bread, with land, with taxes and children and churches. If imperialists and capitalists do thus oppress them, as they most certainly often do, then the condition of those more powerful persons can also be described in few and simple words; such as crime and sin and death and hell. But when complaints are made, as they are sometimes in Palestine and still more in Egypt, in the elaborate and long-winded style of a leading article, the sympathetic European is apt to remember how very little confidence he has ever felt in his own leading articles. If an Arab comes to me and says, "The stranger from across the sea has taxed me, and taken the corn-sheaves from the field of my fathers," I do really feel that he towers over me and my perishing industrial civilisation with a terrible appeal to eternal things. I feel he is a figure more enduring than a statue, like the figure of Naboth or of Nathan. But when that simple son of the desert opens his mouth and says, "The self-determination of proletarian class-conscious solidarity as it functions for international reconstruction," and so on, why then I must confess to the weakness of feeling my sympathies instantly and strangely chilled. I merely feel inclined to tell him that I can talk that sort of pidgin English better than he can. If he modelled himself on the great rebels and revolutionists of the Bible, it would at least be a considerable improvement in his literary style. But as a matter of fact something much more solid is involved than literary style. There is a logic and justice in the distinction, even in the world of ideas. That most people with much more education than the Arab, and therefore much less excuse than the Arab, entirely ignore that distinction, is merely a result of their ignoring ideas, and being satisfied with long words. They like democracy because it is a long word; that is the only thing they do like about it.

People are entitled to self-government; that is, to such

government as is self-made. They are not necessarily entitled to a special and elaborate machinery that somebody else has made. It is their right to make it for themselves, but it is also their duty to think of it for themselves. Self-government of a simple kind has existed in numberless simple societies, and I shall always think it a horrible responsibility to interfere with it. But representative government, or theoretically representative government, of an exceedingly complicated kind, may exist in certain complicated societies without their being bound to transfer it to others, or even to admire it for themselves. At any rate, for good or evil, they have invented it themselves. And there is a moral distinction, which is perfectly rational and democratic, between such inventions and the self-evident rights which no man can claim to have invented. If the Arab says to me, "I don't care a curse for Europe; I demand bread," the reproach is to me both true and terrible. But if he says, "I don't care a curse for Europe; I demand French cookery, Italian confectionery, English audit ale," and so on, I think he is rather an unreasonable Arab. After all, we invented these things; in *auctore auctoritas*.

And of this problem there is a sort of working model in the presence of the snow in Palestine, especially in the light of the old proverb about the impossibility of snow in Egypt. Palestine is wilder, less wealthy and modernised, more religious and therefore more realistic. The issue between the things only a European can do, and the things no European has the right to do, is much sharper and clearer than the confusions of verbosity. On the one hand the things the English can do are more real things, like clearing away the snow; for the very reason that the English are not here, so to speak, building on a French pavement but on the bare rocks of the Eastern wilds, the contact with Islam and Israel is more simple and direct. And on the other side the discontents and revolts are more real. So far from intending to suggest that the Egyptians have no complaints, I am very far from meaning that they have no wrongs. But curiously enough the wrongs seem to me more real than the complaints. The real case against our Egyptian adventure was stated long ago by Randolph Churchill, when he denounced "a bondholder's war"; it is in the whole business of collecting debts due to cosmopolitan finance. But a stranger in Egypt hears little denunciation of cosmopolitan finance, and a great deal of drivel in the way of cosmopolitan idealism. When the Palestinians say that usurers menace their land they mean the land they dig; an old actuality and not a new abstraction. Their revolt may be right or wrong, but it is real; and what applies to their revolt applies to their religion. There may well be doubts about whether Egypt is a nation, but there is no doubt that Jerusalem is a city, and the nations have come to its light.

The problem of the snow proved indeed the text for a tale touching the practical politics of the city. The English soldiers cleared the snow away; the Arabs sat down satisfied or stoical with the snow blocking their own doors or loading their own roofs. But the Jews, as the story went, were at length persuaded to clear away the snow in front of them, and then demanded a handsome salary for having recovered the use of their own front doors. The story is not quite fair; and yet it is not so unfair as it seems. Any rational Anti-Semite will agree that such tales, even when they are true, do not always signify an avaricious tradition in Semitism, but sometimes the healthier and more human suggestion of Bolshevism. The Jews do demand high wages, but it is not always because they are in the old sense money-grabbers, but rather in the new sense money-grabbers (as an enemy would put it) men sincerely and bitterly convinced of their right to the surplus of capitalism. There is the same problem in the Jewish colonies in the country districts; in the Jewish explanation of the employment of Arab and Syrian labour. The Jews argue that this occurs, not because they wish to remain idle capitalists, but because they insist on being properly paid proletarians. With all this I shall deal, however, when I treat of the Jewish problem itself.

The point for the moment is that the episode of the snow did in a superficial way suggest the parts played by the three parties and the tales told about them. To begin with, it is right to say that the English do a great many things, as they clear away the snow, simply because nobody else would do them. They did save the oriental inhabitants from some of the worst consequences of the calamity. Probably they sometimes save the inhabitants from something which the inhabitants do not regard as a calamity. It is the danger of all such foreign efficiency that it often saves men who do not want to be saved. But they do in many cases do things from which Moslems profit, but which Moslems by themselves would not propose, let alone perform. And this has a general significance even in our first survey, for it suggests a truth easy to abuse, but I think impossible to ignore. I mean that there is something non-political about Moslem morality. Perverse as it may appear, I suspect that most of their political movements result from their non-political morality. They become politicians because they know they are not political; and feel their simple and more or less healthy life is at a disadvantage, in face of the political supremacy of the English and the political subtlety of the Jews.

For instance, the tradition of Turkish rule is simply a joke. All the stories about it are jokes, and often very good jokes. My own favourite incident is that which is still comme-morated in the English cathedral by an enormous hole in the floor. The Turks dug up the pavement looking for concealed English artillery; because they had been told that the bishop had given his blessing to two canons. The bishop had indeed recently appointed two canons to the service of the Church, but he had not secreted them under the floor of the chancel. There was another agreeable incident when the Turkish authorities, by an impulsive movement of religious toleration, sent for a Greek priest to bury Greek soldiers, and told him to take his choice in a heap of corpses of all creeds and colours. But at once the most curious and the most common touch of comedy is the perpetual social introduction to solid and smiling citizens who have been nearly hanged by the Turks. The fortunate gentleman seems still to be regarding his escape with a broad grin. If you were introduced to a polite Frenchman who had come straight from the guillotine, or to an affable American who had only just vacated the electrical chair, you would feel a faint curiosity about the whole story. If a friend introduced somebody, saying, "My friend Robinson; his sentence has been commuted to penal servitude," or "My Uncle William, just come from Dartmoor Prison," your mind and perhaps your lips would faintly form the syllables "What for?" But evidently, under Turkish rule, being hanged was like being knocked down by a cab; it might happen to anybody. This is a parenthesis, since I am only dealing here with the superficial experience of the streets, especially in the snow. But it will be well to safe-guard it by saying that this unpolitical carelessness and comprehensiveness of the indiscriminate Turk had its tragic as well as its comic side. It was by no means everybody that escaped hanging; and there was a tree growing outside the Jaffa Gate at which men might still shudder as they pass it in the sunlight. It was what a modern revolutionary poet has called bitterly the Tree of Man's Making; and what a medieval revolutionary poet called the fruit tree in the orchard of the king. It was the gibbet; and lives have dropped from it like leaves from a tree in autumn. Yet even on the sterner side, we can trace the truth about the Moslem fatalism which seems so alien to political actuality. There was a popular legend or proverb that this terrible tree was in some way bound up with the power of the Turk, and perhaps the Moslem over a great part of the earth. There is nothing more strange about that Moslem fatalism than a certain gloomy magnanimity which can invoke omens and oracles against itself. It is astonishing how often the Turks seem to have accepted a legend or prophecy about their own ultimate failure. De Quincey mentions one of them in the blow that half broke the Palladium of

Byzantium. It is said that the Moslems themselves predict the entry of a Christian king of Jerusalem through the Golden Gate. Perhaps that is why they have blocked up the fatal gate; but in any case they dealt in that fashion with the fatal tree. They elaborately bound and riveted it with iron, as if accepting the popular prophecy which declared that so long as it stood the Turkish Empire would stand. It was as if the wicked man of Scripture had daily watered a green bay-tree, to make sure that it should flourish.

In the last chapter I have attempted to suggest a background of the battlemented walls with the low gates and narrow windows which seem to relieve the liveliest of the coloured groups against the neutral tints of the North, and how this was intensified when the neutral tints were touched with the positive hue of snow. In the same merely impressionist spirit I would here attempt to sketch some of the externals of the actors in such a scene, though it is hard to do justice to such a picture even in the superficial matter of the picturesque. Indeed it is hard to be sufficiently superficial; for in the East nearly every external is a symbol. The greater part of it is the gorgeous rag-heap of Arabian humanity, and even about that one could lecture on almost every coloured rag. We hear much of the gaudy colours of the East; but the most striking thing about them is that they are delicate colours. It is rare to see a red that is merely like a pillar-box, or a blue that is Reckitt's blue; the red is sure to have the enrichment of tawny wine or blood oranges, and the blue of peacocks or the sea. In short these people are artistic in the sense that used to be called aesthetic; and it is a nameless instinct that preserves these nameless tints. Like all such instincts, it can be blunted by a bullying rationalism; like all such children, these people do not know why they prefer the better, and can therefore be persuaded by sophists that they prefer the worst. But there are other elements emerging from the coloured crowd, which are more significant, and therefore more stubborn. A stranger entirely ignorant of that world would feel something like a chill to the blood when he first saw the black figures of the veiled Moslem women, sinister figures without faces. It is as if in that world every woman were a widow. When he realised that these were not the masked mutes at a very grisly funeral, but merely ladies literally obeying a convention of wearing veils in public, he would probably have a reaction of laughter. He would be disposed to say flippantly that it must be, a dull life, not only for the women but the men; and that a man might well want five wives if he had to marry them before he could even look at them. But he will be wise not to be satisfied with such flippancy, for the complete veiling of the Moslem women of Jerusalem, though not a finer thing than the freedom of the Christian woman of Bethlehem, is almost certainly a finer thing than the more coquettish compromise of the other Moslem women of Cairo. It simply means that the Moslem religion is here more sincerely observed; and this in turn is part of something that a sympathetic person will soon feel in Jerusalem, if he has come from these more commercial cities of the East; a spiritual tone decidedly more delicate and dignified, like the clear air about the mountain city. Whatever the human vices involved, it is not altogether for nothing that this is the holy town of three great religions. When all is said, he will feel that there are some tricks that could not be played, some trades that could not be plied, some shops that could not be opened, within a stone's throw of the Sepulchre. This indefinable seriousness has its own fantasies of fanaticism or formalism; but if these are vices they are not vulgarities. There is no stronger example of this than the real Jews of Jerusalem, especially those from the ghettoes of eastern Europe. They can be immediately picked out by the peculiar wisps of hair worn on each side of the face, like something between curls and whiskers. Sometimes they look strangely effeminate, like some rococo burlesque of the ringlets of an Early Victorian woman. Sometimes they look considerably more like the horns of a devil; and one need not be an Anti-Semite to say that the face is often made to match. But though they may be ugly, or even horrible, they are not vulgar like the Jews at Brighton; they trail behind them too many primeval traditions and laborious loyalties, along with their grand though often greasy robes of bronze or purple velvet. They often wear on their heads that odd turban of fur worn by the Rabbis in the pictures of Rembrandt. And indeed that great name is not irrelevant; for the whole truth at the back of Zionism is in the difference between the picture of a Jew by Rembrandt and a picture of a Jew by Sargent. For Rembrandt the Rabbi was, in a special and double sense, a distinguished figure. He was something distinct from the world of the artist, who drew a Rabbi as he would a Brahmin. But Sargent had to treat his sitters as solid citizens of England or America; and consequently his pictures are direct provocations to a pogrom. But the light that Rembrandt loved falls not irreverently on the strange hairy haloes that can still be seen on the shaven heads of the Jews of Jerusalem. And I should be sorry for any pogrom that brought down any of their grey wisps or whiskers in sorrow to the grave.

The whole scene indeed, seriousness apart, might be regarded as a fantasia for barbers; for the different ways of dressing the hair would alone serve as symbols of different races and religions. Thus the Greek priests of the Orthodox Church, bearded and robed in black with black towers upon their heads, have for some strange reason their hair bound up behind like a woman's. In any case they have in their pomp a touch of the bearded bulls of Assyrian sculpture; and this strange fashion of curling if not oiling the Assyrian bull gives the newcomer an indescribable and illogical impression of the unnatural sublimity of archaic art. In the Apocalypse somewhere there is an inspiringly unintelligible allusion to men coming on the earth, whose hair is like the hair of women and their teeth like the teeth of lions. I have never been bitten by an Orthodox clergyman, and cannot say whether his teeth are at all leonine; though I have seen seven of them together enjoying their lunch at an hotel with decorum and dispatch. But the twisting of the hair in the womanish fashion does for us touch that note of the abnormal which the mystic meant to convey in his poetry, and which others feel rather as a recoil into humour. The best and last touch to this topsy-turvydom was given when a lady, observing one of these reverend gentlemen who for some reason did not carry this curious coiffure, exclaimed, in a tone of heartrending surprise and distress, "Oh, he's bobbed his hair!"

Here again of course even a superficial glance at the pageant of the street should not be content with its comedy. There is an intellectual interest in the external pomp and air of placid power in these ordinary Orthodox parish priests; especially if we compare them with the comparatively prosaic and jog-trot good nature of the Roman monks, called in this country the Latins. Mingling in the same crowd with these black-robed pontiffs can be seen shaven men in brown habits who seem in comparison to be both busy and obscure. These are the sons of St. Francis, who came to the East with a grand simplicity and thought to finish the Crusades with a smile. The spectator will be wise to accept this first contrast that strikes the eye with an impartial intellectual interest; it has nothing to do with personal character, of course, and many Greek priests are as simple in their tastes as they are charming in their manners; while any Roman priests can find as much ritual as they may happen to want in other aspects of their own religion. But it is broadly true that Roman and Greek Catholicism are contrasted in this way in this country; and the contrast is the flat contrary to all our customary associations in the West. In the East it is Roman Catholicism that stands for much that we associate with Protestantism. It is Roman Catholicism that is by comparison plain and practical and scornful of superstition and concerned for social work. It is Greek Catholicism that is stiff with gold and gorgeous with ceremonial, with its hold on ancient history and its inheritance of imperial tradition. In the cant of our own society, we may say it is the Roman who rationalises and the Greek who Romanises. It is the Roman Catholic who is impatient with Russian and Greek childishness, and perpetually appealing for common sense. It is the Greek who defends such childishness as childlike faith and would rebuke such common sense as common scepticism. I do not speak of the theological tenets or even the deeper emotions involved, but only, as I have said, of contrasts visible even in the street. And the whole difference is sufficiently suggested in two phrases I heard within a few days. A distinguished Anglo-Catholic, who has himself much sympathy with the Greek Orthodox traditions, said to me, "After all, the Romans were the first Puritans." And I heard that a Franciscan, being told that this Englishman and perhaps the English generally were disposed to make an alliance with the Greek Church, had only said by way of comment, "And a good thing too, the Greeks might do something at last."

Anyhow the first impression is that the Greek is more gorgeous in black than the Roman in colours. But the Greek of course can also appear in colours, especially in those eternal forms of frozen yet fiery colours which we call jewels. I have seen the Greek Patriarch, that magnificent old gentleman, walking down the street like an emperor in the *Arabian Nights*, hung all over with historic jewels as thick as beads or buttons, with a gigantic cross of solid emeralds that might have been given him by the green genii of the sea, if any of the genii are Christians. These things are toys, but I am entirely in favour of toys; and rubies and emeralds are almost as intoxicating as that sort of lustrous coloured paper they put inside Christmas crackers. This beauty has been best achieved in the North in the glory of coloured glass; and I have seen great Gothic windows in which one could really believe that the robes of martyrs were giant rubies or the starry sky a single enormous sapphire. But the colours of the West are transparent, the colours of the East opaque. I have spoken of the *Arabian*

G. K. CHESTERTON

Nights, and there is really a touch of them even in the Christian churches, perhaps increased with a tradition of early Christian secrecy. There are glimpses of gorgeously tiled walls, of blue curtains and green doors and golden inner chambers, that are just like the entrance to an Eastern tale. The Orthodox are at least more oriental in the sense of being more ornamental; more flat and decorative. The Romans are more Western, I might even say more modern, in the sense of having more realism even in their ritualism. The Greek cross is a cross; the Roman cross is a crucifix.

But these are deeper matters; I am only trying to suggest a sort of silhouette of the crowd like the similar silhouette of the city, a profile or outline of the heads and hats, like the profile of the towers and spires. The tower that makes the Greek priest look like a walking catafalque is by no means alone among the horns thus fantastically exalted. There is the peaked hood of the Armenian priest, for instance; the stately survival of that strange Monophysite heresy which perpetuated itself in pomp and pride mainly through the sublime accident of the Crusades. That black cone also rises above the crowd with something of the immemorial majesty of a pyramid; and rightly so, for it is typical of the prehistoric poetry by which these places live that some say it is a surviving memory of Ararat and the Ark.

Again the high white headgear of the Bethlehem women, or to speak more strictly of the Bethlehem wives, has already been noted in another connection; but it is well to remark it again among the colours of the crowd, because this at least has a significance essential to all criticism of such a crowd. Most travellers from the West regard such an Eastern city far too much as a Moslem city, like the lady whom Mr. Maurice Baring met who travelled all over Russia, and thought all the churches were mosques. But in truth it is very hard to generalise about Jerusalem, precisely because it contains everything, and its contrasts are real contrasts. And anybody who doubts that its Christianity is

Christian, a thing fighting for our own culture and morals on the borders of Asia, need only consider the concrete fact of these women of Bethlehem and their costume. There is no need to sneer in any unsympathetic fashion at all the domestic institutions of Islam; the sexes are never quite so stupid as some feminists represent; and I dare say a woman often has her own way in a harem as well as in a household. But the broad difference does remain. And if there be one thing, I think, that can safely be said about all Asia and all oriental tribes, it is this; that if a married woman wears any distinctive mark, it is always meant to prevent her from receiving the admiration or even the notice of strange men. Often it is only made to disguise her; sometimes it is made to disfigure her. It may be the masking of the face as among the Moslems; it may be the shaving of the head as among the Jews; it may, I believe, be the blackening of the teeth and other queer expedients among the people of the Far East. But is never meant to make her look magnificent in public; and the Bethlehem wife is made to look magnificent in public. She not only shows all the beauty of her face; and she is often very beautiful. She also wears a towering erection which is as unmistakably meant to give her consequence as the triple tiara of the Pope. A woman wearing such a crown, and wearing it without a veil, does stand, and can only conceivably stand, for what we call the Western view of women, but should rather call the Christian view of women. This is the sort of dignity which must of necessity come from some vague memory of chivalry. The woman may or may not be, as the legend says, a lineal descendant of a Crusader. But whether or no she is his daughter, she is certainly his heiress.

She may be put last among the local figures I have here described, for the special reason that her case has this rather deeper significance. For it is not possible to remain content with the fact that the crowd offers such varied shapes and colours to the eye, when it also offers much deeper divisions and even dilemmas to the intelligence. The black dress of the Moslem woman and the white dress of the Christian woman are in sober truth as different as black and white. They stand for real principles in a real opposition; and the black and white will not easily disappear in the dull grey of our own compromises. The one tradition will defend what it regards as modesty, and the other what it regards as dignity, with passions far deeper than most of our paltry political appetites. Nor do I see how we can deny such a right of defence, even in the case we consider the less enlightened. It is made all the more difficult by the fact that those who consider themselves the pioneers of enlightenment generally also consider themselves the protectors of native races and aboriginal rights. Whatever view we take of the Moslem Arab, we must at least admit that the greater includes the less. It is manifestly absurd to say we have no right to interfere in his country, but have a right to interfere in his home.

It is the intense interest of Jerusalem that there can thus be two universes in the same street. Indeed there are ten rather than two; and it is a proverb that the fight is not only between Christian and Moslem, but between Christian and Christian. At this moment, it must be admitted, it is almost entirely a fight of Christian and Moslem allied against Jew. But of that I shall have to speak later; the point for the moment is that the varied colours of the streets are a true symbol of the varied colours of the souls. It is perhaps the only modern place where the war waged between ideas has such a visible and vivid heraldry.

And that fact alone may well leave the spectator with one final reflection; for it is a matter in which the modern world may well have to learn something from the motley rabble of this remote Eastern town.

It may be an odd thing to suggest that a crowd in Bond Street or Piccadilly should model itself on this masquerade of religions. It would be facile and fascinating to turn it into a satire or an extravaganza. Every good and innocent mind would be gratified with the image of a bowler hat in the precise proportions of the Dome of St. Paul's, and surmounted with a little ball and cross, symbolising the loyalty of some Anglican to his mother church. It might even be pleasing to see the street dominated with a more graceful top-hat modelled on the Eiffel Tower, and signifying the wearer's faith in scientific enterprise, or perhaps in its frequent concomitant of political corruption. These would be fair Western parallels to the head-dresses of Jerusalem; modelled on Mount Ararat or Solomon's Temple, and some may insinuate that we are not very likely ever to meet them in the Strand. A man wearing whiskers is not even compelled to plead some sort of excuse or authority for wearing whiskers, as the Jew can for wearing ringlets; and though the Anglican clergyman may indeed be very loyal to his mother church, there might be considerable hesitation if his mother bade him bind his hair. Nevertheless a more historical view of the London and Jerusalem crowds will show as far from impossible to domesticate such symbols; that some day a lady's jewels might mean something like the sacred jewels of the Patriarch, or a lady's furs mean something like the furred turban of the Rabbi. History indeed will show us that we are not so much superior to them as inferior to ourselves.

When the Crusaders came to Palestine, and came riding up that road from Jaffa where the orange plantations glow on either side, they came with motives which may have been mixed and are certainly disputed. There may have been different theories among the Crusaders; there are certainly different theories among the critics of the Crusaders. Many sought God, some gold, some perhaps black magic. But whatever else they were in search of, they were not in search of the picturesque. They were not drawn from a drab civilisation by that mere thirst for colour that draws so many modern artists to the bazaars of the East. In those days there were colours in the West as well as in the East;

and a glow in the sunset as well as in the sunrise. Many of the men who rode up that road were dressed to match the most glorious orange garden and to rival the most magnificent oriental king. King Richard cannot have been considered dowdy, even by comparison, when he rode on that high red saddle graven with golden lions, with his great scarlet hat and his vest of silver crescents. That squire of the comparatively unobtrusive household of Joinville, who was clad in scarlet striped with yellow, must surely have been capable (if I may be allowed the expression) of knocking them in the most magnificent Asiatic bazaar. Nor were these external symbols less significant, but rather more significant than the corresponding symbols of the Eastern civilisation. It is true that heraldry began beautifully as an art and afterwards degenerated into a science. But even in being a science it had to possess a significance; and the Western colours were often allegorical where the Eastern were only accidental. To a certain extent this more philosophical ornament was doubtless imitated; and I have remarked elsewhere on the highly heraldic lions which even the Saracens carved over the gate of St. Stephen. But it is the extraordinary and even exasperating fact that it was not imitated as the most meaningless sort of modern vulgarity is imitated. King Richard's great red hat embroidered with beasts and birds has not overshadowed the earth so much as the billycock, which no one has yet thought of embroidering with any such natural and universal imagery. The cockney tourist is not only more likely to set out with the intention of knocking them, but he has actually knocked them; and Orientals are imitating the tweeds of the tourist more than they imitated the stripes of the squire. It is a curious and perhaps melancholy truth that the world is imitating our worst, our weariness and our dingy decline, when it did not imitate our best and the high moment of our morning.

Perhaps it is only when civilisation becomes a disease that it becomes an infection. Possibly it is only when it becomes a very virulent disease that it becomes an epidemic. Possibly again that is the meaning both of cosmopolitanism and imperialism. Anyhow the tribes sitting by Afric's sunny fountains did not take up the song when Francis of Assisi stood on the very mountain of the Middle Ages, singing the Canticle of the Sun. When Michael Angelo carved a statue in snow, Eskimos did not copy him, despite their large natural quarries or resources. Laplanders never made a model of the Elgin Marbles, with a frieze of reindeers instead of horses; nor did Hottentots try to paint Mumbo Jumbo as Raphael had painted Madonnas. But many a savage king has worn a top-hat, and the barbarian has sometimes been so debased as to add to it a pair of trousers. Explosive bullets and the brutal factory system numbers of advanced natives are anxious to possess. And it was this reflection, arising out of the mere pleasure of the eye in the parti-coloured crowd before me, that brought back my mind to the chief problem and peril of our position in Palestine, on which I touched earlier in this chapter; the peril which is largely at the back both of the just and of the unjust objections to Zionism. It is the fear that the West, in its modern mercantile mood, will send not its best but its worst. The artisan way of putting it, from the point of view of the Arab, is that it will mean not so much the English merchant as the Jewish money-lender. I shall write else-where of better types of Jew and the truths they really represent; but the Jewish money-lender is in a curious and complex sense the representative of this unfortunate paradox. He is not only unpopular both in the East and West, but he is unpopular in the West for being Eastern and in the East for being Western. He is accused in Europe of Asiatic crookedness and secrecy, and in Asia of European vulgarity and bounce. I have said *a propos* of the Arab that the dignity of the oriental is in his long robe; the merely mercantile Jew is the oriental who has lost his long robe, which leads to a dangerous liveliness in the legs. He bustles and hustles too much; and in Palestine some of the unpopularity even of the better sort of Jew is simply due to his restlessness. But there remains a fear that it will not be a question of the better sort of Jew, or of the better sort of British influence. The same ignominious inversion which reproduces everywhere the factory chimney without the church tower, which spreads a cockney commerce but not a Christian culture, has given many men a vague feeling that the influence of modern civilisation will surround these ragged but coloured groups with something as dreary and discoloured, as unnatural and as desolate as the unfamiliar snow in which they were shivering as I watched them. There seemed a sort of sinister omen in this strange visitation that the north had sent them; in the fact that when the north wind blew at last, it had only scattered on them this silver dust of death.

It may be that this more melancholy mood was intensified by that pale landscape and those impassable ways. I do not dislike snow; on the contrary I delight in it; and if it had drifted as deep in my own country against my own door I should have thought it the triumph of Christmas, and a thing as comic as my own dog and donkey. But the people in the coloured rags did dislike it; and the effects of it were not comic but tragic. The news that came in seemed in that little lonely town like the news of a great war, or even of a great defeat. Men fell to regarding it, as they have fallen too much to regarding the war, merely as an unmixed misery, and here the misery was really unmixed. As the snow began to melt corpses were found in it, homes were hopelessly buried, and even the gradual clearing of the roads only brought him stories of the lonely hamlets lost in the hills. It seemed as if a breath of the aimless destruction that wanders in the world had drifted across us; and no task remained for men but the weary rebuilding of ruins and the numbering of the dead.

Only as I went out of the Jaffa Gate, a man told me that the tree of the hundred deaths, that was the type of the eternal Caliphate of the Crescent, was cast down and lying broken in the snow.

CHAPTER VI

THE GROUPS OF THE CITY

Palestine is a striped country; that is the first effect of landscape on the eye. It runs in great parallel lines wavering into vast hills and valleys, but preserving the parallel pattern; as if drawn boldly but accurately with gigantic chalks of green and grey and red and yellow. The natural explanation or (to speak less foolishly) the natural process of this is simple enough. The stripes are the strata of the rock, only they are stripped by the great rains, so that everything has to grow on ledges, repeating yet again that terraced character to be seen in the vineyards and the staircase streets of the town. But though the cause is in a sense in the ruinous strength of the rain, the hues are not the dreary hues of ruin. What earth there is is commonly a red clay richer than that of Devon; a red clay of which it would be easy to believe that the giant limbs of the first man were made. What grass there is is not only an enamel of emerald, but is literally crowded with those crimson anemones which might well have called forth the great saying touching Solomon in all his glory. And even what rock there is is coloured with a thousand secondary and tertiary tints, as are the walls and streets of the Holy City which is built from the quarries of these hills. For the old stones of the old Jerusalem are as precious as the precious stones of the New Jerusalem; and at certain moments of morning or of sunset, every pebble might be a pearl.

And all these coloured strata rise so high and roll so far that they might be skies rather than slopes. It is as if we looked up at a frozen sunset; or a daybreak fixed for ever with its fleeting bars of cloud. And indeed the fancy is not without a symbolic suggestiveness. This is the land of eternal things; but we tend too much to forget that recurrent things are eternal things. We tend to forget that subtle tones and delicate hues, whether in the hills or the heavens, were to the primitive poets and sages as visible as they are to us; and the strong and simple words in which they describe them do not prove that they did not realise them. When Wordsworth speaks of "the clouds that gather round the setting sun," we assume that he has seen every shadow of colour and every curve of form; but when the Hebrew poet says "He hath made the clouds his chariot"; we do not always realise that he was full of indescribable emotions aroused by indescribable sights. We vaguely assume that the very sky was plainer in primitive times. We feel as if there had been a fashion in sunsets; or as if dawn was always grey in the Stone Age or brown in the Bronze Age.

But there is another parable written in those long lines of many-coloured clay and stone. Palestine is in every sense a stratified country. It is not only true in the natural sense, as here where the clay has fallen away and left visible the very ribs of the hills. It is true in the quarries where men dig, in the dead cities where they excavate, and even in the living cities where they still fight and pray. The sorrow of all Palestine is that its divisions in culture, politics and theology are like its divisions in geology. The dividing line is horizontal instead of vertical. The frontier does not run between states but between stratified layers. The Jew did not appear beside the Canaanite but on top of the Canaanite; the Greek not beside the Jew but on top of the Jew; the Moslem not beside the Christian but on top of the Christian. It is not merely a house divided against itself, but one divided across itself. It is a house in which the first floor is fighting the second floor, in which the basement is oppressed from above and attics are besieged from below.

There is a great deal of gunpowder in the cellars; and people are by no means comfortable even on the roof. In days of what some call Bolshevism, it may be said that most states are houses in which the kitchen has declared war on the drawing-room. But this will give no notion of the toppling pagoda of political and religious and racial differences, of which the name is Palestine. To explain that it is necessary to give the traveller's first impressions more particularly in their order, and before I return to this view of the society as stratified, I must state the problem more practically as it presents itself while the society still seems fragmentary.

We are always told that the Turk kept the peace between the Christian sects. It would be nearer the nerve of vital truth to say that he made the war between the Christian sects. But it would be nearer still to say that the war is something not made by Turks but made up by infidels. The tourist visiting the churches is often incredulous about the tall tales told about them; but he is completely credulous about the tallest of all the tales, the tale that is told against them. He believes in a frantic fraticidal war perpetually waged by Christian against Christian in Jerusalem. It freshens the free sense of adventure to wander through those crooked and cavernous streets, expecting every minute to see the Armenian Patriarch trying to stick a knife into the Greek Patriarch; just as it would add to the romance of London to linger about Lambeth and West-minster in the hope of seeing the Archbishop of Canterbury locked in a deadly grapple with the President of the Wesleyan Conference. And if we return to our homes at evening without having actually seen these things with the eye of flesh, the vision has none the less shone on our path, and led us round many corners with alertness and with hope. But in bald fact religion does not involve perpetual war in the East, any more than patriotism involves perpetual war in the West. What it does involve in both cases is a defensive attitude; a vigilance on the frontiers.

There is no war; but there is an armed peace.

I have already explained the sense in which I say that the Moslems are unhistoric or even anti-historic. Perhaps it would be near the truth to say that they are prehistoric. They attach themselves to the tremendous truisms which men might have realised before they had any political experience at all; which might have been scratched with primitive knives of flint upon primitive pots of clay. Being simple and sincere, they do not escape the need for legends; I might almost say that, being honest, they do not escape the need for lies. But their mood is not historic, they do not wish to grapple with the past; they do not love its complexities; nor do they understand the enthusiasm for its details and even its doubts. Now in all this the Moslems of a place like Jerusalem are the very opposite of the Christians of Jerusalem. The Christianity of Jerusalem is highly historic, and cannot be understood without historical imagination. And this is not the strong point perhaps of those among us who generally record their impressions of the place. As the educated Englishman does not know the history of England, it would be unreasonable to expect him to know the history of Moab or of Mesopotamia. He receives the impression, in visiting the shrines of Jerusalem, of a number of small sects squabbling about small things. In short, he has before him a tangle of trivialities, which include the Roman Empire in the West and in the East, the Catholic Church in its two great divisions, the Jewish race, the memories of Greece and Egypt, and the whole Mahometan world in Asia and Africa. It may be that he regards these as small things; but I should be glad if he would cast his eye over human history, and tell me what are the large things. The truth is that the things that meet to-day in Jerusalem are by far the greatest things that the world has yet seen. If they are not important nothing on this earth is important, and certainly not the impressions of those who happen to be bored by them. But to understand them it is necessary to have something which is much commoner in Jerusalem than in Oxford or Boston; that sort of living history which we call tradition.

For instance, the critic generally begins by dismissing these conflicts with the statement that they are all about small points of theology. I do not admit that theological points are small points. Theology is only thought applied to religion; and those who prefer a thoughtless religion need not be so very disdainful of others with a more rationalistic taste. The old joke that the Greek sects only differed about a single letter is about the lamest and most illogical joke in the world. An atheist and a theist only differ by a single letter; yet theologians are so subtle as to distinguish definitely between the two. But though I do not in any case allow that it is idle to be concerned about theology, as a matter of actual fact these quarrels are not chiefly concerned about theology. They are concerned about history. They are concerned with the things about which the only human sort of history is concerned; great memories of great men, great battles for great ideas, the love of brave people for beautiful places, and the faith by which the dead are alive. It is quite true that with this historic sense men inherit heavy responsibilities and revenges, fury and sorrow and shame. It is also true that without it men die, and nobody even digs their graves.

The truth is that these quarrels are rather about patriotism than about religion, in the sense of theology. That is, they are just such heroic passions about the past as we call in the West by the name of nationalism; but they are conditioned by the extraordinarily complicated position of the nations, or what corresponds to the nations. We of the West, if we wish to understand it, must imagine ourselves as left with all our local loves and family memories unchanged, but the places affected by them intermingled and tumbled about by some almost inconceivable convulsion. We must imagine cities and landscapes to have turned on some unseen pivots, or been shifted about by some unseen machinery, so that our nearest was furthest and our remotest enemy our neighbour. We must imagine monuments on the wrong sites, and the antiquities of one county emptied out on top of another. And we must imagine through all this the thin but tough threads of tradition everywhere tangled and yet everywhere unbroken. We must picture a new map made out of the broken fragments of the old map; and yet with every one remembering the old map and ignoring the new. In short we must try to imagine, or rather we must try to hope, that our own memories would be as long and our own loyalties as steady as the memories and loyalties of the little crowd in Jerusalem; and hope, or pray, that we could only be as rigid, as rabid and as bigoted as are these benighted people. Then perhaps we might preserve all our distinctions of truth and falsehood in a chaos of time and space.

We have to conceive that the Tomb of Napoleon is in the middle of Stratford-on-Avon, and that the Nelson Column is erected on the field of Bannockburn; that Westminster Abbey has taken wings and flown away to the most romantic situation on the Rhine, and that the wooden "Victory" is stranded, like the Ark on Ararat, on the top of the Hill of Tara; that the pilgrims to the shrine of Lourdes have to look for it in the Island of Runnymede, and that the only existing German statue of Bismarck is to be found in the Pantheon at Paris. This intolerable topsy-turvydom is no exaggeration of the way in which stories cut across each other and sites are imposed on each other in the historic chaos of the Holy City. Now we in the West are very lucky in having our nations normally distributed into their native lands; so that good patriots can talk about themselves without perpetually annoying their neighbours. Some of the pacifists tell us that national frontiers and divisions are evil because they exasperate us to war. It would be far truer to say that national frontiers and divisions keep us at peace. It would be far truer to say that we can always love each other so long as we do not see each other. But the people of

Jerusalem are doomed to have difference without division. They are driven to set pillar against pillar in the same temple, while we can set city against city across the plains of the world. While for us a church rises from its foundations as naturally as a flower springs from a flower-bed, they have to bless the soil and curse the stones that stand on it. While the land we love is solid under our feet to the earth's centre, they have to see all they love and hate lying in strata like alternate night and day, as incompatible and as inseparable. Their entanglements are tragic, but they are not trumpery or accidental. Everything has a meaning; they are loyal to great names as men are loyal to great nations; they have differences about which they feel bound to dispute to the death; but in their death they are not divided.

Jerusalem is a small town of big things; and the average modern city is a big town full of small things. All the most important and interesting powers in history are here gathered within the area of a quiet village; and if they are not always friends, at least they are necessarily neighbours. This is a point of intellectual interest, and even intensity, that is far too little realised. It is a matter of modern complaint that in a place like Jerusalem the Christian groups do not always regard each other with Christian feelings. It is said that they fight each other; but at least they meet each other. In a great industrial city like London or Liverpool, how often do they even meet each other? In a large town men live in small cliques, which are much narrower than classes; but in this small town they live at least by large contacts, even if they are conflicts. Nor is it really true, in the daily humours of human life, that they are only conflicts. I have heard an eminent English clergyman from Cambridge bargaining for a brass lamp with a Syrian of the Greek Church, and asking the advice of a Franciscan friar who was standing smiling in the same shop. I have met the same representative of the Church of England, at a luncheon party with the wildest Zionist Jews, and with the Grand Mufti, the head of the Moslem religion. Suppose the same Englishman had been, as he might well have been, an eloquent and popular vicar in Chelsea or Hampstead. How often would he have met a Franciscan or a Zionist? Not once in a year. How often would he have met a Moslem or a Greek Syrian? Not once in a lifetime. Even if he were a bigot, he would be bound in Jerusalem to become a more interesting kind of bigot. Even if his opinions were narrow, his experiences would be wide. He is not, as a fact, a bigot, nor, as a fact, are the other people bigots, but at the worst they could not be unconscious bigots. They could not live in such uncorrected complacency as is possible to a larger social set in a larger social system. They could not be quite so ignorant as a broad-minded person in a big suburb. Indeed there is something fine and distinguished about the very delicacy, and even irony, of their diplomatic relations. There is something of chivalry in the courtesy of their armed truce, and it is a great school of manners that includes such differences in morals.

This is an aspect of the interest of Jerusalem which can easily be neglected and is not easy to describe. The normal life there is intensely exciting, not because the factions fight, but rather because they do not fight. Of the abnormal crisis when they did fight, and the abnormal motives that made them fight, I shall have something to say later on. But it was true for a great part of the time that what was picturesque and thrilling was not the war but the peace. The sensation of being in this little town is rather like that of being at a great international congress. It is like that moving and glittering social satire, in which diplomatists can join in a waltz who may soon be joining in a war. For the religious and political parties have yet another point in common with separate nations; that even within this narrow space the complicated curve of their frontiers is really more or less fixed, and certainly not particularly fluctuating. Persecution is impossible and conversion is not at all common. The very able Anglo-Catholic leader, to whom I have already referred, uttered to me a paradox that was a very practical truth. He said he felt exasperated with the Christian sects, not for their fanaticism but for their lack of fanaticism. He meant their lack of any fervour and even of any hope, of converting each other to their respective religions. An Armenian may be quite as proud of the Armenian Church as a Frenchman of the French nation, yet he may no more expect to make a Moslem an Armenian than the Frenchman expects to make an Englishman a Frenchman. If, as we are told, the quarrels could be condemned as merely theological, this would certainly be the very reverse of logical. But as I say, we get much nearer to them by calling them national; and the leaders of the great religions feel much more like the ambassadors of great nations. And, as I have also said, that ambassadorial atmosphere can be best expressed on the word irony, sometimes a rather tragic irony. At any tea-party or talk in the street, between the rival leaders, there is a natural tendency to that sort of wit which consists in veiled allusion to a very open secret. Each mail feels that there are heavy forces behind a small point, as the weight of the fencer is behind the point of the rapier. And the point can be yet more pointed because the politics of the city, when I was there, included several men with a taste and talent for such polished intercourse; including especially two men whose experience and culture would have been remarkable in any community in the world; the American Consul and the Military Governor of Jerusalem.

If in cataloguing the strata of the society we take first the topmost layer of Western officialism, we might indeed find it not inconvenient to take these two men as representing the chief realities about it. Dr. Glazebrook, the representative of the United States, has the less to do with the internal issues of the country; but his mere presence and history is so strangely picturesque that he might be put among the first reasons for finding the city interesting. He is an old man now, for he actually began life as a soldier in the Southern and Secessionist army, and still keeps alive in every detail, not merely the virtues but the very gestures of the old Southern and Secessionist aristocrat.

He afterward became a clergyman of the Episcopalian Church, and served as a chaplain in the Spanish-American war, then, at an age when most men have long retired from the most peaceful occupations, he was sent out by President Wilson to the permanent battlefield of Palestine. The brilliant services he performed there, in the protection of British and American subjects, are here chiefly interesting as throwing a backward light on the unearthly topsy-turvydom of Turkish rule. There appears in his experiences something in such rule which we are perhaps apt to forget in a vision of stately Eastern princes and gallant Eastern warriors, something more tyrannical even than the dull pigheadedness of Prussianism. I mean the most atrocious of all tortures, which is called caprice. It is the thing we feel in the Arabian tales, when no man knows whether the Sultan is good or bad, and he gives the same Vizier a thousand pounds or a thousand lashes. I have heard Dr. Glazebrook describe a whole day of hideous hesitation, in which fugitives for whom he pleaded were allowed four times to embark and four times were brought back again to their prison. There is something there dizzy as well as dark, a whirlpool in the very heart of Asia; and something wilder than our own worst oppressions in the peril of those men who looked up and saw above all the power of Asiatic arms, their hopes hanging on a rocking mind like that of a maniac. The tyrant let them go at last, avowedly out of a simple sentiment for the white hair of the consul, and the strange respect that many Moslems feel for the minister of any religion. Once at least the trembling rock of barbaric rule nearly fell on him and killed him. By a sudden movement of lawlessness the Turkish military authorities sent to him, demanding the English documents left in his custody. He refused to give them up; and he knew what he was doing. In standing firm he was not even standing like

Nurse Cavell against organised Prussia under the full criticism of organised Europe. He was rather standing in a den of brigands, most of whom had never heard of the international rules they violated. Finally by another freak of friendliness they left him and his papers alone; but the old man had to wait many days in doubt, not knowing what they would do, since they did not know themselves. I do not know what were his thoughts, or whether they were far from Palestine and all possibilities that tyranny might return and reign for ever. But I have sometimes fancied that, in that ghastly silence, he may have heard again only the guns of Lee and the last battle in the Wilderness.

If the mention of the American Consul refers back to the oppression of the past, the mention of the Military Governor brings back all the problems of the present. Here I only sketch these groups as I first found them in the present; and it must be remembered that my present is already past. All this was before the latest change from military to civil government, but the mere name of Colonel Storrs raises a question which is rather misunderstood in relation to that change itself. Many of our journalists, especially at the time of the last and worst of the riots, wrote as if it would be a change from some sort of stiff militarism to a liberal policy akin to parliamentarism. I think this a fallacy, and a fallacy not uncommon in journalism, which is professedly very much up to date, and actually very much behind the times. As a fact it is nearly four years behind the times, for it is thinking in terms of the old small and rigidly professional army. Colonel Storrs is the very last man to be called militaristic in the narrow sense; he is a particularly liberal and enlightened type of the sort of English gentleman who readily served his country in war, but who is rather particularly fitted to serve her in politics or literature. Of course many purely professional soldiers have liberal and artistic tastes; as General Shea, one of the organisers of Palestinian victory, has a fine taste in poetry, or Colonel Popham, then deputy Governor of

Jerusalem, an admirable taste in painting. But while it is sometimes forgotten that many soldiers are men, it is now still more strange to forget that most men are soldiers. I fancy there are now few things more representative than the British Army; certainly it is much more representative than the British Parliament. The men I knew, and whom I remember with so much gratitude, working under General Bols at the seat of government on the Mount of Olives, were certainly not narrowed by any military profession-alism, and had if anything the mark of quite different professions. One was a very shrewd and humorous lawyer employed on legal problems about enemy property, another was a young schoolmaster, with keen and clear ideas, or rather ideals, about education for all the races in Palestine. These men did not cease to be themselves because they were all dressed in khaki; and if Colonel Storrs recurs first to the memory, it is not because he had become a colonel in the trade of soldiering, but because he is the sort of man who could talk equally about all these other trades and twenty more. Incidentally, and by way of example, he can talk about them in about ten languages. There is a story, which whether or no it be true is very typical, that one of the Zionist leaders made a patriotic speech in Hebrew, and broke off short in his recollection of this partially revived national tongue; whereupon the Governor of Jerusalem finished his Hebrew speech for him - whether to exactly the same effect or not it would be impertinent to inquire. He is a man rather recalling the eighteenth century aristocrat, with his love of wit and classical learning; one of that small group of the governing class that contains his uncle, Harry Cust, and was warmed with the generous culture of George Wyndham. It was a purely mechanical distinction between the military and civil government that would lend to such figures the stiffness of a drumhead court martial. And even those who differed with him accused him in practice, not of militarist lack of sympathy with any of those he ruled, but rather with too imaginative a sympathy with some of them. To know these things, however slightly, and then read the

English newspapers afterwards is often amusing enough; but I have only mentioned the matter because there is a real danger in so crude a differentiation. It would be a bad thing if a system military in form but representative in fact gave place to a system representative in form but financial in fact. That is what the Arabs and many of the English fear; and with the mention of that fear we come to the next stratum after the official. It must be remembered that I am not at this stage judging these groups, but merely very rapidly sketching them, like figures and costumes in the street.

The group standing nearest to the official is that of the Zionists; who are supposed to have a place at least in our official policy. Among these also I am happy to have friends; and I may venture to call the official head of the Zionists an old friend in a matter quite remote from Zionism. Dr. Eder, the President of the Zionist Commission, is a man for whom I conceived a respect long ago when he protested, as a professional physician, against the subjection of the poor to medical interference to the destruction of all moral independence. He criticised with great effect the proposal of legislators to kidnap anybody else's child whom they chose to suspect of a feeblemindedness they were themselves too feeble-minded to define. It was defended, very characteristically, by a combination of precedent and progress; and we were told that it only extended the principle of the lunacy laws. That is to say, it only extended the principle of the lunacy laws to people whom no sane man would call lunatics. It is as if they were to alter the terms of a quarantine law from "lepers" to "light-haired persons"; and then say blandly that the principle was the same. The humour and human sympathy of a Jewish doctor was very welcome to us when we were accused of being Anti-Semites, and we afterwards asked Dr. Eder for his own views on the Jewish problem. We found he was then a very strong Zionist; and this was long before he had the faintest chance of figuring as a leader of

Zionism. And this accident is important; for it stamps the sincerity of the small group of original Zionists, who were in favour of this nationalist ideal when all the international Jewish millionaires were against it. To my mind the most serious point now against it is that the millionaires are for it. But it is enough to note here the reality of the ideal in men like Dr. Eder and Dr. Weizmann, and doubtless many others. The only defect that need be noted, as a mere detail of portraiture, is a certain excessive vigilance and jealousy and pertinacity in the wrong place, which sometimes makes the genuine Zionists unpopular with the English, who themselves suffer unpopularity for supporting them. For though I am called an Anti-Semite, there were really periods of official impatience when I was almost the only Pro-Semite in the company. I went about pointing out what was really to be said for Zionism, to people who were represented by the Arabs as the mere slaves of the Zionists.

This group of Arab Anti-Semites may be taken next, but very briefly; for the problem itself belongs to a later page; and the one thing to be said of it here is very simple. I never expected it, and even now I do not fully understand it. But it is the fact that the native Moslems are more Anti-Semitic than the native Christians. Both are more or less so; and have formed a sort of alliance out of the fact. The banner carried by the mob bore the Arabic inscription "Moslems and Christians are brothers." It is as if the little wedge of Zionism had closed up the cracks of the Crusades.

Of the Christian crowds in that partnership, and the Christian creeds they are proud to inherit, I have already suggested something; it is only as well to note that I have put them out of their strict order in the stratification of history. It is too often forgotten that in these countries the Christian culture is older than the Moslem culture. I for one regret that the old Pax Romana was broken up by the Arabs; and hold that in the long run there was more life in that Byzantine decline than in that Semitic revival. And I will add what I cannot here develop or defend; that in the long run it is best that the Pax Romana should return; and that the suzerainty of those lands at least will have to be Christian, and neither Moslem nor Jewish. To defend it is to defend a philosophy; but I do hold that there is in that philosophy, for all the talk of its persecutions in the past, a possibility of comprehension and many-sided sympathy which is not in the narrow intensity either of the Moslem or the Jew. Christianity is really the right angle of that triangle, and the other two are very acute angles.

But in the meetings that led up to the riots it is the more Moslem part of the mixed crowds that I chiefly remember; which touches the same truth that the Christians are the more potentially tolerant. But many of the Moslem leaders are as dignified and human as many of the Zionist leaders; the Grand Mufti is a man I cannot imagine as either insulting anybody, or being conceivably the object of insult. The Moslem Mayor of Jerusalem was another such figure, belonging also I believe to one of the Arab aristocratic houses (the Grand Mufti is a descendant of Mahomet) and I shall not forget his first appearance at the first of the riotous meetings in which I found myself. I will give it as the first of two final impressions with which I will end this chapter, I fear on a note of almost anarchic noise, the unearthly beating and braying of the Eastern gongs and horns of two fierce desert faiths against each other.

I first saw from the balcony of the hotel the crowd of rioters come rolling up the street. In front of them went two fantastic figures turning like teetotums in an endless dance and twirling two crooked and naked scimitars, as the Irish were supposed to twirl shillelaghs. I thought it a delightful way of opening a political meeting; and I wished we could do it at home at the General Election. I wish that instead of the wearisome business of Mr. Bonar Law taking the chair, and Mr. Lloyd George addressing the meeting, Mr. Law and Mr. Lloyd George would only hop and caper in front of a procession, spinning round and round till they were dizzy, and waving and crossing a pair of umbrellas in a thousand invisible patterns. But this political announcement or advertisement, though more intelligent than our own, had, as I could readily believe, another side to it. I was told that it was often a prelude to ordinary festivals, such as weddings; and no doubt it remains from some ancient ritual dance of a religious character. But I could imagine that it might sometimes seem to a more rational taste to have too religious a character. I could imagine that those dancing men might indeed be dancing dervishes, with their heads going round in a more irrational sense than their bodies. I could imagine that at some moments it might suck the soul into what I have called in metaphor the whirlpool of Asia, or the whirlwind of a world whipped like a top with a raging monotony; the cyclone of eternity. That is not the sort of rhythm nor the sort of religion by which I myself should hope to save the soul; but it is intensely interesting to the mind and even the eye, and I went downstairs and wedged myself into the thick and thronging press. It surged through the gap by the gate, where men climbed lamp-posts and roared out speeches, and more especially recited national poems in rich resounding voices; a really moving effect, at least for one who could not understand a word that was said. Feeling had already gone as far as knocking Jews' hats off and other popular sports, but not as yet on any universal and systematic scale; I saw a few of the antiquated Jews with wrinkles and ringlets, peering about here and there; some said as spies or representatives of the Zionists, to take away the Anti-Semitic colour from the meeting. But I think this unlikely; especially as it would have been pretty hard to take it away. It is more likely, I think, that the archaic Jews were really not unamused and perhaps not unsympathetic spectators; for the Zionist problem is complicated by a real quarrel in the Ghetto about Zionism. The old religious Jews do not welcome the new nationalist Jews; it would sometimes be hardly an exaggeration to say that one party stands for the religion without the nation, and the other for the nation without the religion. Just as the old agricultural Arabs hate the Zionists as the instruments of new Western business grab and sharp practice; so the old peddling and pedantic but intensely pious Jews hate the Zionists as the instruments of new Western atheism of free thought. Only I fear that when the storm breaks, such distinctions are swept away.

The storm was certainly rising. Outside the Jaffa Gate the road runs up steeply and is split in two by the wedge of a high building, looking as narrow as a tower and projecting like the prow of a ship. There is something almost theatrical about its position and stage properties, its one high-curtained window and balcony, with a sort of pole or flag-staff; for the place is official or rather municipal. Round it swelled the crowd, with its songs and poems and passionate rhetoric in a kind of crescendo, and then suddenly the curtain of the window rose like the curtain of the theatre, and we saw on that high balcony the red fez and the tall figure of the Mahometan Mayor of Jerusalem.

I did not understand his Arabic observations; but I know when a man is calming a mob, and the mob did become calmer. It was as if a storm swelled in the night and gradually died away in a grey morning; but there are perpetual mutterings of that storm. My point for the moment is that the exasperations come chiefly from the two extremes of the two great Semitic traditions of mono-theism; and certainly not primarily from those poor Eastern Christians of whose fanaticism we have been taught to make fun. From time to time there are gleams of the extremities of Eastern fanaticism which are almost ghastly to Western feeling. They seem to crack the polish of the dignified leaders of the Arab aristocracy and the Zionist school of culture, and reveal a volcanic substance of which only oriental creeds have been made. One day a wild Jewish proclamation is passed from hand to hand, denouncing disloyal Jews who refuse the teaching Hebrew; telling doctors to let them die and hospitals to let them rot, ringing with the old unmistakable and awful accent that bade men dash their children against the stones. Another day the city would be placarded with posters printed in Damascus, telling the Jews who looked to Palestine for a national home that they should find it a national cemetery. And when these cries clash it is like the clash of those two crooked Eastern swords, that crossed and recrossed and revolved like blazing wheels, in the vanguard of the marching mob.

I felt the fullest pressure of the problem when I first walked round the whole of the Haram enclosure, the courts of the old Temple, where the high muezzin towers now stand at every corner, and heard the clear voices of the call to prayer. The sky was laden with a storm that became the snow-storm; and it was the time at which the old Jews beat their hands and mourn over what are believed to be the last stones of the Temple. There was a movement in my own mind that was attuned to these things, and impressed by the strait limits and steep sides of that platform of the mountains; for the sense of crisis is not only in the intensity of the ideals, but in the very conditions of the reality, the reality with which this chapter began. And the burden of it is the burden of Palestine; the narrowness of the boundaries and the stratification of the rock. A voice not of my reason but rather sounding heavily in my heart, seemed to be repeating sentences like pessimistic proverbs. There is no place for the Temple of Solomon but on the ruins of the Mosque of Omar. There is no place for the nation of the Jews but in the country of the Arabs. And these whispers came to me first not as intellectual conclusions upon the conditions of the case, of which I should have much more to say and to hope; but rather as hints of something immediate and menacing and yet mysterious. I felt almost a momentary impulse to flee from the place, like one who has received an omen. For two voices had met in my ears; and

G. K. CHESTERTON

within the same narrow space and in the same dark hour, electric and yet eclipsed with cloud, I had heard Islam crying from the turret and Israel wailing at the wall.

CHAPTER VII

THE SHADOW OF THE PROBLEM

A traveller sees the hundred branches of a tree long before he is near enough to see its single and simple root; he generally sees the scattered or sprawling suburbs of a town long before he has looked upon the temple or the market-place. So far I have given impressions of the most motley things merely as they came, in chronological and not in logical order; the first flying vision of Islam as a sort of sea, with something both of the equality and the emptiness and the grandeur of its purple seas of sand; the first sharp silhouette of Jerusalem, like Mount St. Michael, lifting above that merely Moslem flood a crag still crowned with the towers of the Crusaders; the mere kaleidoscope of the streets, with little more than a hint of the heraldic meaning of the colours; a merely personal impression of a few of the leading figures whom I happened to meet first, and only the faintest suggestion of the groups for which they stood. So far I have not even tidied up my own first impressions of the place; far less advanced a plan for tidying up the place itself.

In any case, to begin with, it is easy to be in far too much of a hurry about tidying up. This has already been noted in the more obvious case, of all that religious art that bewildered the tourist with its churches full of flat and gilded ikons. Many a man has had the sensation of something as full as a picture gallery and as futile as a lumber-room, merely by not happening to know what is really of value, or

G. K. CHESTERTON

especially in what way it is really valued. An Armenian or a Syrian might write a report on his visit to England, saying that our national and especially our naval heroes were neglected, and left to the lowest dregs of the rabble; since the portraits of Benbow and Nelson, when exhibited to the public, were painted on wood by the crudest and most incompetent artists. He would not perhaps fully appreciate the fine shade of social status and utility implied in a public-house sign. He might not realise that the sign of Nelson could be hung on high everywhere, because the reputation of Nelson was high everywhere, not because it was low anywhere; that his bad portrait was really a proof of his good name. Yet the too rapid reformer may easily miss even the simple and superficial parallel between the wooden pictures of admirals and the wooden pictures of angels. Still less will he appreciate the intense spiritual atmosphere, that makes the real difference between an ikon and an inn-sign, and makes the inns of England, noble and national as they are, relatively the homes of Christian charity but hardly a Christian faith. He can hardly bring himself to believe that Syrians can be as fond of religion as Englishmen of beer.

Nobody can do justice to these cults who has not some sympathy with the power of a mystical idea to transmute the meanest and most trivial objects with a kind of magic. It is easy to talk of superstitiously attaching importance to sticks and stones, but the whole poetry of life consists of attaching importance to sticks and stones; and not only to those tall sticks we call the trees or those large stones we call the mountains. Anything that gives to the sticks of our own furniture, or the stones of our own backyard, even a reflected or indirect divinity is good for the dignity of life; and this is often achieved by the dedication of similar and special things. At least we should desire to see the profane things transfigured by the sacred, rather than the sacred disenchanted by the profane; and it was a prophet walking on the walls of this mountain city, who said that in his vision all the bowls should be as the bowls before the altar, and on every pot in Jerusalem should be written Holy unto the Lord.

Anyhow, this intensity about trifles is not always understood. Several quite sympathetic Englishmen told me merely as a funny story (and God forbid that I should deny that it is funny) the fact of the Armenians or some such people having been allowed to suspend a string of lamps from a Greek pillar by means of a nail, and their subsequent alarm when their nail was washed by the owners of the pillar; a sort of symbol that their nail had finally fallen into the hands of the enemy. It strikes us as odd that a nail should be so valuable or so vivid to the imagination. And yet, to men so close to Calvary, even nails are not entirely commonplace.

All this, regarding a decent delay and respect for religion or even for superstition, is obvious and has already been observed. But before leaving it, we may note that the same argument cuts the other way; I mean that we should not insolently impose our own ideas of what is picturesque any more than our own ideas of what is practical. The aesthete is sometimes more of a vandal than the vandal. The proposed reconstructions of Jerusalem have been on the whole reasonable and sympathetic; but there is always a danger from the activities, I might almost say the antics, of a sort of antiquary who is more hasty than an anarchist. If the people of such places revolt against their own limitations, we must have a reasonable respect for their revolt, and we must not be impatient even with their impatience.

It is their town; they have to live in it, and not we. As they are the only judges of whether their antiquities are really authorities, so they are the only judges of whether their novelties are really necessities. As I pointed out more than once to many of my friends in Jerusalem, we should be very much annoyed if artistic visitors from Asia took similar liberties in London. It would be bad enough if they proposed to conduct excavations in Pimlico or Paddington, without much reference to the people who lived there; but it would be worse if they began to relieve them of the mere utilitarianism of Chelsea Bridge or Paddington Station. Suppose an eloquent Abyssinian Christian were to hold up his hand and stop the motor-omnibuses from going down Fleet Street on the ground that the thoroughfare was sacred to the simpler locomotion of Dr. Johnson. We should be pleased at the African's appreciation of Johnson; but our pleasure would not be unmixed. Suppose when you or I are in the act of stepping into a taxi-cab, an excitable Coptic Christian were to leap from behind a lamp-post, and implore us to save the grand old growler or the cab called the gondola of London. I admit and enjoy the poetry of the hansom; I admit and enjoy the personality of the true cabman of the old four-wheeler, upon whose massive man-hood descended something of the tremendous tradition of Tony Weller. But I am not so certain as I should like to be, that I should at that moment enjoy the personality of the Copt. For these reasons it seems really desirable, or at least defensible, to defer any premature reconstruction of disputed things, and to begin this book as a mere note-book or sketch-book of things as they are, or at any rate as they appear. It was in this irregular order, and in this illogical disproportion, that things did in fact appear to me, and it was some time before I saw any real generalisation that would reduce my impressions to order. I saw that the groups disagreed, and to some extent why they disagreed, long before I could seriously consider anything on which they would be likely to agree. I have therefore confined the first section of this book to a mere series of such impressions, and left to the last section a study of the problem and an attempt at the solution. Between these two I have inserted a sort of sketch of what seemed to me the deter-mining historical events that make the problem what it is. Of these I will only say for the moment that, whether by a coincidence or for some deeper cause, I feel it myself to be a case of first thoughts being best; and that some further study of history served rather to solidify what had seemed merely a sort of vision. I might almost say that I fell in love with Jerusalem at first sight; and the final impression, right or wrong, served only to fix the fugitive fancy which had seen, in the snow on the city, the white crown of a woman of Bethlehem.

But there is another cause for my being content for the moment, with this mere chaos of contrasts. There is a very real reason for emphasising those contrasts, and for shunning the temptation to shut our eyes to them even considered as contrasts. It is necessary to insist that the contrasts are not easy to turn into combinations; that the red robes of Rome and the green scarves of Islam will not very easily fade into a dingy russet; that the gold of Byzantium and the brass of Babylon will require a hot furnace to melt them into any kind of amalgam. The reason for this is akin to what has already been said about Jerusalem as a knot of realities. It is especially a knot of popular realities. Although it is so small a place, or rather because it is so small a place, it is a domain and a dominion for the masses. Democracy is never quite democratic except when it is quite direct; and it is never quite direct except when it is quite small. So soon as a mob has grown large enough to have delegates it has grown large enough to have despots; indeed the despots are often much the more representative of the two. Now in a place so small as Jerusalem, what we call the rank and file really counts. And it is generally true, in religions especially, that the real enthusiasm or even fanaticism is to be found in the rank and file. In all intense religions it is the poor who are more religious and the rich who are more irreligious. It is certainly so with the creeds and causes that come to a collision in Jerusalem. The great Jewish population throughout the world did hail Mr. Balfour's declaration with something almost of the tribal triumph they might have shown when the Persian conqueror broke the Babylonian bondage. It was rather the plutocratic princes of Jewry who long hung back and hesitated about Zionism. The mass of Mahometans really are ready to combine against the Zionists as they might have combined against the Crusades. It is rather the responsible Mahometan leaders who will naturally be found more moderate and diplomatic. This popular spirit may take a good or a bad form; and a mob may cry out many things, right and wrong. But a mob cries out "No Popery"; it does not cry out "Not so much Popery," still less "Only a moderate admixture of Popery." It shouts "Three cheers for Gladstone," it does not shout "A gradual and evolutionary social tendency towards some ideal similar to that of Gladstone." It would find it quite a difficult thing to shout; and it would find exactly the same difficulty with all the advanced formulae about nationalisation and internationalisation and class-conscious solidarity. No rabble could roar at the top of its voice the collectivist formula of "The nationalisation of all the means of production, distribution, and exchange." The mob of Jerusalem is no exception to the rule, but rather an extreme example of it. The mob of Jerusalem has cried some remarkable things in its time; but they were not pedantic and they were not evasive. There was a day when it cried a single word; "Crucify." It was a thing to darken the sun and rend the veil of the temple; but there was no doubt about what it meant.

This is an age of minorities; of minorities powerful and predominant, partly through the power of wealth and partly through the idolatry of education. Their powers appeared in every crisis of the Great War, when a small group of pacifists and internationalists, a microscopic minority in every country, were yet constantly figuring as diplomatists and intermediaries and men on whose attitude great issues might depend. A man like Mr. Macdonald, not a workman nor a formal or real representative of workmen, was followed everywhere by the limelight; while the millions of workmen who worked and fought were out of focus and therefore looked like a fog. Just as such figures give a fictitious impression of unity between the crowds fighting for different flags and frontiers, so there are similar figures giving a fictitious unity to the crowds following different creeds. There are already Moslems who are Modernists; there have always been a ruling class of Jews who are Materialists. Perhaps it would be true to say about much of the philosophical controversy in Europe, that many Jews tend to be Materialists, but all tend to be Monists, though the best in the sense of being Monotheists. The worst are in a much grosser sense materialists, and have motives very different from the dry idealism of men like Mr. Macdonald, which is probably sincere enough in its way. But with whatever motives, these intermediaries everywhere bridge the chasm between creeds as they do the chasm between countries. Everywhere they exalt the minority that is indifferent over the majority that is interested. Just as they would make an international congress out of the traitors of all nations, so they would make an ecumenical council out of the heretics of all religions.

Mild constitutionalists in our own country often discuss the possibility of a method of protecting the minority. If they will find any possible method of protecting the majority, they will have found something practically unknown to the modern world. The majority is always at a disadvantage; the majority is difficult to idealise, because it is difficult to imagine. The minority is generally idealised, sometimes by its servants, always by itself. But my sympathies are gene-rally, I confess, with the impotent and even invisible majority. And my sympathies, when I go beyond the things I myself believe, are with all the poor Jews who do believe in Judaism and all the Mahometans who do believe in Mahometanism, not to mention so obscure a crowd as the Christians who do believe in Christianity. I feel I have more morally and even intellectually in common with these people, and even the religions of these people, than with the supercilious negations that make up the most part of what is called enlightenment. It is these masses whom we ought to consider everywhere; but it is especially these masses whom we must consider in Jerusalem. And the reason is in the reality I have described; that the place is like a Greek city or a medieval parish; it is sufficiently small and simple to be a democracy. This is not a university town full of philosophies; it is a Zion of the hundred sieges raging with religions; not a place where resolutions can be voted and amended, but a place where men can be crowned and crucified.

There is one small thing neglected in all our talk about self-determination; and that is determination. There is a great deal more difference than there is between most motions and amendments between the things for which a demo-cracy will vote and the things on which a democracy is determined. You can take a vote among Jews and Christians and Moslems about whether lamp-posts should be painted green or portraits of politicians painted at all, and even their solid unanimity may be solid indifference. Most of what is called self-determination is like that; but there is no self-determination about it. The people are not determined. You cannot take a vote when the people are determined. You accept a vote, or something very much more obvious than a vote.

Now it may be that in Jerusalem there is not one people but rather three or four; but each is a real people, having its public opinion, its public policy, its flag and almost, as I have said, its frontier. It is not a question of persuading weak and wavering voters, at a vague parliamentary election, to vote on the other side for a change, to choose afresh between two middle-class gentlemen, who look exactly alike and only differ on a question about which nobody knows or cares anything. It is a question of contrasts that will almost certainly remain contrasts, except under the flood of some spiritual conversion which cannot be foreseen and certainly cannot be enforced. We cannot enrol these people under our religion, because we have not got one. We can enrol them under our government, and if we are obliged to do that, the obvious essential is that like Roman rule before Christianity, or the English rule in India it should profess to be impartial if only by being irreligious. That is why I willingly set down for the moment only the first impressions of a stranger in a strange country. It is because our first safety is in seeing that it is a strange country; and our present preliminary peril that we may fall into the habit of thinking it a familiar country. It does no harm to put the facts in a fashion that seems disconnected; for the first fact of all is that they are disconnected. And the first danger of all is that we may allow some international nonsense or newspaper cant to imply that they are connected when they are not. It does no harm, at any rate to start with, to state the differences as irreconcilable. For the first and most unfamiliar fact the English have to learn in this strange land is that differences can be irreconcilable. And again the chief danger is that they may be persuaded that the wordy compromises of Western politics can reconcile them; that such abysses can be filled up with rubbish, or such chasms bridged with cobwebs. For we have created in England a sort of compromise which may up to a certain point be workable in England; though there are signs that even in England that point is approaching or is past. But in any case we could only do with that compromise as we could do without conscription; because an accident had made us insular and even provincial. So in India where we have treated the peoples as different from ourselves and from each other we have at least partly succeeded. So in Ireland, where we have tried to make them agree with us and each other, we have made one never-ending nightmare.

We can no more subject the world to the English compromise than to the English climate; and both are things of incalculable cloud and twilight. We have grown used to a habit of calling things by the wrong names and supporting them by the wrong arguments; and even doing the right thing for the wrong cause. We have party governments which consist of people who pretend to agree when they really disagree. We have party debates which consist of people who pretend to disagree when they really agree. We have whole parties named after things they no longer support, or things they would never dream of proposing. We have a mass of meaningless parliamentary ceremonials that are no longer even symbolic; the rule by which a parliamentarian possesses a constituency but not a surname; or the rule by which he becomes a minister in order to cease to be a member. All this would seem the most superstitious and idolatrous mummery to the simple worshippers in the shrines of Jerusalem. You may think what they say fantastic, or what they mean fanatical, but they do not say one thing and mean another. The Greek may or may not have a right to say he is Orthodox, but he means that he is Orthodox; in a very different sense from that in which a man supporting a new Home Rule Bill means that he is Unionist. A Moslem would stop the sale of strong drink because he is a Moslem. But he is not quite so muddleheaded as to profess to stop it because he is a Liberal, and a particular supporter of the party of liberty. Even in England indeed it will generally be found that there is something more clear and rational about the terms of theology than those of politics and popular science. A man has at least a more logical notion of what he means when he calls himself an Anglo-Catholic than when he calls himself an Anglo-Saxon. But the old Jew with the drooping ringlets, shuffling in and out of the little black booths of Jerusalem, would not condescend to say he is a child of anything like the Anglo-Saxon race. He does not say he is a child of the Aramaico-Semitic race. He says he is a child of the Chosen Race, brought with thunder and with miracles and with mighty battles out of the land of Egypt and out of the house of bondage. In other words, he says something that means something, and something that he really means. One of the white Dominicans or brown Franciscans, from the great monasteries of the Holy City, may or may not be right in maintaining that a Papacy is necessary to the unity of Christendom. But he does not pass his life in proving that the Papacy is not a Papacy, as many of our liberal constitutionalists pass it in proving that the Monarchy is not a Monarchy. The Greek priests spend an hour on what seems to the sceptic mere meaningless formalities of the preparation of the Mass. But they would not spend a minute if they were themselves sceptics and thought them meaningless formalities, as most modern people do think of the formalities about Black Rod or the Bar of the House. They would be far less ritualistic than we are, if they cared as little for the Mass as we do for the Mace. Hence it is necessary for us to realise that these rude and simple worshippers, of all the different forms of worship, really would be bewildered by the ritual dances and elaborate ceremonial antics of John Bull, as by the superstitious forms and almost supernatural incantations of most of what we call plain English.

Now I take it we retain enough realism and common sense not to wish to transfer these complicated conventions and compromises to a land of such ruthless logic and such rending divisions. We may hope to reproduce our laws, we do not want to reproduce our legal fictions. We do not want to insist on everybody referring to Mr. Peter or Mr. Paul, as the honourable member for Waddy Walleh; because a retiring Parliamentarian has to become Steward of the Chiltern Hundreds, we shall not insist on a retiring Palestinian official becoming Steward of the Moabitic Hundreds. But yet in much more subtle and more dangerous ways we are making that very mistake. We are transferring the fictions and even the hypocrisies of our own insular institutions from a place where they can be tolerated to a place where they will be torn in pieces. I have confined myself hitherto to descriptions and not to criticisms, to stating the elements of the problem rather than attempting as yet to solve it; because I think the danger is rather that we shall underrate the difficulties than overdo the description; that we shall too easily deny the problem rather than that we shall too severely criticise the solution. But I would conclude this chapter with one practical criticism which seems to me to follow directly from all that is said here of our legal fictions and local anomalies. One thing at least has been done by our own Government, which is entirely according to the ritual or routine of our own Parliament. It is a parliament of Pooh Bah, where anybody may be Lord High Everything Else. It is a parliament of Alice in Wonderland, where the name of a thing is different from what it is called, and even from what its name is called. It is death and destruction to send out these fictions into a foreign daylight, where they will be seen as things and not theories. And knowing all this, I cannot conceive the reason, or even the meaning, of sending out Sir Herbert Samuel as the British representative in Palestine.

I have heard it supported as an interesting experiment in Zionism. I have heard it denounced as a craven concession to Zionism. I think it is quite obviously a flat and violent contradiction to Zionism. Zionism, as I have always understood it, and indeed as I have always defended it, consists in maintaining that it would be better for all parties if Israel had the dignity and distinctive responsibility of a separate nation; and that this should be effected, if possible, or so far as possible, by giving the Jews a national home, preferably in Palestine. But where is Sir Herbert Samuel's national home? If it is in Palestine he cannot go there as a representative of England. If it is in England, he is so far a living proof that a Jew does not need a national home in Palestine. If there is any point in the Zionist argument at all, you have chosen precisely the wrong man and sent him to precisely the wrong country. You have asserted not the independence but the dependence of Israel, and yet you have ratified the worst insinuations about the dependence of Christendom. In reason you could not more strongly state that Palestine does not belong to the Jews, than by sending a Jew to claim it for the English. And yet in practice, of course, all the Anti-Semites will say he is claiming it for the Jews. You combine all possible disadvantages of all possible courses of action; you run all the risks of the hard Zionist adventure, while actually denying the high Zionist ideal. You make a Jew admit he is not a Jew but an Englishman; even while you allow all his enemies to revile him because he is not an Englishman but a Jew.

Now this sort of confusion or compromise is as local as a London fog. A London fog is tolerable in London, indeed I think it is very enjoyable in London. There is a beauty in that brown twilight as well as in the clear skies of the Orient and the South. But it is simply horribly dangerous for a Londoner to carry his cloud of fog about with him, in the crystalline air about the crags of Zion, or under the terrible stars of the desert. There men see differences with almost unnatural clearness, and call things by savagely simple names. We in England may consider all sorts of aspects of a man like Sir Herbert Samuel; we may consider him as a Liberal, or a friend of the Fabian Socialists, or a cadet of one of the great financial houses, or a Member of Parliament who is supposed to represent certain miners in Yorkshire, or in twenty other more or less impersonal ways. But the people in Palestine will see only one aspect, and it will be a very personal aspect indeed. For the enthusiastic Moslems he will simply be a Jew; for the enthusiastic Zionists he will not really be a Zionist. For them he will always be the type of Jew who would be willing to remain in London, and who is ready to represent Westminster. Meanwhile, for the masses of Moslems and Christians, he will only be the aggravation in practice of the very thing of which he is the denial in theory. He will not mean that Palestine is not surrendered to the Jews, but only that England is. Now I have nothing as yet to do with the truth of that suggestion; I merely give it as an example of the violent and unexpected reactions we shall produce if we thrust our own unrealities amid the red-hot realities of the

Near East; it is like pushing a snow man into a furnace. I have no objection to a snow man as a part of our own Christmas festivities; indeed, as has already been suggested, I think such festivities a great glory of English life. But I have seen the snow melting in the steep places about Jerusalem; and I know what a cataract it could feed.

As I considered these things a deepening disquiet possessed me, and my thoughts were far away from where I stood. After all, the English did not indulge in this doubling of parts and muddling of mistaken identity in their real and unique success in India. They may have been wrong or right but they were realistic about Moslems and Hindoos; they did not say Moslems were Hindoos, or send a highly intelligent Hindoo from Oxford to rule Moslems as an Englishman. They may not have cared for things like the ideal of Zionism; but they understood the common sense of Zionism, the desirability of distinguishing between entirely different things. But I remembered that of late their tact had often failed them even in their chief success in India; and that every hour brought worse and wilder news of their failure in Ireland. I remembered that in the Early Victorian time, against the advice only of the wisest and subtlest of the Early Victorians, we had tied ourselves to the triumphant progress of industrial capitalism; and that progress had now come to a crisis and what might well be a crash. And now, on the top of all, our fine patriotic tradition of foreign policy seemed to be doing these irrational and random things. A sort of fear took hold of me; and it was not for the Holy Land that I feared.

A cold wave went over me, like that unreasonable change and chill with which a man far from home fancies his house has been burned down, or that those dear to him are dead. For one horrible moment at least I wondered if we had come to the end of compromise and comfortable nonsense, and if at last the successful stupidity of England would topple over like the successful wickedness of Prussia;

because God is not mocked by the denial of reason any more than the denial of justice. And I fancied the very crowds of Jerusalem retorted on me words spoken to them long ago; that a great voice crying of old along the Via Dolorosa was rolled back on me like thunder from the mountains; and that all those alien faces are turned against us to-day, bidding us weep not for them, who have faith and clarity and a purpose, but weep for ourselves and for our children.

G. K. CHESTERTON

CHAPTER VIII

THE OTHER SIDE OF THE DESERT

There was a story in Jerusalem so true or so well told that I can see the actors in it like figures in coloured costumes on a lighted stage. It occurred during the last days of Turkish occupation, while the English advance was still halted before Gaza, and heroically enduring the slow death of desert warfare. There were German and Austrian elements present in the garrison with the Turks, though the three allies seem to have held strangely aloof from each other. In the Austrian group there was an Austrian lady, "who had some dignity or other," like Lord Lundy's grandmother. She was very beautiful, very fashionable, somewhat frivolous, but with fits of Catholic devotion. She had some very valuable Christian virtues, such as indiscriminate charity for the poor and indiscriminate loathing for the Prussians. She was a nurse; she was also a nuisance. One day she was driving just outside the Jaffa Gate, when she saw one of those figures which make the Holy City seem like the eternal crisis of an epic. Such a man will enter the gate in the most ghastly rags as if he were going to be crowned king in the city; with his head lifted as if he saw apocalyptic stars in heaven, and a gesture at which the towers might fall. This man was ragged beyond all that moving rag-heap; he was as gaunt as a gallows tree, and the thing he was uttering with arms held up to heaven was evidently a curse. The lady sent an inquiry by her German servant, whom also I can see in a vision, with his face of wood and his air of still trailing all the heraldic trappings of the Holy Roman Empire. This ambassador soon returned in state and said, "Your Serene High Sublimity (or whatever it is), he says he is cursing the English." Her pity and patriotism were alike moved; and she again sent the plenipotentiary to discover why he cursed the English, or what tale of wrong or ruin at English hands lay behind the large gestures of his despair. A second time the wooden intermediary returned and said, "Your Ecstatic Excellency (or whatever be the correct form), he says he is cursing the English because they don't come."

There are a great many morals to this story, besides the general truth to which it testifies; that the Turkish rule was not popular even with Moslems, and that the German war was not particularly popular even with Turks. When all deductions are made for the patriot as a partisan, and his way of picking up only what pleases him, it remains true that the English attack was very widely regarded rather as a rescue than an aggression. And what complaint there was really was, in many cases, a complaint that the rescue did not come with a rush; that the English forces had to fall back when they had actually entered Gaza, and could not for long afterwards continue their advance on Jerusalem. This kind of criticism of military operations is always, of course, worthless. In journalists it is generally worthless without being even harmless. There were some in London whose pessimistic wailing was less excusable than that of the poor Arab in Jerusalem; who cursed the English with the addition of being English themselves, who did it, not as he did, before one foreigner, but before all foreign opinion; and who advertised their failure in a sort of rags less reputable than his. No one can judge of a point like the capture and loss of Gaza, unless he knows a huge mass of technical and local detail that can only be known to the staff on the spot; it is not a question of lack of water but of exactly how little water; not of the arrival of reinforcements but of exactly how much reinforcement; not of whether time presses, but of exactly how much time there is.

Nobody can know these things who is editing a newspaper at the other end of the world; and these are the things which, for the soldier on the spot, make all the difference between jumping over a paling and jumping over a precipice. Even the latter, as the philosophic relativist will eagerly point out, is only a matter of degree. But this is a parenthesis; for the purpose with which I mentioned the anecdote is something different. It is the text of another and somewhat more elusive truth; some appreciation of which is necessary to a sympathy with the more profound problems of Palestine. And it might be expressed thus; it is a proverb that the Eastern methods seem to us slow; that the Arabs trail along on labouring camels while the Europeans flash by on motors or mono-planes. But there is another and stranger sense in which we do seem to them slow, and they do seem to themselves to have a secret of swiftness. There is a sense in which we here touch the limits of a land of lightning; across which, as in a dream, the motor-car can be seen crawling like a snail.

I have said that there is another side to the desert; though there is something queer in talking of another side to something so bare and big and oppressively obvious. But there is another side besides the big and bare truths, like giant bones, that the Moslem has found there; there is, so to speak, an obverse of the obvious. And to suggest what I mean I must go back again to the desert and the days I spent there, being carted from camp to camp and giving what were courteously described as lectures. All I can say is that if those were lectures, I cannot imagine why everybody is not a lecturer. Perhaps the secret is already out; and multitudes of men in evening dress are already dotted about the desert, wandering in search of an audience. Anyhow in my own wanderings I found myself in the high narrow house of the Base Commandant at Kantara, the only house in the whole circle of the horizon; and from the wooden balustrade and verandah, running round the top of it, could be seen nine miles of tents. Sydney Smith said that the bulbous domes of the Brighton Pavilion looked as if St. Paul's Cathedral had come down there and littered; and that grey vista of countless cones looked rather as if the Great Pyramid had multiplied itself on the prolific scale of the herring. Nor was even such a foolish fancy without its serious side; for though these pyramids would pass, the plan of them was also among the mightiest of the works of man; and the king in every pyramid was alive. For this was the great camp that was the pivot of the greatest campaign; and from that balcony I had looked on something all the more historic because it may never be seen again. As the dusk fell and the moon brightened above that great ghostly city of canvas, I had fallen into talk with three or four of the officers at the base; grizzled and hard-headed men talking with all the curious and almost colourless common sense of the soldier. All that they said was objective; one felt that everything they mentioned was really a thing and not merely a thought; a thing like a post or a palm-tree. I think there is something in this of a sympathy between the English and the Moslems, which may have helped us in India and elsewhere. For they mentioned many Moslem proverbs and traditions, lightly enough but not contemptuously, and in particular another of the proverbial prophecies about the term of Turkish power. They said there was an old saying that the Turk would never depart until the Nile flowed through Palestine; and this at least was evidently a proverb of pride and security, like many such; as who should say until the sea is dry or the sun rises in the west. And one of them smiled and made a small gesture as of attention. And in the silence of that moonlit scene we heard the clanking of a pump. The water from the Nile had been brought in pipes across the desert.

And I thought that the symbol was a sound one, apart from all vanities; for this is indeed the special sort of thing that Christendom can do, and that Islam by itself would hardly care to do. I heard more afterwards of that water, which was eventually carried up the hills to Jerusalem, when I myself followed it thither; and all I heard bore testimony to this truth so far as it goes; the sense among the natives themselves of something magic in our machinery, and that in the main a white magic; the sense of all the more solid sort of social service that belongs rather to the West than to the East. When the fountain first flowed in the Holy City in the mountains, and Father Waggett blessed it for the use of men, it is said that an old Arab standing by said, in the plain and powerful phraseology of his people: "The Turks were here for five hundred years, and they never gave us a cup of cold water."

I put first this minimum of truth about the validity of Western work because the same conversation swerved slowly, as it were, to the Eastern side. These same men, who talked of all things as if they were chairs and tables, began to talk quite calmly of things more amazing than table-turning. They were as wonderful as if the water had come there like the wind, without any pipes or pumps; or if Father Waggett had merely struck the rock like Moses. They spoke of a solitary soldier at the end of a single telephone wire across the wastes, hearing of something that had that moment happened hundreds of miles away, and then coming upon a casual Bedouin who knew it already. They spoke of the whole tribes moving and on the march, upon news that could only come a little later by the swiftest wires of the white man. They offered no explanation of these things; they simply knew they were there, like the palm-trees and the moon. They did not say it was "telepathy"; they lived much too close to realities for that. That word, which will instantly leap to the lips of too many of my readers, strikes me as merely an evidence of two of our great modern improvements; the love of long words and the loss of common sense. It may have been telepathy, whatever that is; but a man must be almost stunned with stupidity if he is satisfied to say telepathy as if he were saying telegraphy. If everybody is satisfied about how it is done, why does not everybody do it? Why does not a cultivated clergyman in Cornwall make a casual remark to an old friend of his at the University of Aberdeen? Why does not a harassed commercial traveller in Barcelona settle a question by merely thinking about his business partner in Berlin? The common sense of it is, of course, that the name makes no sort of difference; the mystery is why some people can do it and others cannot; and why it seems to be easy in one place and impossible in another. In other words it comes back to that very mystery which of all mysteries the modern world thinks most superstitious and senseless; the mystery of locality. It works back at last to the hardest of all the hard sayings of supernaturalism; that there is such a thing as holy or unholy ground, as divinely or diabolically inspired people; that there may be such things as sacred sites or even sacred stones; in short that the airy nothing of spiritual essence, evil or good, can have quite literally a local habitation and a name.

It may be said in passing that this *genius loci* is here very much the presiding genius. It is true that everywhere to-day a parade of the theory of pantheism goes with a considerable practice of particularism; and that people everywhere are beginning to wish they were somewhere. And even where it is not true of men, it seems to be true of the mysterious forces which men are once more studying. The words we now address to the unseen powers may be vague and universal, but the words they are said to address to us are parochial and even private. While the Higher Thought Centre would widen worship everywhere to a temple not made with hands, the Psychical Research Society is conducting practical experiments round a haunted house. Men may become cosmopolitans, but ghosts remain patriots. Men may or may not expect an act of healing to take place at a holy well, but nobody expects it ten miles from the well; and even the sceptic who comes to expose the ghost-haunted churchyard has to haunt the churchyard like a ghost. There may be something faintly amusing about the idea of demi-gods with door-knockers and dinner tables, and demons, one may almost say, keeping the home fires burning. But the driving force of this dark mystery of locality is all the more indisputable because it drives against most modern theories and associations. The truth is that, upon a more transcendental consideration, we do not know what place is any more than we know what time is. We do not know of the unknown powers that they cannot concentrate in space as in time, or find in a spot something that corresponds to a crisis. And if this be felt everywhere, it is necessarily and abnormally felt in those alleged holy places and sacred spots. It is felt supremely in all those lands of the Near East which lie about the holy hill of Zion.

In these lands an impression grows steadily on the mind much too large for most of the recent religious or scientific definitions. The bogus heraldry of Haeckel is as obviously insufficient as any quaint old chronicle tracing the genealogies of English kings through the chiefs of Troy to the children of Noah. There is no difference, except that the tale of the Dark Ages can never be proved, while the travesty of the Darwinian theory can sometimes be disproved. But I should diminish my meaning if I suggested it as a mere score in the Victorian game of Scripture versus Science. Some much larger mystery veils the origins of man than most partisans on either side have realised; and in these strange primeval plains the traveller does realise it. It was never so well expressed as by one of the most promising of those whose literary possibilities were gloriously broken off by the great war; Lieutenant Warre-Cornish who left a strange and striking fragment, about a man who came to these lands with a mystical idea of forcing himself back against the stream of time into the very fountain of creation. This is a parenthesis; but before resuming the more immediate matter of the supernormal tricks of the tribes of the East, it is well to recognise this very real if much more general historic impression about the particular lands in which they lived. I have called it a historic impression; but it might more truly be called a prehistoric impression. It is best expressed in symbol by saying that the legendary site of the Garden of Eden is in Mesopotamia. It is equally well expressed in concrete experience by saying that, when I was in these parts, a learned man told me that the primitive form of wheat had just, for the first time, been discovered in Palestine.

The feeling that fills the traveller may be faintly suggested thus; that here, in this legendary land between Asia and Europe, may well have happened whatever did happen; that through this Eastern gate, if any, entered whatever made and changed the world. Whatever else this narrow strip of land may seem like, it does really seem, to the spirit and almost to the senses, like the bridge that may have borne across archaic abysses the burden and the mystery of man. Here have been civilisations as old as any barbarism; to all appearance perhaps older than any barbarism. Here is the camel; the enormous unnatural friend of man; the prehistoric pet. He is never known to have been wild, and might make a man fancy that all wild animals had once been tame. As I said elsewhere, all might be a runaway menagerie; the whale a cow that went swimming and never came back, the tiger a large cat that took the prize (and the prize-giver) and escaped to the jungle. This is not (I venture to think) true; but it is true as Pithecanthropus and Primitive Man and all the other random guesses from dubious bits of bone and stone. And the truth is some third thing, too tremendous to be remembered by men. Whatever it was, perhaps the camel saw it; but from the expression on the face of that old family servant, I feel sure that he will never tell.

I have called this the other side of the desert; and in another sense it is literally the other side. It is the other shore of that shifting and arid sea. Looking at it from the West and considering mainly the case of the Moslem, we feel the desert is but a barren border-land of Christendom; but seen from the other side it is the barrier between us and a heathendom far more mysterious and even monstrous than anything Moslem can be. Indeed it is necessary to realise this more vividly in order to feel the virtue of the Moslem movement. It belonged to the desert, but in one sense it was rather a clearance in the cloud that rests upon the desert; a rift of pale but clean light in volumes of vapour rolled on it like smoke from the strange lands beyond. It conceived a fixed hatred of idolatry, partly because its face was turned towards the multitudinous idolatries of the lands of sunrise; and as I looked Eastward I seemed to be conscious of the beginnings of that other world; and saw, like a forest of arms or a dream full of faces, the gods of Asia on their thousand thrones.

It is not a mere romance that calls it a land of magic, or even of black magic. Those who carry that atmosphere to us are not the romanticists but the realists. Every one can feel it in the work of Mr. Rudyard Kipling; and when I once remarked on his repulsive little masterpiece called "The Mark of the Beast," to a rather cynical Anglo-Indian officer, he observed moodily, "It's a beastly story. But those devils really can do jolly queer things." It is but to take a commonplace example out of countless more notable ones to mention the many witnesses to the mango trick. Here again we have from time to time to weep over the weak-mindedness that hurriedly dismisses it as the practice of hypnotism. It is as if people were asked to explain how one unarmed Indian had killed three hundred men, and they said it was only the practice of human sacrifice. Nothing that we know as hypnotism will enable a man to alter the eyes in the heads of a huge crowd of total strangers; wide awake in broad daylight; and if it is hypnotism, it is something so appallingly magnified as to need a new magic to explain the explanation; certainly something that explains it better than a Greek word for sleep. But the impression of these special instances is but one example of a more universal impression of the Asiatic atmosphere; and that atmosphere itself is only an example of something vaster still for which I am trying to find words. Asia stands for something which the world in the West as well as the East is more and more feeling as a presence, and even a pressure. It might be called the spiritual world let loose; or a sort of psychical anarchy; a jungle of mango plants. And it is pressing upon the West also to-day because of the breaking down of certain materialistic barriers that have hitherto held it back. In plain words the attitude of science is not only modified; it is now entirely reversed. I do not say it with mere pleasure; in some ways I prefer our materialism to their spiritualism. But for good or evil the scientists are now destroying their own scientific world.

The agnostics have been driven back on agnosticism; and are already recovering from the shock. They find themselves in a really unknown world under really unknown gods; a world which is more mystical, or at least more mysterious. For in the Victorian age the agnostics were not really agnostics. They might be better described as reverent materialists; or at any rate monists. They had at least at the back of their minds a clear and consistent concept of their rather clockwork cosmos; that is why they could not admit the smallest speck of the supernatural into their clockwork. But to-day it is very hard for a scientific man to say where the supernatural ends or the natural begins, or what name should be given to either. The word agnostic has ceased to be a polite word for atheist. It has become a real word for a very real state of mind, conscious of many possibilities beyond that of the atheist, and not excluding that of the polytheist. It is no longer a question of defining or denying a simple central power, but of balancing the brain in a bewilderment of new powers which seem to overlap and might even conflict. Nature herself has become unnatural. The wind is blowing from the other side of the desert, not now with noble truism "There is no God but God," but rather with that other motto out of the deeper anarchy of Asia, drawn out by Mr. Kipling, in the shape of a native proverb, in the very story already mentioned; "Your gods and my gods, do you or I know which is the stronger?" There was a mystical story I read somewhere in my boyhood, of which the only image that remains is that of a rose-bush growing mysteriously in the middle of a room. Taking this image for the sake of argument, we can easily fancy a man half-conscious and convinced that he is delirious, or still partly in a dream, because he sees such a magic bush growing irrationally in the middle of his bedroom. All the walls and furniture are familiar and solid, the table, the clock, the telephone, the looking glass or what not; there is nothing unnatural but this one hovering hallucination or optical delusion of green and red. Now that was very much the view taken of the Rose of Sharon, the mystical rose of the sacred tradition of Palestine, by any educated man about 1850, when the rationalism of the eighteenth century was supposed to have found full support in the science of the nineteenth. He had a sentiment about a rose: he was still glad it had fragrance or atmosphere; though he remembered with a slight discomfort that it had thorns. But what bothered him about it was that it was impossible. And what made him think it impossible was it was inconsistent with everything else. It was one solitary and monstrous exception to the sort of rule that ought to have no exceptions. Science did not convince him that there were few miracles, but that there were no miracles; and why should there be miracles only in Palestine and only for one short period? It was a single and senseless contra-diction to an otherwise complete cosmos. For the furniture fitted in bit by bit and better and better; and the bedroom seemed to grow more and more solid. The man recognised the portrait of himself over the mantelpiece or the medicine bottles on the table, like the dying lover in Browning. In other words, science so far had steadily solidified things; Newton had measured the walls and ceiling and made a calculus of their three dimensions. Darwin was already arranging the animals in rank as neatly as a row of chairs, or Faraday the chemical elements as clearly as a row of medicine bottles. From the middle of the eighteenth century to the middle of the nineteenth, science was not only making discoveries, but all the discoveries were in one direction. Science is still making discoveries; but they are in the opposite direction.

For things are rather different when the man in the bed next looks at the bedroom. Not only is the rose-bush still very obvious; but the other things are looking very odd. The perspective seems to have gone crooked; the walls seem to vary in measurement till the man thinks he is going mad. The wall-paper has a new pattern, of strange spirals instead of round dots. The table seems to have moved by itself across the room and thrown the medicine bottles out of the window. The telephone has vanished from the wall; the mirror does not reflect what is in front of it. The portrait of himself over the mantelpiece has a face that is not his own.

That is something like a vision of the vital change in the whole trend of natural philosophy in the last twenty or thirty years. It matters little whether we regard it as the deepening or the destruction of the scientific universe. It matters little whether we say that grander abysses have opened in it, or merely that the bottom has fallen out of it. It is quite self-evident that scientific men are at war with wilder and more unfathomable fancies than the facts of the age of Huxley. I attempt no controversy about any of the particular cases: it is the cumulative effect of all of them that makes the impression one of common sense. It is really true that the perspective and dimensions of the man's bedroom have altered; the disciples of Einstein will tell him that straight lines are curved and perhaps measure more one way than the other; if that is not a nightmare, what is? It is really true that the clock has altered, for time has turned into the fourth dimension or something entirely different; and the telephone may fairly be said to have faded from view in favour of the invisible telepath. It is true that the pattern of the paper has changed, for the very pattern of the world has changed; we are told that it is not made of atoms like the dots but of electrons like the spirals. Scientific men of the first rank have seen a table move by itself, and walk upstairs by itself. It does not matter here whether it was done by the spirits; it is enough that few still pretend that is entirely done by the spiritualists. I am not dealing with doctrines but with doubts; with the mere fact that all these things have grown deeper and more bewildering. Some people really are throwing their medicine bottles out of the window; and some of them at least are working purely psychological cures of a sort that would once have been called miraculous healing. I do not say we know how far this could go; it is my whole point that we do not know, that we are in contact with numbers of new things of which we know uncommonly little. But the vital point is, not that science deals with what we do not know, but that science is destroying what we thought we did know. Nearly all the latest discoveries have been destructive, not of the old dogmas of religion, but rather of the recent dogmas of science. The conservation of energy could not itself be entirely conserved. The atom was smashed to atoms. And dancing to the tune of Professor Einstein, even the law of gravity is behaving with lamentable levity.

And when the man looks at the portrait of himself he really does not see himself. He sees his Other Self, which some say is the opposite of his ordinary self; his Subconscious Self or his Subliminal Self, said to rage and rule in his dreams, or a suppressed self which hates him though it is hidden from him; or the Alter Ego of a Dual Personality. It is not to my present purpose to discuss the merit of these specu-lations, or whether they be medicinal or morbid. My purpose is served in pointing out the plain historical fact; that if you had talked to a Utilitarian and Rationalist of Bentham's time, who told men to follow "enlightened self-interest," he would have been considerably bewildered if you had replied brightly and briskly, "And to which self do you refer; the sub-conscious, the conscious, the latently criminal or suppressed, or others that we fortunately have in stock?" When the man looks at his own portrait in his own bedroom, it does really melt into the face of a stranger or flicker into the face of a fiend. When he looks at the bedroom itself, in short, it becomes clearer and clearer that it is exactly this comfortable and solid part of the vision that is altering and breaking up. It is the walls and furniture that are only a dream or memory. And when he looks again at the incongruous rose-bush, he seems to smell as well as see; and he stretches forth his hand, and his finger bleeds upon a thorn.

It will not be altogether surprising if the story ends with the man recovering full consciousness, and finding he has been convalescing in a hammock in a rose-garden. It is not so very unreasonable when you come to think of it; or at least when you come to think of the whole of it. He was not wrong in thinking the whole must be a consistent whole, and that one part seemed inconsistent with the other. He was only wrong about which part was wrong through being inconsistent with the other. Now the whole of the rationalistic doubt about the Palestinian legends, from its rise in the early eighteenth century out of the last movements of the Renascence, was founded on the fixity of facts. Miracles were monstrosities because they were against natural law, which was necessarily immutable law. The prodigies of the Old Testament or the mighty works of the New were extravagances because they were exceptions; and they were exceptions because there was a rule, and that an immutable rule. In short, there was no rose-tree growing out of the carpet of a trim and tidy bedroom; because rose-trees do not grow out of carpets in trim and tidy bedrooms. So far it seemed reasonable enough. But it left out one possibility; that a man can dream about a room as well as a rose; and that a man can doubt about a rule as well as an exception.

As soon as the men of science began to doubt the rules of the game, the game was up. They could no longer rule out all the old marvels as impossible, in face of the new marvels which they had to admit as possible. They were themselves dealing now with a number of unknown quantities; what is the power of mind over matter; when is matter an illusion of mind; what is identity, what is individuality, is there a limit to logic in the last extremes of mathematics? They knew by a hundred hints that their non-miraculous world was no longer watertight; that floods were coming in from somewhere in which they were already out of their depth, and down among very fantastical deep-sea fishes. They could hardly feel certain even about the fish that swallowed Jonah, when they had no test except the very true one that there are more fish in the sea than ever came out of it. Logically they would find it quite as hard to draw the line at the miraculous draught of fishes. I do not mean that they, or even I, need here depend on those particular stories; I mean that the difficulty now is to draw a line, and a new line, after the obliteration of an old and much more obvious line. Any one can draw it for himself, as a matter of mere taste in probability; but we have not made a philosophy until we can draw it for others. And the modern men of science cannot draw it for others. Men could easily mark the contrast between the force of gravity and the fable of the Ascension. They cannot all be made to see any such contrast between the levitation that is now discussed as a possibility and the ascension which is still derided as a miracle. I do not even say that there is not a great difference between them; I say that science is now plunged too deep in new doubts and possibilities to have authority to define the difference. I say the more it knows of what seems to have happened, or what is said to have happened, in many modern drawing-rooms, the less it knows what did or did not happen on that lofty and legendary hill, where a spire rises over Jerusalem and can be seen beyond Jordan.

But with that part of the Palestinian story which is told in the New Testament I am not directly concerned till the next chapter; and the matter here is a more general one. The truth is that through a thousand channels something has returned to the modern mind. It is not Christianity. On the contrary, it would be truer to say that it is paganism. In reality it is in a very special sense paganism; because it is polytheism. The word will startle many people, but not the people who know the modern world best. When I told a distinguished psychologist at Oxford that I differed from his view of the universe, he answered, "Why universe? Why should it not be a multiverse?" The essence of polytheism is the worship of gods who are not God; that is, who are not necessarily the author and the authority of all things. Men are feeling more and more that there are many spiritual forces in the universe, and the wisest men feel that some are to be trusted more than others. There will be a tendency, I think, to take a favourite force, or in other words a familiar spirit. Mr. H. G. Wells, who is, if anybody is, a genius among moderns and a modern among geniuses, really did this very thing; he selected a god who was really more like a daemon. He called his book *God, the Invisible King*; but the curious point was that he specially insisted that his God differed from other people's God in the very fact that he was not a king. He was very particular in explaining that his deity did not rule in any almighty or infinite sense; but merely influenced, like any wandering spirit. Nor was he particularly invisible, if there can be said to be any degrees in invisibility. Mr. Wells's Invisible God was really like Mr. Wells's Invisible Man. You almost felt he might appear at any moment, at any rate to his one devoted worshipper; and that, as if in old Greece, a glad cry might ring through the woods of Essex, the voice of Mr. Wells crying, "We have seen, he hath seen us, a visible God." I do not mean this disrespectfully, but on the contrary very sympatheti-cally; I think it worthy of so great a man to appreciate and answer the general sense of a richer and more adventurous spiritual world around us. It is a great emancipation from the leaden materialism which weighed on men of imagi-nation forty years ago. But my point for the moment is that the mode of the emancipation was pagan or even polytheistic, in the real philosophical sense that it was the selection of a single spirit, out of many there might be in the spiritual world. The point is that while Mr. Wells worships his god (who is not his creator or even necessarily his overlord) there is nothing to prevent Mr. William Archer, also emancipated, from adoring another god in another temple; or Mr. Arnold Bennett, should he similarly liberate his mind, from bowing down to a third god in a third temple. My imagination rather fails me, I confess, in evoking the image and symbolism of Mr. Bennett's or Mr. Archer's idolatries; and if I had to choose between the three, I should probably be found as an acolyte in the shrine of Mr. Wells. But, anyhow, the trend of all this is to polytheism, rather as it existed in the old civilisation of paganism.

There is the same modern mark in Spiritualism. Spiritualism also has the trend of polytheism, if it be in a form more akin to ancestor-worship. But whether it be the invocation of ghosts or of gods, the mark of it is that it invokes something less than the divine; nor am I at all quarrelling with it on that account. I am merely describing the drift of the day; and it seems clear that it is towards the summoning of spirits to our aid whatever their position in the unknown world, and without any clear doctrinal plan of that world. The most probable result would seem to be a multitude of psychic cults, personal and impersonal, from the vaguest reverence for the powers of nature to the most concrete appeal to crystals or mascots. When I say that the agnostics have discovered agnosticism, and have now recovered from the shock, I do not mean merely to sneer at the identity of the word agnosticism with the word ignorance. On the contrary, I think ignorance the greater thing; for ignorance can be creative. And the thing it can create, and soon probably will create, is one of the lost arts of the world; a mythology.

In a word, the modern world will probably end exactly where the Bible begins. In that inevitable setting of spirit against spirit, or god against god, we shall soon be in a position to do more justice not only to the New Testament, but to the Old Testament. Our descendants may very possibly do the very thing we scoff at the old Jews for doing; grope for and cling to their own deity as one rising above rivals who seem to be equally real. They also may feel him not primarily as the sole or even the supreme but only as the best; and have to abide the miracles of ages to prove that he is also the mightiest. For them also he may at first be felt as their own, before he is extended to others; he also, from the collision with colossal idolatries and towering spiritual tyrannies, may emerge only as a God of Battles and a Lord of Hosts. Here between the dark wastes and the clouded mountain was fought out what must seem even to the indifferent a wrestle of giants driving the world out of its course; Jehovah of the mountains casting down Baal of the desert and Dagon of the sea. Here wandered and endured that strange and terrible and tenacious people who held high above all their virtues and their vices one indestructible idea; that they were but the tools in that tremendous hand. Here was the first triumph of those who, in some sense beyond our understanding, had rightly chosen among the powers invisible, and found their choice a great god above all gods. So the future may suffer not from the loss but the multiplicity of faith; and its fate be far more like the cloudy and mythological war in the desert than like the dry radiance of theism or monism. I have said nothing here of my own faith, or of that name on which, I am well persuaded, the world will be most wise to call. But I do believe that the tradition founded in that far tribal battle, in that far Eastern land, did indeed justify itself by leading up to a lasting truth; and that it will once again be justified of all its children. What has survived through an age of atheism as the most indestructible would survive through an age of polytheism as the most indispensable. If among many gods it could not presently be proved to be the strongest, some would still know it was the best. Its central presence would endure through times of cloud and confusion, in which it was judged only as a myth among myths or a man among men. Even the old heathen test of humanity and the apparition of the body, touching which I have quoted the verse about the pagan polytheist as sung by the neo-pagan poet, is a test which that incarnate mystery will abide the best. And however much or little our spiritual inquirers may lift the veil from their invisible kings, they will not find a vision more vivid than a man walking unveiled upon the mountains, seen of men and seeing; a visible god.

CHAPTER IX

THE BATTLE WITH THE DRAGON

Lydda or Ludd has already been noted as the legendary birthplace of St. George, and as the camp on the edge of the desert from which, as it happened, I caught the first glimpse of the coloured fields of Palestine that looked like the fields of Paradise. Being an encampment of soldiers, it seems an appropriate place for St. George; and indeed it may be said that all that red and empty land has resounded with his name like a shield of copper or of bronze. The name was not even confined to the cries of the Christians; a curious imaginative hospitality in the Moslem mind, a certain innocent and imitative enthusiasm, made the Moslems also half-accept a sort of Christian mythology, and make an abstract hero of St. George. It is said that Coeur de Lion on these very sands first invoked the soldier saint to bless the English battle-line, and blazon his cross on the English banners. But the name occurs not only in the stories of the victory of Richard, but in the enemy stories that led up to the great victory of Saladin. In that obscure and violent quarrel which let loose the disaster of Hattin, when the Grand Master of the Templars, Gerard the Englishman from Bideford in Devon, drove with demented heroism his few lances against a host, there fell among those radiant fanatics one Christian warrior, who had made with his single sword such a circle of the slain, that the victorious Moslems treated even his dead body as something supernatural; and bore it away with them with honour, saying it was the body of St. George.

G. K. CHESTERTON

But if the purpose of the camp be appropriate to the story of St. George, the position of the camp might be considered appropriate to the more fantastic story of St. George and the Dragon. The symbolic struggle between man and monster might very well take place somewhere where the green culture of the fields meets the red desolation of the desert. As a matter of fact, I dare say, legend locates the duel itself somewhere else, but I am only making use of the legend as a legend, or even as a convenient figure of speech. I would only use it here to make a kind of picture which may clarify a kind of paradox, very vital to our present attitude towards all Palestinian traditions, including those that are more sacred even than St. George. This paradox has already been touched on in the last chapter about polytheistic spirits or superstitions such as surrounded the Old Testament, but it is yet more true of the criticisms and apologetics surrounding the New Testament. And the paradox is this; that we never find our own religion so right as when we find we are wrong about it. I mean that we are finally convinced not by the sort of evidence we are looking for, but by the sort of evidence we are not looking for. We are convinced when we come on a ratification that is almost as abrupt as a refutation. That is the point about the wireless telegraphy or wordless telepathy of the Bedouins. A supernatural trick in a dingy tribe wandering in dry places is not the sort of supernaturalism we should expect to find; it is only the sort that we do find. These rocks of the desert, like the bones of a buried giant, do not seem to stick out where they ought to, but they stick out, and we fall over them.

Whatever we think of St. George, most people would see a mere fairy-tale in St. George and the Dragon. I dare say they are right; and I only use it here as a figure for the sake of argument. But suppose, for the sake of argument, that a man has come to the conclusion that there probably was such a person as St. George, in spite of all the nonsense about dragons and the chimera with wings and claws that has somehow interwreathed itself with his image. Perhaps he is a little biased by patriotism or other ethical aims; and thinks the saint a good social ideal. Perhaps he knows that early Christianity, so far from being a religion of pacifists, was largely a religion of soldiers. Anyhow he thinks St. George himself a quite sufficiently solid and historical figure; and has little doubt that records or traces can be found of him. Now the point is this; suppose that man goes to the land of the legendary combat; and finds comparatively few or faint traces of the personality of St. George. But suppose he *does* find, on that very field of combat, the bones of a gigantic monster unlike every other creature except the legendary dragon. Or suppose he only finds ancient Eastern sculptures and hieroglyphics representing maidens, being sacrificed to such a monster, and making it quite clear that even within historic times one of those sacrificed was a princess. It is surely clear that he will be considerably impressed by this confirmation, not of the part he did believe, but actually of the part he did not believe. He has not found what he expected but he has found what he wanted, and much more than he wanted. He has not found a single detail directly in support of St. George. But he had found a very considerable support of St. George and the Dragon.

It is needless to inform the reader, I trust, that I do not think this particular case in the least likely; or that I am only using it for the sake of lucidity. Even as it stands, it would not necessarily make a man believe the traditional story, but it would make him guess that it was some sort of tradition of some sort of truth; that there was something in it, and much more in it than even he himself had imagined. And the point of it would be precisely that his reason had not anticipated the extent of his revelation. He has proved the improbable, not the probable thing. Reason had already taught him the reasonable part; but facts had taught him the fantastic part. He will certainly conclude that the whole story is very much more valid than anybody has supposed.

G. K. CHESTERTON

Now as I have already said, it is not in the least likely that this will happen touching this particular tale of Palestine. But this is precisely what really has happened touching the most sacred and tremendous of all the tales of Palestine. This is precisely what has happened touching that central figure, round which the monster and the champion are alike only ornamental symbols; and by the right of whose tragedy even St. George's Cross does not belong to St. George. It is not likely to be true of the desert duel between George and the Dragon; but it is already true of the desert duel between Jesus and the Devil. St. George is but a servant and the Dragon is but a symbol, but it is precisely about the central reality, the mystery of Christ and His mastery of the powers of darkness, that this very paradox has proved itself a fact.

Going down from Jerusalem to Jericho I was more than once moved by a flippant and possibly profane memory of the swine that rushed down a steep place into the sea. I do not insist on the personal parallel; for whatever my points of resemblance to a pig I am not a flying pig, a pig with wings of speed and precipitancy; and if I am possessed of a devil, it is not the blue devil of suicide. But the phrase came back into my mind because going down to the Dead Sea does really involve rushing down a steep place. Indeed it gives a strange impression that the whole of Palestine is one single steep place. It is as if all other countries lay flat under the sky, but this one country had been tilted sideways. This gigantic gesture of geography or geology, this sweep as of a universal landslide, is the sort of thing that is never conveyed by any maps or books or even pictures. All the pictures of Palestine I have seen are descriptive details, groups of costume or corners of architecture, at most views of famous places; they cannot give the bottomless vision of this long descent. We went in a little rocking Ford car down steep and jagged roads among ribbed and columned cliffs; but the roads below soon failed us altogether; and the car had to tumble like a tank over rocky banks and into empty river-beds, long before it came to the sinister and discoloured landscapes of the Dead Sea. And the distance looks far enough on the map, and seems long enough in the motor journey, to make a man feel he has come to another part of the world; yet so much is it all a single fall of land that even when he gets out beyond Jordan in the wild country of the Shereef he can still look back and see, small and faint as if in the clouds, the spire of the Russian church (I fancy) upon the hill of the Ascension. And though the story of the swine is attached in truth to another place, I was still haunted with its fanciful appropriateness to this one, because of the very steepness of this larger slope and the mystery of that larger sea. I even had the fancy that one might fish for them and find them in such a sea, turned into monsters; sea-swine or four-legged fishes, swollen and with evil eyes, grown over with sea-grass for bristles; the ghosts of Gadara.

And then it came back to me, as a curiosity and almost a coincidence, that the same strange story had actually been selected as the text for the central controversy of the Victorian Age between Christianity and criticism. The two champions were two of the greatest men of the nineteenth century; Huxley representing scientific scepticism and Gladstone scriptural orthodoxy. The scriptural champion was universally regarded as standing for the past, if not for the dead past; and the scientific champion as standing for the future, if not the final judgment of the world. And yet the future has been entirely different to anything that anybody expected; and the final judgment may yet reverse all the conceptions of their contemporaries and even of themselves. The philosophical position now is in a very curious way the contrary of the position then. Gladstone had the worst of the argument, and has been proved right. Huxley had the best of the argument, and has been proved wrong. At any rate he has been ultimately proved wrong about the way the world was going, and the probable position of the next generation. What he thought indisputable is disputed; and what he thought dead is rather too much alive.

Huxley was not only a man of genius in logic and rhetoric; he was a man of a very manly and generous morality. Morally he deserves much more sympathy than many of the mystics who have supplanted him. But they have supplanted him. In the more mental fashions of the day, most of what he thought would stand has fallen, and most of what he thought would fall is standing yet. In the Gadarene controversy with Gladstone, he announced it as his purpose to purge the Christian ideal, which he thought self-evidently sublime, of the Christian demonology, which he thought self-evidently ridiculous. And yet if we take any typical man of the next generation, we shall very probably find Huxley's sublime thing scoffed at, and Huxley's ridiculous thing taken seriously. I imagine a very typical child of the age succeeding Huxley's may be found in Mr. George Moore. He has one of the most critical, appreciative and atmospheric talents of the age. He has lived in most of the sets of the age, and through most of the fashions of the age. He has held, at one time or another, most of the opinions of the age. Above all, he has not only thought for himself, but done it with peculiar pomp and pride; he would consider himself the freest of all freethinkers. Let us take him as a type and a test of what has really happened to Huxley's analysis of the gold and the dross. Huxley quoted as the indestructible ideal the noble passage in Micah, beginning "He hath shewed thee, O man, that which is good"; and asked scornfully whether anybody was ever likely to suggest that justice was worthless or that mercy was unlovable, and whether anything would diminish the distance between ourselves and the ideals that we reverence. And yet already, perhaps, Mr. George Moore was anticipating Nietzsche, sailing near, as he said, "the sunken rocks about the cave of Zarathustra." He said, if I remember right, that Cromwell should be admired for his injustice. He implied that Christ should be condemned, not because he destroyed the swine, but because he delivered the sick. In short he found justice quite worthless and mercy quite unlovable; and as for humility and the distance between himself and his ideals, he seemed rather to suggest (at this time at least) that his somewhat varying ideals were only interesting because they had belonged to himself. Some of this, it is true, was only in the *Confessions of a Young Man*; but it is the whole point here that they were then the confessions of a young man, and that Huxley's in comparison were the confessions of an old man. The trend of the new time, in very varying degrees, was tending to undermine, not merely the Christian demonology, not merely the Christian theology, not merely the Christian religion, but definitely the Christian ethical ideal, which had seemed to the great agnostic as secure as the stars.

But while the world was mocking the morality he had assumed, it was bringing back the mysticism he had mocked. The next phase of Mr. George Moore himself, whom I have taken as a type of the time, was the serious and sympathetic consideration of Irish mysticism, as embodied in Mr. W. B. Yeats. I have myself heard Mr. Yeats, about that time, tell a story, to illustrate how concrete and even comic is the reality of the supernatural, saying that he knew a farmer whom the fairies had dragged out of bed and beaten. Now suppose Mr. Yeats had told Mr. Moore, then moving in this glamorous atmosphere, another story of the same sort. Suppose he had said that the farmer's pigs had fallen under the displeasure of some magician of the sort he celebrates, who had conjured bad fairies into the quadrupeds, so that they went in a wild dance down to the village pond. Would Mr. Moore have thought that story any more incredible than the other? Would he have thought it worse than a thousand other things that a modern mystic may lawfully believe? Would he have risen to his feet and told Mr. Yeats that all was over between them? Not a bit of it. He would at least have listened with a serious, nay, a solemn face. He would think it a grim little grotesque of rustic diablerie, a quaint tale of goblins, neither less nor more improbable than hundreds of psychic fantasies or farces for which there is really a good deal of evidence. He would be ready to entertain the idea if he found it anywhere except in the New Testament. As for the more vulgar and universal fashions that have followed after the Celtic movement, they have left such trifles far behind. And they have been directed not by imaginative artists like Mr. Yeats or even Mr. Moore, but by solid scientific students like Sir William Crookes and Sir Arthur Conan Doyle. I find it easier to imagine an evil spirit agitating the legs of a pig than a good spirit agitating the legs of a table. But I will not here enter into the argument, since I am only trying to describe the atmosphere. Whatever has happened in more recent years, what Huxley expected has certainly not happened. There has been a revolt against Christian morality, and where there has not been a return of Christian mysticism, it has been a return of the mysticism without the Christianity. Mysticism itself has returned, with all its moons and twilights, its talismans and spells. Mysticism itself has returned, and brought with it seven devils worse than itself.

But the scientific coincidence is even more strict and close. It affects not only the general question of miracles, but the particular question of possession. This is the very last element in the Christian story that would ever have been selected by the enlightened Christian apologist. Gladstone would defend it, but he would not go out of his way to dwell on it. It is an excellent working model of what I mean by finding an unexpected support, and finding it in an unexpected quarter. It is not theological but psychological study that has brought us back into this dark underworld of the soul, where even identity seems to dissolve or divide, and men are not even themselves. I do not say that psychologists admit the discovery of demoniacs; and if they did they would doubtless call them something else, such as demono-maniacs. But they admit things which seem almost as near to a new supernaturalism, and things quite as incredible to the old rationalism. Dual personality is not so very far from diabolic possession. And if the dogma of subconsciousness allows of agnosticism, the agnosticism cuts both ways. A man cannot say there is a part of him of which he is quite unconscious, and only conscious that it is not in contact with the unknown. He cannot say there is a sealed chamber or cellar under his house, of which he knows nothing whatever; but that he is quite certain that it cannot have an underground passage leading anywhere else in the world. He cannot say he knows nothing whatever about its size or shape or appearance, except that it certainly does not contain a relic of the finger-joint of St. Catherine of Alexandria, or that it certainly is not haunted by the ghost of King Herod Agrippa. If there is any sort of legend or tradition or plausible probability which says that it is, he cannot call a thing impossible where he is not only ignorant but even unconscious. It comes back therefore to the same reality, that the old compact cosmos depended on a compact consciousness. If we are dealing with unknown quantities, we cannot deny their connection with other unknown quantities. If I have a self of which I can say nothing, how can I even say that it is my own self? How can I even say that I always had it, or that it did not come from somewhere else? It is clear that we are in very deep waters, whether or no we have rushed down a steep place to fall into them.

It will be noted that what we really lack here is not the supernatural but only the healthy supernatural. It is not the miracle, but only the miracle of healing. I warmly sympathise with those who think most of this rather morbid, and nearer the diabolic than the divine, but to call a thing diabolic is hardly an argument against the existence of diabolism. It is still more clearly the case when we go outside the sphere of science into its penumbra in literature and conversation. There is a mass of fiction and fashionable talk of which it may truly be said, that what we miss in it is not demons but the power to cast them out. It combines the occult with the obscene; the sensuality of materialism with the insanity of spiritualism. In the story of Gadara we have left out nothing except the Redeemer, we have kept the devils and the swine.

In other words, we have not found St. George; but we have found the Dragon. We have found in the desert, as I have said, the bones of the monster we did not believe in, more plainly than the footprints of the hero we did. We have found them not because we expected to find them, for our progressive minds look to the promise of something much brighter and even better; not because we wanted to find them, for our modern mood, as well as our human nature, is entirely in favour of more amiable and reassuring things; not because we thought it even possible to find them, for we really thought it impossible so far as we ever thought of it at all. We have found them because they are *there*; and we are bound to come on them even by falling over them. It is Huxley's method that has upset Huxley's conclusion. As I have said, that conclusion itself is completely reversed. What he thought indisputable is disputed; and what he thought impossible is possible. Instead of Christian morals surviving in the form of humanitarian morals, Christian demonology has survived in the form of heathen demonology. But it has not survived by scholarly traditionalism in the style of Gladstone, but rather by obstinate objective curiosity according to the advice of Huxley. We in the West have "followed our reason as far as it would go," and our reason has led us to things that nearly all the rationalists would have thought wildly irrational. Science was supposed to bully us into being rationalists; but it is now supposed to be bullying us into being irrationalists. The science of Einstein might rather be called following our unreason as far as it will go, seeing whether the brain will crack under the conception that space is curved, or that parallel straight lines always meet. And the science of Freud would make it essentially impossible to say how far our reason or unreason does go, or where it stops. For if a man is ignorant of his other self, how can he possibly know that the other self is ignorant? He can no longer say with pride that at least he knows that he knows nothing. That is exactly what he does not know. The floor has fallen out of his mind and the abyss below may contain subconscious certainties as well as subconscious doubts. He is too ignorant even to ignore; and he must confess himself an agnostic about whether he is an agnostic.

That is the coil or tangle, at least, which the dragon has reached even in the scientific regions of the West. I only describe the tangle; I do not delight in it. Like most people with a taste for Catholic tradition, I am too much of a rationalist for that; for Catholics are almost the only people now defending reason. But I am not talking of the true relations of reason and mystery, but of the historical fact that mystery has invaded the peculiar realms of reason; especially the European realms of the motor and the telephone. When we have a man like Mr. William Archer, lecturing mystically on dreams and psychoanalysis, and saying it is clear that God did not make man a reasonable creature, those acquainted with the traditions and distinguished record of that dry and capable Scot will consider the fact a prodigy. I confess it never occurred to me that Mr. Archer was of such stuff as dreams are made of; and if he is becoming a mystic in his old age (I use the phrase in a mystical and merely relative sense) we may take it that the occult oriental flood is rising fast, and reaching places that are not only high but dry. But the change is much more apparent to a man who has chanced to stray into those orient hills where those occult streams have always risen, and especially in this land that lies between Asia, where the occult is almost the obvious, and Europe, where it is always returning with a fresher and younger vigour. The truth becomes strangely luminous in this wilderness between two worlds, where the rocks stand out stark like the very bones of the Dragon.

As I went down that sloping wall or shoulder of the world from the Holy City on the mountain to the buried Cities of the Plain, I seemed to see more and more clearly all this Western evolution of Eastern mystery, and how on this one high place, as on a pivot, the whole purpose of mankind had swerved. I took up again the train of thought which I had trailed through the desert, as described in the last chapter, about the gods of Asia and of the ancient dispensation, and I found it led me along these hills to a sort of vista or vision of the new dispensation and of Christendom. Considered objectively, and from the outside, the story is something such as has already been loosely outlined; the emergence in this immemorial and mysterious land of what was undoubtedly, when thus considered, one tribe among many tribes worshipping one god among many gods, but it is quite as much an evident external fact that the god has become God. Still stated objectively, the story is that the tribe having this religion produced a new prophet, claiming to be more than a prophet. The old religion killed the new prophet; but the new prophet killed the old religion. He died to destroy it, and it died in destroying him. Now it may be reaffirmed equally realistically that there was nothing normal about the case or its consequences. The things that took part in that tragedy have never been the same since, and have never been like anything else in the world. The Church is not like other religions; its very crimes were unique. The Jews are not like other races; they remain as unique to everybody else as they are to themselves. The Roman Empire did not pass like other empires; it did not perish like Babylon and Assyria. It went through a most extraordinary remorse amounting to madness and resuscitation into sanity, which is equally strange in history whether it seems as ghastly as a galvanised corpse or as glorious as a god risen from the dead. The very land and city are not like other lands and cities. The concentration and conflict in Jerusalem to-day, whether we regard them as a reconquest by Christendom or a conspiracy of Jews or a part of the lingering quarrel with Moslems, are alike the effect of forces gathered and loosened in that one mysterious moment in the history of the city. They equally proclaim the paradox of its insignificance and its importance.

But above all the prophet was not and is not like other prophets; and the proof of it is to be found not primarily among those who believe in him, but among those who do not. He is not dead, even where he is denied. What is the use of a modern man saying that Christ is only a thing like Atys or Mithras, when the next moment he is reproaching Christianity for not following Christ? He does not suddenly lose his temper and talk about our most unmithraic conduct, as he does (very justly as a rule) about our most unchristian conduct. We do not find a group of ardent young agnostics, in the middle of a great war, tried as traitors for their extravagant interpretation of remarks attributed to Atys. It is improbable that Tolstoy wrote a book to prove that all modern ills could be cured by literal obedience to all the orders of Adonis. We do not find wild Bolshevists calling themselves Mithraic Socialists as many of them call themselves Christian Socialists. Leaving orthodoxy and even sanity entirely on one side, the very heresies and insanities of our time prove that after nearly two thousand years the issue is still living and the name is quite literally one to conjure with. Let the critics try to conjure with any of the other names. In the real centres of modern inquiry and mental activity, they will not move even a mystic with the name of Mithras as they will move a materialist with the name of Jesus. There are men who deny God and accept Christ.

But this lingering yet living power in the legend, even for those to whom it is little more than a legend, has another relevancy to the particular point here. Jesus of Nazareth, merely humanly considered, has thus become a hero of humanitarianism. Even the eighteenth-century deists in denying his divinity generally took pains to exalt his humanity. Of the nineteenth-century revolutionists it is really an understatement to say that they exalted him as a man; for indeed they rather exalted him as a superman. That is to say, many of them represented him as a man preaching a decisively superior and ever strange morality, not only in advance of his age but practically in advance of our age. They made of his mystical counsels of perfection a sort of Socialism or Pacifism or Communism, which they themselves still see rather as something that ought to be or that will be; the extreme limit of universal love. I am not discussing here whether they are right or not; I say they have in fact found in the same figure a type of humanitarianism and the care for human happiness. Every one knows the striking and sometimes staggering utterances that do really support and illustrate this side of the teaching. Modern idealists are naturally moved by such things as the intensely poetic paradox about the lilies of the field; which for them has a joy in life and living things like that of Shelley or Whitman, combined with a return to simplicity beyond that of Tolstoy or Thoreau. Indeed I rather wonder that those, whose merely historic or humanistic view of the case would allow of such criticism without incongruity, have not made some study of the purely poetical or oratorical structure of such passages. Certainly there are few finer examples of the swift architecture of style than that single fragment about the flowers; the almost idle opening of a chance reference to a wild flower, the sudden unfolding of the small purple blossom into pavilions and palaces and the great name of the national history; and then with a turn of the hand like a gesture of scorn, the change to the grass that to-day is and to-morrow is cast into the oven. Then follows, as so often in the Gospels, the "how much more" which is like a celestial flight of stairs, a ladder of imaginative logic. Indeed this *a fortiori*, and this power of thinking on three levels, is (I may remark incidentally) a thing very much needed in modern discussion. Many minds apparently cannot stretch to three dimensions, or to thinking that a cube can go beyond a surface as a surface goes beyond a line; for instance, that the citizen is infinitely above all ranks, and yet the soul is infinitely above the citizen. But we are only concerned at the moment with the sides of this many-sided mystery which happen to be really in sympathy with the modern mood. Judged even by our modern tests of emancipated art or ideal economics, it is admitted that Christ understood all that is rather crudely embodied in Socialism or the Simple Life. I purposely insist first on this optimistic, I might almost say this pantheistic or even this pagan aspect of the Christian Gospels. For it is only when we understand that Christ, considered merely as a prophet, can be and is a popular leader in the love of natural things, that we can feel that tremendous and tragic energy of his testimony to an ugly reality, the existence of unnatural things. Instead of taking a text as I have done, take a whole Gospel and read it steadily and honestly and straight through at a sitting, and you will certainly have one impression, whether of a myth or of a man. It is that the exorcist towers above the poet and even the prophet; that the story between Cana and Calvary is one long war with demons. He understood better than a hundred poets the beauty of the flowers of the battle-field; but he came out to battle. And if most of his words mean anything they do mean that there is at our very feet, like a chasm concealed among the flowers, an unfathomable evil.

In short, I would here only hint delicately that perhaps the mind which admittedly knew much of what we think we know about ethics and economics, knew a little more than we are beginning to know about psychology and psychic phenomena. I remember reading, not without amusement, a severe and trenchant article in the *Hibbert Journal,* in which Christ's admission of demonology was alone thought enough to dispose of his divinity. The one sentence of the article, which I cherish in my memory through all the changing years, ran thus: "If he was God, he knew there was no such thing as diabolical possession." It did not seem to strike the *Hibbert* critic that this line of criticism raises the question, not of whether Christ is God, but of whether the critic in the *Hibbert Journal* is God. About that mystery as about the other I am for the moment agnostic; but I should have thought that the meditations of Omniscience on the problem of evil might be allowed, even by an agnostic, to be a little difficult to discover. Of Christ in the Gospels and in modern life I will merely for the moment say this; that if he was God, as the critic put it, it seems possible that he knew the next discovery in science, as well as the last, not to mention (what is more common in rationalistic culture) the last but three. And what will be the next discovery in psychological science nobody can imagine; and we can only say that if it reveals demons and their name is Legion, we can hardly be much surprised now. But at any rate the days are over of Omniscience like that of the *Hibbert* critic, who knows exactly what he would know if he were God Almighty. What is pain? What is evil? What did they mean by devils? What do we mean by madness? The rising generation, when asked by a venerable Victorian critic and catechist, "What does God know?" will hardly think it unreasonably flippant to answer, "God knows."

There was something already suggested about the steep scenery through which I went as I thought about these things; a sense of silent catastrophe and fundamental cleavage in the deep division of the cliffs and crags. They were all the more profoundly moving, because my sense of them was almost as subconscious as the subconsciousness about which I was reflecting. I had fallen again into the old habit of forgetting where I was going, and seeing things with one eye off, in a blind abstraction. I awoke from a sort of trance of absentmindedness in a landscape that might well awaken anybody. It might awaken a man sleeping; but he would think he was still in a nightmare. It might wake the dead, but they would probably think they were in hell. Halfway down the slope the hills had taken on a certain pallor which had about it something primitive, as if the colours were not yet created. There was only a kind of cold and wan blue in the level skies which contrasted with wild sky-line. Perhaps we are accustomed to the contrary condition of the clouds moving and mutable and the hills solid and serene; but anyhow there seemed something of the making of a new world about the quiet of the skies and the cold convulsion of the landscape. But if it was between chaos and creation, it was creation by God or at least by the gods, something with an aim in its anarchy. It was very different in the final stage of the descent, where my mind woke up from its meditations. One can only say that the whole landscape was like a leper. It was of a wasting white and silver and grey, with mere dots of decadent vegetation like the green spots of a plague. In shape it not only rose into horns and crests like waves or clouds, but I believe it actually alters like waves or clouds, visibly but with a loathsome slowness. The swamp is alive. And I found again a certain advantage in forgetfulness; for I saw all this incredible country before I even remembered its name, or the ancient tradition about its nature. Then even the green plague-spots failed, and everything seemed to fall away into a universal blank under the staring sun, as I came, in the great spaces of the circle of a lifeless sea, into the silence of Sodom and Gomorrah.

For these are the foundations of a fallen world, and a sea below the seas on which men sail. Seas move like clouds and fishes float like birds above the level of the sunken land. And it is here that tradition has laid the tragedy of the mighty perversion of the imagination of man; the monstrous birth and death of abominable things. I say such things in no mood of spiritual pride; such things are hideous not because they are distant but because they are near to us; in all our brains, certainly in mine, were buried things as bad as any buried under that bitter sea, and if He

G. K. CHESTERTON

did not come to do battle with them, even in the darkness of the brain of man, I know not why He came. Certainly it was not only to talk about flowers or to talk about Socialism. The more truly we can see life as a fairy-tale, the more clearly the tale resolves itself into war with the Dragon who is wasting fairyland. I will not enter on the theology behind the symbol; but I am sure it was of this that all the symbols were symbolic. I remember distinguished men among the liberal theologians, who found it more difficult to believe in one devil than in many. They admitted in the New Testament an attestation to evil spirits, but not to a general enemy of mankind. As some are said to want the drama of Hamlet without the Prince of Denmark, they would have the drama of Hell without the Prince of Darkness. I say nothing of these things, save that the language of the Gospel seems to me to go much more singly to a single issue. The voice that is heard there has such authority as speaks to an army; and the highest note of it is victory rather than peace. When the apostles were first sent forth with their faces to the four corners of the earth, and turned again to acclaim their master, he did not say in that hour of triumph, "All are aspects of one harmonious whole" or "The universe evolves through progress to perfection" or "All things find their end in Nirvana" or "The dewdrop slips into the shining sea." He looked up and said, "I saw Satan fall like lightning from heaven."

Then I looked up and saw in the long jagged lines of road and rock and cleft something of the swiftness of such a thunderbolt. What I saw seemed not so much a scene as an act; as when abruptly Michael barred the passage of the Lord of Pride. Below me all the empire of evil was splashed and scattered upon the plain, like a wine-cup shattered into a star. Sodom lay like Satan, flat upon the floor of the world. And far away and aloft, faint with height and distance, small but still visible, stood up the spire of the Ascension like the sword of the Archangel, lifted in salute after a stroke.

CHAPTER X

THE ENDLESS EMPIRE

One of the adventures of travel consists, not so much in finding that popular sayings are false, as that they mean more than they say. We cannot appreciate the full force of the phrase until we have seen the fact. We make a picture of the things we do not know out of the things we know; and suppose the traveller's tale to mean no more abroad than it would at home. If a man acquainted only with English churches is told about certain French churches that they are much frequented, he makes an English picture. He imagines a definite dense crowd of people in their best clothes going all together at eleven o'clock, and all coming back together to lunch. He does not picture the peculiar impression he would gain on the spot; of chance people going in and out of the church all day, sometimes for quite short periods, as if it were a sort of sacred inn. Or suppose a man knowing only English beer-shops hears for the first time of a German beer-garden, he probably does not imagine the slow ritual of the place. He does not know that unless the drinker positively slams down the top of his beer-mug with a resounding noise and a decisive gesture, beer will go on flowing into it as from a natural fountain; the drinking of beer being regarded as the normal state of man, and the cessation of it a decisive and even dramatic departure. I do not give this example in contempt; heaven forbid. I have had so much to say of the inhuman side of Prussianised Germany that I am glad to be able to pay a passing tribute to those more generous German traditions which we hope may revive and make Germany once more a part of Christendom. I merely give it as an instance of the way in which things we have all heard of, like church-going or beer-drinking, in foreign lands, mean much more, and something much more special, than we should infer from our own land. Now this is true of a phrase we have all heard of deserted cities or temples in the Near East: "The Bedouins camp in the ruins." When I have read a hundred times that Arabs camp in some deserted town or temple near the Nile or the Euphrates, I always thought of gipsies near some place like Stonehenge. They would make their own rude shelter near the stones, perhaps sheltering behind them to light a fire; and for the rest, generations of gipsies might camp there without making much difference. The thing I saw more than once in Egypt and Palestine was much more curious. It was as if the gipsies set to work to refurnish Stonehenge and make it a commodious residence. It was as if they spread a sort of giant umbrella over the circle of stones, and elaborately hung curtains between them, so as to turn the old Druid temple into a sort of patchwork pavilion. In one sense there is much more vandalism, and in another sense much more practicality; but it is a practicality that always stops short of the true creative independence of going off and building a house of their own. That is the attitude of the Arab; and it runs through all his history. Noble as is his masterpiece of the Mosque of Omar, there is something about it of that patchwork pavilion. It was based on Christian work, it was built with fragments, it was content with things that fastidious architects call fictions or even shams.

I frequently saw old ruined houses of which there only remained two walls of stone, to which the nomads had added two walls of canvas making an exact cube in form with the most startling incongruity in colour. He needs the form and he does not mind the incongruity, nor does he mind the fact that somebody else has done the solid part and he has only done the ramshackle part. You can say that he is nobly superior to jealousy, or that he is without artistic ambition, or that he is too much of a nomad to mind living half in somebody else's house and half in his own. The real quality is probably too subtle for any simple praise or blame; we can only say that there is in the wandering Moslem a curious kind of limited common sense; which might even be called a short-sighted common sense. But however we define it, that is what can really be traced through Arab conquests and Arab culture in all its ingenuity and insufficiency. That is the note of these nomads in all the things in which they have succeeded and failed. In that sense they are constructive and in that sense unconstructive; in that sense artistic and in that sense inartistic; in that sense practical and in that sense unpractical; in that sense cunning and in that sense innocent. The curtains they would hang round Stonehenge might be of beautifully selected colours. The banners they waved from Stonehenge might be defended with glorious courage and enthusiasm. The prayers they recited in Stonehenge might be essentially worthy of human dignity, and certainly a great improvement on its older associations of human sacrifice. All this is true of Islam and the idolatries and negations are often replaced. But they would not have built Stonehenge; they would scarcely, so to speak, have troubled to lift a stone of Stonehenge. They would not have built Stonehenge; how much less Salisbury or Glastonbury or Lincoln.

That is the element about the Arab influence which makes it, after its ages of supremacy and in a sense of success, remain in a subtle manner superficial. When a man first sees the Eastern deserts, he sees this influence as I first described it, very present and powerful, almost omnipresent and omnipotent. But I fancy that to me and to others it is partly striking only because it is strange. Islam is so different to Christendom that to see it at all is at first like entering a new world. But, in my own case at any rate, as the strange colours became more customary, and especially as I saw more of the established seats of history, the cities and the framework of the different states, I became conscious of something else. It was something underneath, undestroyed and even in a sense unaltered. It was something neither Moslem nor modern; not merely oriental and yet very different from the new occidental nations from which I came. For a long time I could not put a name to this historical atmosphere. Then one day, standing in one of the Greek churches, one of those houses of gold full of hard highly coloured pictures, I fancied it came to me. It was the Empire. And certainly not the raid of Asiatic bandits we call the Turkish Empire. The thing which had caught my eye in that coloured interior was the carving of a two-headed eagle in such a position as to make it almost as symbolic as a cross. Every one has heard, of course, of the situation which this might well suggest, the suggestion that the Russian Church was far too much of an Established Church and the White Czar encroached upon the White Christ. But as a fact the eagle I saw was not borrowed from the Russian Empire; it would be truer to say that the Empire was borrowed from the eagle. The double eagle is the ancient emblem of the double empire of Rome and of Byzantium; the one head looking to the west and the other to the east, as if it spread its wings from the sunrise to the sunset. Unless I am mistaken, it was only associated with Russia as late as Peter the Great, though it had been the badge of Austria as the representative of the Holy Roman Empire. And what I felt brooding over that shrine and that landscape was something older not only than Turkey or Russia but than Austria itself. I began to understand a sort of evening light that lies over Palestine and Syria; a sense of smooth ruts of custom such as are said to give a dignity to the civilisation of China. I even understood a sort of sleepiness about the splendid and handsome Orthodox priests moving fully robed about the streets. They were not aristocrats but officials; still moving with the mighty routine of some far-off official system. In so far as the eagle was an emblem not of such imperial peace but of distant imperial wars, it was of wars that we in the West have hardly heard of; it was the emblem of official ovations.

When Heracleius rode homewards from the rout of Ispahan
With the captives dragged behind him and the eagles in the van.

That is the rigid reality that still underlay the light mastery of the Arab rider; that is what a man sees, in the patchwork pavilion, when he grows used to the coloured canvas and looks at the walls of stone. This also was far too great a thing for facile praise or blame, a vast bureaucracy busy and yet intensely dignified, the most civilised thing ruling many other civilisations. It was an endless end of the world; for ever repeating its rich finality. And I myself was still walking in that long evening of the earth; and Caesar my lord was at Byzantium.

But it is necessary to remember next that this empire was not always at its evening. Byzantium was not always Byzantine. Nor was the seat of that power always in the city of Constantine, which was primarily a mere outpost of the city of Caesar. We must remember Rome as well as Byzantium; as indeed nobody would remember Byzantium if it were not for Rome. The more I saw of a hundred little things the more my mind revolved round that original idea which may be called the Mediterranean; and the fact that it became two empires, but remained one civilisation, just as it has become two churches, but remained one religion.

In this little world there is a story attached to every word; and never more than when it is the wrong word. For instance, we may say that in certain cases the word Roman actually means Greek. The Greek Patriarch is sometimes called the Roman Patriarch; while the real Roman Patriarch, who actually comes from Rome, is only called the Latin Patriarch, as if he came from any little town in

Latium. The truth behind this confusion is the truth about five hundred very vital years, which are concealed even from cultivated Englishmen by two vague falsehoods; the notion that the Roman Empire was merely decadent and the notion that the Middle Ages were merely dark. As a fact, even the Dark Ages were not merely dark. And even the Byzantine Empire was not merely Byzantine. It seems a little unfair that we should take the very title of decay from that Christian city, for surely it was yet more stiff and sterile when it had become a Moslem city. I am not so exacting as to ask any one to popularise such a word as "Constantino-politan." But it would surely be a better word for stiffness and sterility to call it Stamboulish. But for the Moslems and other men of the Near East what counted about Byzantium was that it still inherited the huge weight of the name of Rome. Rome had come east and reared against them this Roman city, and though and priest or soldier who came out of it might be speaking as a Greek, he was ruling as a Roman. Its critics in these days of criticism may regard it as a corrupt civilisation. But its enemies in the day of battle only regarded it as civilisation. Saladin, the greatest of the Saracens, did not call Greek bishops degenerate dreamers or dingy outcasts, he called them, with a sounder historical instinct, "The monks of the imperial race." The survival of the word merely means that even when the imperial city fell behind them, they did not surrender their claim to defy all Asia in the name of the Christian Emperor. That is but one example out of twenty, but that is why in this distant place to this day the Greeks who are separated from the see of Rome sometimes bear the strange name of "The Romans."

Now that civilisation is our civilisation, and we never had any other. We have not inherited a Teutonic culture any more than a Druid culture; not half so much. The people who say that parliaments or pictures or gardens or roads or universities were made by the Teutonic race from the north can be disposed of by the simple question: why did not the

Teutonic race make them in the north? Why was not the Parthenon originally built in the neighbourhood of Potsdam, or did ten Hansa towns compete to be the birthplace of Homer? Perhaps they do by this time; but their local illusion is no longer largely shared. Anyhow it seems strange that the roads of the Romans should be due to the inspiration of the Teutons; and that parliaments should begin in Spain because they came from Germany. If I looked about in these parts for a local emblem like that of the eagle, I might very well find it in the lion. The lion is common enough, of course, in Christian art both hagiological and heraldic. Besides the cavern of Bethlehem of which I shall speak presently, is the cavern of St. Jerome, where he lived with that real or legendary lion who was drawn by the delicate humour of Carpaccio and a hundred other religious painters. That it should appear in Christian art is natural; that it should appear in Moslem art is much more singular, seeing that Moslems are in theory forbidden so to carve images of living things. Some say the Persian Moslems are less particular; but whatever the explanation, two lions of highly heraldic appearance are carved over that Saracen gate which Christians call the gate of St. Stephen; and the best judges seem to agree that, like so much of the Saracenic shell of Zion, they were partly at least copied from the shields and crests of the Crusaders.

And the lions graven over the gate of St. Stephen might well be the text for a whole book on the subject. For if they indicate, however indirectly, the presence of the Latins of the twelfth century, they also indicate the earlier sources from which the Latin life had itself been drawn. The two lions are pacing, passant as the heralds would say, in two opposite directions almost as if prowling to and fro. And this also might well be symbolic as well as heraldic. For if the Crusaders brought the lion southward in spite of the conventional fancy of Moslem decoration, it was only because the Romans had previously brought the lion northward to the cold seas and the savage forests. The image of the lion came from north to south, only because the idea of the lion had long ago come from south to north. The Christian had a symbolic lion he had never seen, and the Moslem had a real lion that he refused to draw. For we could deduce from the case of this single creature the fact that all our civilisation came from the Mediterranean, and the folly of pretending that it came from the North Sea. Those two heraldic shapes over the gate may be borrowed from the Norman or Angevin shield now quartered in the Royal Arms of England. They may have been copied, directly or indirectly, from that great Angevin King of England whose title credited him with the heart of a lion. They may have in some far-off fashion the same ancestry as the boast or jest of our own comic papers when they talk about the British Lion. But why are there lions, though of French or feudal origin, on the flag of England? There might as well be camels or crocodiles, for all the apparent connection with England or with France. Why was an English king described as having the heart of a lion, any more than of a tiger? Why do your patriotic cartoons threaten the world with the wrath of the British Lion; it is really as strange as if they warned it against stimulating the rage of the British rhinoceros. Why did not the French and English princes find in the wild boars, that were the objects of their hunting, the subjects of their heraldry? If the Normans were really the Northmen, the sea-wolves of Scandinavian piracy, why did they not display three wolves on their shields? Why has not John Bull been content with the English bull, or the English bull-dog?

The answer might be put somewhat defiantly by saying that the very name of John Bull is foreign. The surname comes through France from Rome; and the Christian name comes through Rome from Palestine. If there had really been any justification for the Teutonic generalisation, we should expect the surname to be "ox" and not "bull"; and we should expect the hero standing as godfather to be Odin or Siegfried, and not the prophet who lived on locusts in the wilderness of Palestine or the mystic who mused with his burning eyes on the blue seas around Patmos. If our national hero is John Bull and not Olaf the Ox, it is ultimately because that blue sea has run like a blue thread through all the tapestries of our traditions; or in other words because our culture, like that of France or Flanders, came originally from the Mediterranean. And if this is true of our use of the word "bull," it is obviously even truer of our use of the word "lion." The later emblem is enough to show that the culture came, not only from the Mediterranean, but from the southern as well as the northern side of the Mediterranean. In other words, the Roman Empire ran all round the great inland sea; the very name of which meant, not merely the sea in the middle of the land, but more especially the sea in the middle of all the lands that mattered most to civilisation. One of these, and the one that in the long run has mattered most of all, was Palestine.

In this lies the deepest difference between a man like Richard the Lion Heart and any of the countless modern English soldiers in Palestine who have been quite as lion-hearted as he. His superiority was not moral but intellectual; it consisted in knowing where he was and why he was there. It arose from the fact that in his time there remained a sort of memory of the Roman Empire, which some would have re-established as a Holy Roman Empire. Christendom was still almost one commonwealth; and it seemed to Richard quite natural to go from one edge of it that happened to be called England to the opposite edge of it that happened to be called Palestine. We may think him right or wrong in the particular quarrel, we may think him innocent or unscrupulous in his incidental methods; but there is next to no doubt whatever that he did regard himself not merely as conquering but as re-conquering a realm. He was not like a man attacking total strangers on a hitherto undiscovered island. He was not opening up a new country, or giving his name to a new continent, and he could boast none of those ideals of imperial innovation which inspire the more enlightened pioneers, who exterminate tribes or extinguish republics for the sake of a gold-mine or an oil-field. Some day, if our modern educational system is further expanded and enforced, the whole of the past of Palestine may be entirely forgotten; and a traveller in happier days may have all the fresher sentiments of one stepping on a new and nameless soil. Disregarding any dim and lingering legends among the natives, he may then have the honour of calling Sinai by the name of Mount Higgins, or marking on a new map the site of Bethlehem with the name of Brownsville. But King Richard, adventurous as he was, could not experience the full freshness of this sort of adventure. He was not riding into Asia thus romantically and at random; indeed he was not riding into Asia at all. He was riding into Europa Irredenta.

But that is to anticipate what happened later and must be considered later. I am primarily speaking of the Empire as a pagan and political matter; and it is easy to see what was the meaning of the Crusade on the merely pagan and political side. In one sentence, it meant that Rome had to recover what Byzantium could not keep. But something further had happened as affecting Rome than anything that could be understood by a man standing as I have imagined myself standing, in the official area of Byzantium. When I have said that the Byzantian civilisation seemed still to be reigning, I meant a curious impression that, in these Eastern provinces, though the Empire had been more defeated it has been less disturbed. There is a greater clarity in that ancient air; and fewer clouds of real revolution and novelty have come between them and their ancient sun. This may seem an enigma and a paradox; seeing that here a foreign religion has successfully fought and ruled. But indeed the enigma is also the explanation. In the East the continuity of culture has only been interrupted by negative things that Islam has done. In the West it has been interrupted by positive things that Christendom itself has done. In the West the past of Christendom has its perspective blocked up by its own creations; in the East it is a true perspective of interminable corridors, with round Byzantine arches and proud Byzantine pillars. That, I incline to fancy, is the real difference that a man come from the west of Europe feels in the east of Europe, it is a gap or a void. It is the absence of the grotesque energy of Gothic, the absence of the experiments of parliament and popular representation, the absence of medieval chivalry, the absence of modern nationality. In the East the civilisation lived on, or if you will, lingered on; in the West it died and was reborn. But for a long time, it should be remembered, it must have seemed to the East merely that it died. The realms of Rome had disappeared in clouds of barbaric war, while the realms of Byzantium were still golden and gorgeous in the sun. The men of the East did not realise that their splendour was stiffening and growing sterile, and even the early successes of Islam may not have revealed to them that their rule was not only stiff but brittle. It was something else that was destined to reveal it. The Crusades meant many things; but in this matter they meant one thing, which was like a word carried to them on the great west wind. And the word was like that in an old Irish song: "The west is awake." They heard in the distance the cries of unknown crowds and felt the earth shaking with the march of mobs; and behind them came the trampling of horses and the noise of harness and of horns of war; new kings calling out commands and hosts of young men full of hope crying out in the old Roman tongue "Id Deus vult," Rome was risen from the dead.

Almost any traveller could select out of the countless things that he has looked at the few things that he has seen. I mean the things that come to him with a curious clearness; so that he actually sees them to be what he knows them to be. I might almost say that he can believe in them although he has seen them. There can be no rule about this realisation; it seems to come in the most random fashion;

G. K. CHESTERTON

and the man to whom it comes can only speak for himself without any attempt at a critical comparison with others. In this sense I may say that the Church of the Nativity at Bethlehem contains something impossible to describe, yet driving me beyond expression to a desperate attempt at description. The church is entered through a door so small that it it might fairly be called a hole, in which many have seen, and I think truly, a symbol of some idea of humility. It is also said that the wall was pierced in this way to prevent the appearance of a camel during divine service, but even that explanation would only repeat the same suggestion through the parable of the needle's eye. Personally I should guess that, in so far as the purpose was practical, it was meant to keep out much more dangerous animals than camels, as, for instance, Turks. For the whole church has clearly been turned into a fortress, windows are bricked up and walls thickened in some or all of its thousand years of religious war. In the blank spaces above the little doorway hung in old times that strange mosaic of the Magi which once saved the holy place from destruction, in the strange interlude between the decline of Rome and the rise of Mahomet. For when the Persians who had destroyed Jerusalem rode out in triumph to the village of Bethlehem, they looked up and saw above the door a picture in coloured stone, a picture of themselves. They were following a strange star and worshipping an unknown child. For a Christian artist, following some ancient Eastern tradition containing an eternal truth, had drawn the three wise men with the long robes and high head-dresses of Persia. The worshippers of the sun had come westward for the worship of the star. But whether that part of the church were bare and bald as it is now or coloured with the gold and purple images of the Persians, the inside of the church would always be by comparison abruptly dark. As familiarity turns the darkness to twilight, and the twilight to a grey daylight, the first impression is that of two rows of towering pillars. They are of a dark red stone having much of the appearance of a dark red marble; and they are crowned with the acanthus in the manner of the Corinthian school. They were carved and set up at the command of Constantine; and beyond them, at the other end of the church beside the attar, is the dark stairway that descends under the canopies of rock to the stable where Christ was born.

Of all the things I have seen the most convincing, and as it were crushing, were these red columns of Constantine. In explanation of the sentiment there are a thousand things that want saying and cannot be said. Never have I felt so vividly the great fact of our history; that the Christian religion is like a huge bridge across a boundless sea, which alone connects us with the men who made the world, and yet have utterly vanished from the world. To put it curtly and very crudely on this point alone it was possible to sympathise with a Roman and not merely to admire him. All his pagan remains are but sublime fossils; for we can never know the life that was in them. We know that here and there was a temple to Venus or there an altar to Vesta; but who knows or pretends to know what he really felt about Venus or Vesta? Was a Vestal Virgin like a Christian Virgin, or something profoundly different? Was he quite serious about Venus, like a diabolist, or merely frivolous about Venus, like a Christian? If the spirit was different from ours we cannot hope to understand it, and if the spirit was like ours, the spirit was expressed in images that no longer express it. But it is here that he and I meet; and salute the same images in the end.

In any case I can never recapture in words the waves of sympathy with strange things that went through me in that twilight of the tall pillars, like giants robed in purple, standing still and looking down into that dark hole in the ground. Here halted that imperial civilisation, when it had marched in triumph through the whole world; here in the evening of its days it came trailing in all its panoply in the pathway of the three kings. For it came following not only a falling but a fallen star and one that dived before them into a birthplace darker than a grave. And the lord of the laurels, clad in his sombre crimson, looked down into that darkness, and then looked up, and saw that all the stars in his own sky were dead. They were deities no longer but only a brilliant dust, scattered down the vain void of Lucretius. The stars were as stale as they were strong; they would never die for they had never lived; they were cursed with an incurable immortality that was but the extension of mortality; they were chained in the chains of causation and unchangeable as the dead. There are not many men in the modern world who do not know that mood, though it was not discovered by the moderns; it was the final and seemingly fixed mood of nearly all the ancients. Only above the black hole of Bethlehem they had seen a star wandering like a lost spark; and it had done what the eternal suns and planets could not do. It had disappeared.

There are some who resent the presence of such purple beside the plain stable of the Nativity. But it seems strange that they always rebuke it as if it were a blind vulgarity like the red plush of a parvenu; a mere insensibility to a mere incongruity. For in fact the insensibility is in the critics and not the artists. It is an insensibility not to an accidental incongruity but to an artistic contrast. Indeed it is an insensibility of a somewhat tiresome kind, which can often be noticed in those sceptics who make a science of folk-lore. The mark of them is that they fail to see the importance of finding the upshot or climax of a tale, even when it is a fairy-tale. Since the old devotional doctors and designers were never tired of insisting on the sufferings of the holy poor to the point of squalor, and simultaneously insisting on the sumptuousness of the subject kings to the point of swagger, it would really seem not entirely improbable that they may have been conscious of the contrast themselves. I confess this is an insensibility, not to say stupidity, in the sceptics and simplifiers, which I find very fatiguing. I do not mind a man not believing a story, but I confess I am bored stiff (if I may be allowed the expression) by a man who can tell a story without seeing the point of the story, considered as a story or even considered as a lie. And a man who sees the rags and the royal purple as a clumsy inconsistency is merely missing the meaning of a deliberate design. He is like a man who should hear the story of King Cophetua and the beggar maid and say doubtfully that it was hard to recognise it as really *a mariage de convenance*; a phrase which (I may remark in parenthesis but not without passion) is not the French for "a marriage of convenience," any more than *hors d'oeuvre* is the French for "out of work"; but may be more rightly rendered in English as "a suitable match." But nobody thought the match of the king and the beggar maid conventionally a suitable match; and nobody would ever have thought the story worth telling if it had been. It is like saying that Diogenes, remaining in his tub after the offer of Alexander, must have been unaware of the opportunities of Greek architecture; or like saying that Nebuchadnezzar eating grass is clearly inconsistent with court etiquette, or not to be found in any fashionable cookery book. I do not mind the learned sceptic saying it is a legend or a lie; but I weep for him when he cannot see the gist of it, I might even say the joke of it. I do not object to his rejecting the story as a tall story; but I find it deplorable when he cannot see the point or end or upshot of the tall story, the very pinnacle or spire of that sublime tower.

This dull type of doubt clouds the consideration of many sacred things as it does that of the shrine of Bethlehem. It is applied to the divine reality of Bethlehem itself, as when sceptics still sneer at the littleness, the localism, the provincial particularity and obscurity of that divine origin; as if Christians could be confounded and silenced by a contrast which Christians in ten thousand hymns, songs and sermons have incessantly shouted and proclaimed. In this capital case, of course, the same principle holds. A man may think the tale is incredible; but it would never have been told at all if it had not been incongruous. But this particular case of the lesser contrast, that between the imperial pomp and the rustic poverty of the carpenter and the shepherds, is alone enough to illustrate the strange artistic fallacy involved. If it be the point that an emperor came to worship a carpenter, it is as artistically necessary to make the emperor imperial as to make the carpenter humble; if we wish to make plain to plain people that before this shrine kings are no better than shepherds, it is as necessary that the kings should have crowns as that the shepherds should have crooks. And if modern intellectuals do not know it, it is because nobody has really been mad enough even to try to make modern intellectualism popular. Now this conception of pomp as a popular thing, this conception of a concession to common human nature in colour and symbol, has a considerable bearing on many misunderstandings about the original enthusiasm that spread from the cave of Bethlehem over the whole Roman Empire. It is a curious fact that the moderns have mostly rebuked historic Christianity, not for being narrow, but for being broad. They have rebuked it because it did prove itself the desire of all nations, because it did satisfy the cravings of many creeds, because it did prove itself to idolaters as something as magic as their idols, or did prove itself to patriots something as lovable as their native land. In many other matters indeed, besides this popular art, we may find examples of the same illogical prejudice. Nothing betrays more curiously the bias of historians against the Christian faith than the fact that they blame in Christians the very human indulgences that they have praised in heathens. The same arts and allegories, the same phraseologies and philosophies, which appear first as proofs of heathen health turn up later as proofs of Christian corruption. It was noble of pagans to be pagan, but it was unpardonable of Christians to be paganised. They never tire of telling us of the glory that was Greece, the grandeur that was Rome, but the Church was infamous because it satisfied the Greek intellect and wielded the Roman power.

Now on the first example of the attempt of theology to

meet the claims of philosophy I will not here dwell at length. I will only remark in passing that it is an utter fallacy to suggest, as for instance Mr. Wells suggests in his fascinating *Outline of History*, that the subtleties of theology were a mere falling away from the simplicities of religion. Religion may be better simple for those who find it simple; but there are bound to be many who in any case find it subtle, among those who think about it and especially those who doubt about it. To take an example, there is no saying which the humanitarians of a broad religion more commonly offer as a model of simplicity than that most mystical affirmation "God is Love." And there is no theological quarrel of the Councils of the Church which they, especially Mr. Wells, more commonly deride as bitter and barren than that at the Council of Nicea about the Co-eternity of the Divine Son. Yet the subtle statement is simply a metaphysical explanation of the simple statement; and it would be quite possible even to make it a popular explanation, by saying that God could not love when there was nothing to be loved. Now the Church Councils were originally very popular, not to say riotous assemblies. So far from being undemocratic, they were rather too democratic; the real case against them was that they passed by uproarious votes, and not without violence, things that had ultimately to be considered more calmly by experts. But it may reasonably be suggested, I think, that the concentration of the Greek intellect on these things did gradually pass from a popular to a more professional or official thing; and that the traces of it have finally tended to fade from the official religion of the East. It was far otherwise with the more poetical and therefore more practical religion of the West. It was far otherwise with that direct appeal to pathos and affection in the highly coloured picture of the Shepherd and the King. In the West the world not only prolonged its life but recovered its youth. That is the meaning of the movement I have described as the awakening of the West and the resurrection of Rome. And the whole point of that movement, as I propose to suggest, was that it was a popular movement. It had returned with exactly that strange and simple energy that belongs to the story of Bethlehem. Not in vain had Constantine come clad in purple to look down into that dark cave at his feet; nor did the star mislead him when it seemed to end in the entrails of the earth. The men who followed him passed on, as it were, through the low and vaulted tunnel of the Dark Ages; but they had found the way, and the only way, out of that world of death, and their journey ended in the land of the living. They came out into a world more wonderful than the eyes of men have looked on before or after; they heard the hammers of hundreds of happy craftsmen working for once according to their own will, and saw St. Francis walking with his halo a cloud of birds.

CHAPTER XI

THE MEANING OF THE CRUSADE

There are three examples of Western work on the great eastern slope of the Mount of Olives; and they form a sort of triangle illustrating the truth about the different influences of the West on the East. At the foot of the hill is the garden kept by the Franciscans on the alleged site of Gethsemane, and containing the hoary olive that is supposed to be the terrible tree of the agony of Christ. Given the great age and slow growth of the olives, the tradition is not so unreasonable as some may suppose. But whether or not it is historically right, it is not artistically wrong. The instinct, if it was only an instinct, that made men fix upon this strange growth of grey and twisted wood, was a true imaginative instinct. One of the strange qualities of this strange Southern tree is its almost startling hardness; accidentally to strike the branch of an olive is like striking rock. With its stony surface, stunted stature, and strange holes and hollows, it is often more like a grotto than a tree. Hence it does not seem so unnatural that it should be treated as a holy grotto; or that this strange vegetation should claim to stand for ever like a sculptured monument. Even the shimmering or shivering silver foliage of the living olive might well have a legend like that of the aspen; as if it had grown grey with fear from the apocalyptic paradox of a divine vision of death. A child from one of the villages said to me, in broken English, that it was the place where God said his prayers. I for one could not ask for a finer or more defiant statement of all that separates the Christian from the Moslem or the Jew; *credo quia impossibile.*

Around this terrible spot the Franciscans have done something which will strike many good and thoughtful people as quite fantastically inadequate; and which strikes me as fantastically but precisely right. They have laid out the garden simply as a garden, in a way that is completely natural because it is completely artificial. They have made flower-beds in the shape of stars and moons, and coloured them with flowers like those in the backyard of a cottage. The combination of these bright patterns in the sunshine with the awful shadow in the centre is certainly an incongruity in the sense of a contrast. But it is a poetical contrast, like that of birds building in a temple or flowers growing on a tomb. The best way of suggesting what I for one feel about it would be something like this; suppose we imagine a company of children, such as those whom Christ blessed in Jerusalem, afterwards put permanently in charge of a field full of his sorrow; it is probable that, if they could do anything with it, they would do something like this. They might cut it up into quaint shapes and dot it with red daisies or yellow marigolds. I really do not know that there is anything better that grown up people could do, since anything that the greatest of them could do must be, must look quite as small. "Shall I, the gnat that dances in Thy ray, dare to be reverent?" The Franciscans have not dared to be reverent; they have only dared to be cheerful. It may be too awful an adventure of the imagination to imagine Christ in that garden. But there is not the smallest difficulty about imagining St. Francis there; and that is something to say of an institution which is eight hundred years old.

Immediately above this little garden, overshadowing and almost overhanging it, is a gorgeous gilded building with golden domes and minarets glittering in the sun, and filling a splendid situation with almost shameless splendour; the Russian church built over the upper part of the garden, belonging to the Orthodox-Greeks. Here again many

Western travellers will be troubled; and will think that golden building much too like a fairy palace in a pantomime. But here again I shall differ from them, though perhaps less strongly. It may be that the pleasure is childish rather than childlike; but I can imagine a child clapping his hands at the mere sight of those great domes like bubbles of gold against the blue sky. It is a little like Aladdin's Palace, but it has a place in art as Aladdin has a place in literature; especially since it is oriental literature. Those wise missionaries in China who were not afraid to depict the Twelve Apostles in the costume of Chinamen might have built such a church in a land of glittering mosques. And as it is said that the Russian has in him something of the child and something of the oriental, such a style may be quite sincere, and have even a certain simplicity in its splendour. It is genuine of its kind; it was built for those who like it; and those who do not like it can look at something else. This sort of thing may be called tawdry, but it is not what I call meretricious. What I call really meretricious can be found yet higher on the hill; towering to the sky and dominating all the valleys.

The nature of the difference, I think, is worth noting. The German Hospice, which served as a sort of palace for the German Emperor, is a very big building with a very high tower, planned I believe with great efficiency, solidity and comfort, and fitted with a thousand things that mark its modernity compared with the things around, with the quaint garden of the Franciscans or the fantastic temple of the Russians. It is what I can only describe as a handsome building; rather as the more vulgar of the Victorian wits used to talk about a fine woman. By calling it a handsome building I mean that from the top of its dizzy tower to the bottom of its deepest foundations there is not one line or one tint of beauty. This negative fact, however, would be nothing; it might be honestly ugly and utilitarian like a factory or a prison; but it is not. It is as pretentious as the gilded dome below it; and it is pretentious in a wicked way where the other is pretentious in a good and innocent way. What annoys me about it is that it was not built by children, or even by savages, but by professors; and the professors could profess the art and could not practise it. The architects knew everything about a Romanesque building except how to build it. We feel that they accumulated on that spot all the learning and organisation and information and wealth of the world, to do this one particular thing; and then did it wrong. They did it wrong, not through superstition, not through fanatical exaggeration, not through provincial ignorance, but through pure, profound, internal, intellectual incompetence; that intellectual incompetence which so often goes with intellectual pride. I will mention only one matter out of a hundred. All the columns in the Kaiser's Chapel are in one way very suitable to their place; every one of them has a swelled head. The column itself is slender but the capital is not only big but bulging; and it has the air of bulging *downwards*, as if pressing heavily on something too slender to support it. This is false, not to any of the particular schools of architecture about which professors can read in libraries, but to the inmost instinctive idea of architecture itself. A Norman capital can be heavy because the Norman column is thick, and the whole thing expresses an elephantine massiveness and repose. And a Gothic column can be slender, because its strength is energy; and is expressed in its line, which shoots upwards like the life of a tree, like the jet of a fountain or even like the rush of a rocket. But a slender thing beneath, obviously oppressed by a bloated thing above, suggests weakness by one of those miraculous mistakes that are as precisely wrong as masterpieces are precisely right. And to all this is added the intolerable intuition; that the Russians and the Franciscans, even if we credit them with fantastic ignorance, are at least looking up at the sky; and we know how the learned Germans would look down upon them, from their monstrous tower upon the hill.

And this is as true of the moral as of the artistic elements in the modern Jerusalem. To show that I am not unjustly partisan, I will say frankly that I see little to complain of in that common subject of complaint; the mosaic portrait of the Emperor on the ceiling of the chapel. It is but one among many figures; and it is not an unknown practice to include a figure of the founder in such church decorations. The real example of that startling moral stupidity which marked the barbaric imperialism can be found in another figure of which, curiously enough, considerably less notice seems to have been taken. It is the more remarkable because it is but an artistic shadow of the actual fact; and merely records in outline and relief the temporary masquerade in which the man walked about in broad daylight. I mean the really astounding trick of dressing himself up as a Crusader. That was, under the circumstances, far more ludicrous and lunatic a proceeding than if he had filled the whole ceiling with cherub heads with his own features, or festooned all the walls with one ornamental pattern of his moustaches.

The German Emperor came to Jerusalem under the escort of the Turks, as the ally of the Turks, and solely because of the victory and supremacy of the Turks. In other words, he came to Jerusalem solely because the Crusaders had lost Jerusalem; he came there solely because the Crusaders had been routed, ruined, butchered before and after the disaster of Hattin: because the Cross had gone down in blood before the Crescent, under which alone he could ride in with safety. Under those circumstances to dress up as a Crusader, as if for a fancy dress ball, was a mixture of madness and vulgarity which literally stops the breath. There is no need whatever to blame him for being in alliance with the Turks; hundreds of people have been in alliance with the Turks; the English especially have been far too much in alliance with them. But if any one wants to appreciate the true difference, distinct from all the cant of newspaper nationality, between the English and the Germans (who were classed together by the same

G. K. CHESTERTON

newspapers a little time before the war) let him take this single incident as a test. Lord Palmerston, for instance, was a firm friend of the Turks. Imagine Lord Palmerston appearing in chain mail and the shield of a Red Cross Knight.

It is obvious enough that Palmerston would have said that he cared no more for the Crusade than for the Siege of Troy; that his diplomacy was directed by practical patriotic considerations of the moment; and that he regarded the religious wars of the twelfth century as a rubbish heap of remote superstitions. In this he would be quite wrong, but quite intelligible and quite sincere; an English aristocrat of the nineteenth century inheriting from the English aristo-crats of the eighteenth century; whose views were simply those of Voltaire. And these things are something of an allegory. For the Voltairian version of the Crusades is still by far the most reasonable of all merely hostile views of the Crusades. If they were not a creative movement of religion, then they were simply a destructive movement of super-stition; and whether we agree with Voltaire in calling it superstition or with Villehardouin in calling it religion, at least both these very clear-headed Frenchmen would agree that the motive did exist and did explain the facts. But just as there is a clumsy German building with statues that at once patronise and parody the Crusaders, so there is a clumsy German theory that at once patronises and minimises the Crusades. According to this theory the essential truth about a Crusade was that it was not a Crusade. It was something that the professors, in the old days before the war, used to call a Teutonic Folk-Wande-ring. Godfrey and St. Louis were not, as Villehardouin would say, fighting for the truth; they were not even, as Voltaire would say, fighting for what they thought was the truth; this was only what they thought they thought, and they were really thinking of something entirely different. They were not moved either by piety or priestcraft, but by a new and unexpected nomadism. They were not inspired either by faith or fanaticism, but by an unusually aimless taste for foreign travel. This theory that the war of the two great religions could be explained by "Wanderlust" was current about twenty years ago among the historical professors of Germany, and with many of their other views, was often accepted by the historical professors of England. It was swallowed by an earthquake, along with other rubbish, in the year 1914.

Since then, so far as I know, the only person who has been patient enough to dig it up again is Mr. Ezra Pound. He is well known as an American poet; and he is, I believe, a man of great talent and information. His attempt to recover the old Teutonic theory of the Folk-Wandering of Peter the Hermit was expressed, however, in prose; in an article in the *New Age*. I have no reason to doubt that he was to be counted among the most loyal of our allies; but he is evidently one of those who, quite without being Pro-German, still manage to be German. The Teutonic theory was very Teutonic; like the German Hospice on the hill it was put together with great care and knowledge and it is rotten from top to bottom. I do not understand, for that matter, why that alliance which we enjoy with Mr. Pound should not be treated in the same way as the other historical event; or why the war should not be an example of the Wanderlust. Surely the American Army in France must have drifted eastward merely through the same vague nomadic need as the Christian Army in Palestine. Surely Pershing as well as Peter the Hermit was merely a rather restless gentleman who found his health improved by frequent change of scene. The Americans said, and perhaps thought, that they were fighting for democracy; and the Crusaders said, and perhaps thought, that they were fighting for Christianity. But as we know what the Crusaders meant better than they did themselves, I cannot quite understand why we do not enjoy the same valuable omniscience about the Americans. Indeed I do not see why we should not enjoy it (for it would be very enjoyable) about any individual American. Surely it was this vague vagabond spirit that moved Mr. Pound, not only to come to England, but in a fashion to come to Fleet Street. A dim tribal tendency, vast and invisible as the wind, carried him and his article like an autumn leaf to alight on the *New Age* doorstep. Or a blind aboriginal impulse, wholly without rational motive, led him one day to put on his hat, and go out with his article in an envelope and put it in a pillar-box. It is vain to correct by cold logic the power of such primitive appetites; nature herself was behind the seemingly random thoughtlessness of the deed. And now that it is irrevocably done, he can look back on it and trace the large lines of an awful law of averages; wherein it is ruled by a ruthless necessity that a certain number of such Americans should write a certain number of such articles, as the leaves fall or the flowers return.

In plain words, this sort of theory is a blasphemy against the intellectual dignity of man. It is a blunder as well as a blasphemy; for it goes miles out of its way to find a bestial explanation when there is obviously a human explanation. It is as if a man told me that a dim survival of the instincts of a quadruped was the reason of my sitting on a chair with four legs. I answer that I do it because I foresee that there may be grave disadvantages in sitting on a chair with one leg. Or it is as if I were told that I liked to swim in the sea, solely because some early forms of amphibian life came out of the sea on to the shore. I answer that I know why I swim in the sea; and it is because the divine gift of reason tells me that it would be unsatisfactory to swim on the land. In short this sort of vague evolutionary theorising simply amounts to finding an unconvincing explanation of something that needs no explanation. And the case is really quite as simple with great political and religious movements by which man has from time to time changed the world in this or that respect in which he happened to think it would be the better for a change. The Crusade was a religious movement, but it was also a perfectly rational movement;

one might almost say a rationalist movement. I could quite understand Mr. Pound saying that such a campaign for a creed was immoral; and indeed it often has been, and now perhaps generally is, quite horribly immoral. But when he implies that it is irrational he has selected exactly the thing which it is not.

It is not enlightenment, on the contrary it is ignorance and insularity, which causes most of us to miss this fact. But it certainly is the fact that religious war is in itself much more rational than patriotic war. I for one have often defended and even encouraged patriotic war, and should always be ready to defend and encourage patriotic passion. But it cannot be denied that there is more of mere passion, of mere preference and prejudice, in short of mere personal accident, in fighting another nation than in fighting another faith. The Crusader is in every sense more rational than the modern conscript or professional soldier. He is more rational in his object, which is the intelligent and intelligible object of conversion; where the modern militarist has an object much more confused by momentary vanity and one-sided satisfaction. The Crusader wished to make Jerusalem a Christian town; but the Englishman does not wish to make Berlin an English town. He has only a healthy hatred of it as a Prussian town. The Moslem wished to make the Christian a Moslem; but even the Prussian did not wish to make the Frenchman a Prussian. He only wished to make the Frenchman admire a Prussian; and not only were the means he adopted somewhat ill-considered for this purpose, but the purpose itself is looser and more irrational. The object of all war is peace; but the object of religious war is mental as well as material peace; it is agreement. In short religious war aims ultimately at equality, where national war aims relatively at superiority. Conversion is the one sort of conquest in which the conquered must rejoice.

In that sense alone it is foolish for us in the West to sneer at those who kill men when a foot is set in a holy place, when we ourselves kill hundreds of thousands when a foot is put across a frontier. It is absurd for us to despise those who shed blood for a relic when we have shed rivers of blood for a rag. But above all the Crusade, or, for that matter, the Jehad, is by far the most philosophical sort of fighting, not only in its conception of ending the difference, but in its mere act of recognising the difference, as the deepest kind of difference. It is to reverse all reason to suggest that a man's politics matter and his religion does not matter. It is to say he is affected by the town he lives in, but not by the world he lives in. It is to say that he is altered when he is a fellow-citizen walking under new lamp-posts, but not altered when he is another creature walking under strange stars. It is exactly as if we were to say that two people ought to live in the same house, but it need not be in the same town. It is exactly as if we said that so long as the address included York it did not matter whether it was New York; or that so long as a man is in Essex we do not care whether he is in England.

Christendom would have been entirely justified in the abstract in being alarmed or suspicious at the mere rise of a great power that was not Christian. Nobody nowadays would think it odd to express regret at the rise of a power because it was Militarist or Socialist or even Protectionist. But it is far more natural to be conscious of a difference, not about the order of battle but the battle of life; not about our definable enjoyment of possessions, but about our much more doubtful possession of enjoyment; not about the fiscal divisions between us and foreigners but about the spiritual divisions even between us and friends. These are the things that differ profoundly with differing views of the ultimate nature of the universe. For the things of our country are often distant; but the things of our cosmos are always near; we can shut our doors upon the wheeled traffic of our native town; but in our own inmost chamber we hear the sound that never ceases; that wheel which Dante and a popular proverb have dared to christen as the love that makes the world go round. For this is the great paradox of life; that there are not only wheels within wheels, but the larger wheels within the smaller. When a whole community rests on one conception of life and death and the origin of things, it is quite entitled to watch the rise of another community founded on another conception as the rise of something certain to be different and likely to be hostile. Indeed, as I have pointed out touching certain political theories, we already admit this truth in its small and questionable examples. We only deny the large and obvious examples.

Christendom might quite reasonably have been alarmed if it had not been attacked. But as a matter of history it had been attacked. The Crusader would have been quite justified in suspecting the Moslem even if the Moslem had merely been a new stranger; but as a matter of history he was already an old enemy. The critic of the Crusade talks as if it had sought out some inoffensive tribe or temple in the interior of Thibet, which was never discovered until it was invaded. They seem entirely to forget that long before the Crusaders had dreamed of riding to Jerusalem, the Moslems had almost ridden into Paris. They seem to forget that if the Crusaders nearly conquered Palestine, it was but a return upon the Moslems who had nearly conquered Europe. There was no need for them to argue by an appeal to reason, as I have argued above, that a religious division must make a difference; it had already made a difference. The difference stared them in the face in the startling transformation of Roman Barbary and of Roman Spain. In short it was something which must happen in theory and which did happen in practice; all expectation suggested that it would be so and all experience said it was so. Having thought it out theoretically and experienced it practically, they proceeded to deal with it equally practically. The first division involved every principle of the science of thought; and the last developments followed out every principle of the science of war. The Crusade was the counter-attack. It was the defensive army taking the offensive in its turn, and driving back the enemy to his base. And it is this process, reasonable from its first axiom to its last act, that Mr. Pound actually selects as a sort of automatic wandering of an animal. But a man so intelligent would not have made a mistake so extraordinary but for another error which it is here very essential to consider. To suggest that men engaged, rightly or wrongly, in so logical a military and political operation were only migrating like birds or swarming like bees is as ridiculous as to say that the Prohibition campaign in America was only an animal reversion towards lapping as the dog lappeth, or Rowland Hill's introduction of postage stamps an animal taste for licking as the cat licks. Why should we provide other people with a remote reason for their own actions, when they themselves are ready to tell us the reason, and it is a perfectly reasonable reason?

I have compared this pompous imposture of scientific history to the pompous and clumsy building of the scientific Germans on the Mount of Olives, because it substitutes in the same way a modern stupidity for the medieval simplicity. But just as the German Hospice after all stands on a fine site, and might have been a fine building, so there is after all another truth, somewhat analogous, which the German historians of the Folk-Wanderings might possibly have meant, as distinct from all that they have actually said. There is indeed one respect in which the case of the Crusade does differ very much from modern political cases like prohibition or the penny post. I do not refer to such incidental peculiarities as the fact that Prohibition could only have succeeded through the enormous power of modern plutocracy, or that even the convenience of the postage goes along with an extreme coercion by the police. It is a somewhat deeper difference that I mean; and it may possibly be what these critics mean. But the difference is not in the evolutionary, but rather the revolutionary spirit.

The First Crusade was not a racial migration; it was something much more intellectual and dignified; a riot. In order to understand this religious war we must class it, not so much with the wars of history as with the revolutions of history. As I shall try to show briefly on a later page, it not only had all the peculiar good and the peculiar evil of things like the French Revolution or the Russian Revolution, but it was a more purely popular revolution than either of them. The truly modern mind will of course regard the contention that it was popular as tantamount to a confession that it was animal. In these days when papers and speeches are full of words like democracy and self-determination, anything really resembling the movement of a mass of angry men is regarded as no better than a stampede of bulls or a scurry of rats. The new sociologists call it the herd instinct, just as the old reactionaries called it the many-headed beast. But both agree in implying that it is hardly worth while to count how many head there are of such cattle. In face of such fashionable comparisons it will seem comparatively mild to talk of migration as it occurs among birds or insects. Nevertheless we may venture to state with some confidence that both the sociologists and the reactionaries are wrong. It does not follow that human beings become less than human because their ideas appeal to more and more of humanity. Nor can we deduce that men are mindless solely from the fact that they are all of one mind. In plain fact the virtues of a mob cannot be found in a herd of bulls or a pack of wolves, any more than the crimes of a mob can be committed by a flock of sheep or a shoal of herrings. Birds have never been known to besiege and capture an empty cage of an aviary, on a point of principle, merely because it had kept a few other birds in captivity, as the mob besieged and captured the almost empty Bastille, merely because it was the fortress of a historic tyranny. And rats have never been known to die by thousands merely in order to visit a particular trap in which a particular rat had perished, as the poor peasants of the First Crusade died in thousands for a far-off sight of the Sepulchre or a fragment of the true cross. In this sense indeed the Crusade was not rationalistic, if the rat is the only rationalist. But it will seem more truly rational to point out that the inspiration of such a crowd is not in such instincts as we share with the animals, but precisely in such ideas as the animals never (with all their virtues) understand.

What is peculiar about the First Crusade is that it was in quite a new and abnormal sense a popular movement. I might almost say it was the only popular movement there ever was in the world. For it was not a thing which the populace followed; it was actually a thing which the populace led. It was not only essentially a revolution, but it was the only revolution I know of in which the masses began by acting alone, and practically without any support from any of the classes. When they had acted, the classes came in; and it is perfectly true, and indeed only natural, that the masses alone failed where the two together succeeded. But it was the uneducated who educated the educated. The case of the Crusade is emphatically not a case in which certain ideas were first suggested by a few philosophers, and then preached by demagogues to the democracy. This was to a great extent true of the French Revolution; it was probably yet more true of the Russian Revolution; and we need not here pause upon the fine shade of difference that Rousseau was right and Karl Marx was wrong. In the First Crusade it was the ordinary man who was right or wrong. He came out in a fury at the insult to his own little images or private prayers, as if he had come out to fight with his own domestic poker or private carving-knife. He was not armed with new weapons of wit and logic served round from the arsenal of an academy. There was any amount of wit and logic in the academies of the Middle Ages; but the typical leader of the Crusade was not Abelard or Aquinas but Peter the Hermit, who can hardly be called even a popular leader, but rather a popular flag. And it was his army, or rather his enormous rabble, that first marched across the world to die for the deliverance of Jerusalem.

Historians say that in that huge host of thousands there were only nine knights. To any one who knows even a little of medieval war the fact seems astounding. It is indeed a long exploded fallacy to regard medievalism as identical with feudalism. There were countless democratic institutions, such as the guilds; sometimes as many as twenty guilds in one small town. But it is really true that the military organization of the Middle Ages was almost entirely feudal; indeed we might rather say that feudalism was the name of their military organisation. That so vast a military mass should have attempted to move at all, with only nine of the natural military leaders, seems to me a prodigy of popular initiative. It is as if a parliament were elected at the next general election, in which only two men could afford to read a daily newspaper.

This mob marched against the military discipline of the Moslems and was massacred; or, might I so mystically express it, martyred. Many of the great kings and knights who followed in their tracks did not so clearly deserve any haloes for the simplicity and purity of their motives. The canonisation of such a crowd might be impossible, and would certainly be resisted in modern opinion; chiefly because they indulged their democratic violence on the way by killing various usurers; a course which naturally fills modern society with an anger verging on alarm. A perversity leads me to weep rather more over the many slaughtered peasants than over the few slaughtered usurers; but in any case the peasants certainly were not slaughtered in vain. The common conscience of all classes, in a time when all had a common creed, was aroused, and a new army followed of a very different type of skill and training; led by most of the ablest captains and by some of the most chivalrous gentlemen of the age. For curiously enough, the host contained more than one cultured gentleman who was as simple a Christian as any peasant, and as recklessly ready to be butchered or tortured for the mere name of Christ.

It is a tag of the materialists that the truth about history rubs away the romance of history. It is dear to the modern mind because it is depressing; but it does not happen to be true. Nothing emerges more clearly from a study that is truly realistic, than the curious fact that romantic people were really romantic. It is rather the historical novels that will lead a modern man vaguely to expect to find the leader of the new knights, Godfrey de Bouillon, to have been merely a brutal baron. The historical facts are all in favour of his having been much more like a knight of the Round Table. In fact he was a far better man than most of the knights of the Round Table, in whose characters the fabulist, knowing that he was writing a fable, was tactful enough to introduce a larger admixture of vice. Truth is not only stranger than fiction, but often saintlier than fiction. For truth is real, while fiction is bound to be realistic. Curiously enough Godfrey seems to have been heroic even in those admirable accidents which are generally and perhaps rightly regarded as the trappings of fiction. Thus he was of heroic stature, a handsome red-bearded man of great personal strength and daring; and he was himself the first man over the wall of Jerusalem, like any boy hero in a boy's adventure story. But he was also, the realist will be surprised to hear, a perfectly honest man, and a perfectly genuine practiser of the theoretical magnanimity of knighthood. Everything about him suggests it; from his first conversion from the imperial to the papal (and popular) cause, to his great refusal of the kinghood of the city he had taken; "I will not wear a crown of gold where my Master wore a crown of thorns." He was a just ruler, and the laws he made were full of the plainest public spirit. But even if we dismiss all that was written of him by Christian chroniclers because they might be his friends (which would be a pathetic and exaggerated compliment to the harmonious unity of Crusaders and of Christians) he would still remain sufficiently assoiled and crowned with the words of his enemies. For a Saracen chronicler wrote of him, with a fine simplicity, that if all truth and honour had otherwise withered off the earth, there would still remain enough of them so long as Duke Godfrey was alive.

Allied with Godfrey were Tancred the Italian, Raymond of Toulouse with the southern French and Robert of Normandy, the adventurous son of the Conqueror, with the Normans and the English. But it would be an error, I think, and one tending to make the whole subsequent story a thing not so much misunderstood as unintelligible, to suppose that the whole crusading movement had been suddenly and unnaturally stiffened with the highest chivalric discipline. Unless I am much mistaken, a great mass of that army was still very much of a mob. It is probable *a priori*, since the great popular movement was still profoundly popular. It is supported by a thousand things in the story of the campaign; the extraordinary emotionalism that made throngs of men weep and wail together, the importance of the demagogue, Peter the Hermit, in spite of his unmilitary character, and the wide differences between the designs of the leaders and the actions of the rank and file. It was a crowd of rude and simple men that cast themselves on the sacred dust at the first sight of the little mountain town which they had tramped for two thousand miles to see. Tancred saw it first from the slope by the village of Bethlehem, which had opened its gates willingly to his hundred Italian knights; for Bethlehem then as now was an island of Christendom in the sea of Islam. Meanwhile Godfrey came up the road from Jaffa, and crossing the mountain ridge, saw also with his living eyes his vision of the world's desire. But the poorest men about him probably felt the same as he; all ranks knelt together in the dust, and the whole story is one wave of numberless and nameless men. It was a mob that had risen like a man for the faith. It was a mob that had truly been tortured like a man for the faith. It was already transfigured by pain as well as passion. Those that know war in those deserts through the summer months, even with modern supplies and appliances and modern maps and calculations, know that it could only be described as a hell full of heroes. What it must have been to those little local serfs and peasants from the Northern villages, who had never dreamed in nightmares of such landscapes or such a sun, who knew not how men lived at all in such a furnace and could neither guess the alleviations nor get them, is beyond the imagination of man. They arrived dying with thirst, dropping with weariness, lamenting the loss of the dead that rotted along their road; they arrived shrivelled to rags or already raving with fever and they did what they had come to do.

Above all, it is clear that they had the vices as well as the virtues of a mob. The shocking massacre in which they indulged in the sudden relaxation of success is quite obviously a massacre by a mob. It is all the more profoundly revolutionary because it must have been for the most part a French mob. It was of the same order as the Massacre of September, and it is but a part of the same truth that the First Crusade was as revolutionary as the French Revolution. It was of the same order as the Massacre of St. Bartholomew, which was also a piece of purely popular fanaticism, directed against what was also regarded as an anti-national aristocracy. It is practically self-evident that the Christian commanders were opposed to it, and tried to stop it. Tancred promised their lives to the Moslems in the mosque, but the mob clearly disregarded him. Raymond of Toulouse himself saved those in the Tower of David, and managed to send them safely with their property to Ascalon. But revolution with all its evil as well as its good was loose and raging in the streets of the Holy City. And in nothing do we see that spirit of revolution more clearly than in the sight of all those peasants and serfs and vassals, in that one wild moment in revolt, not only against the conquered lords of Islam, but even against the conquering lords of Christendom.

The whole strain of the siege indeed had been one of high and even horrible excitement. Those who tell us to-day about the psychology of the crowd will agree that men who have so suffered and so succeeded are not normal; that their brains are in a dreadful balance which may turn either way. They entered the city at last in a mood in which they might all have become monks; and instead they all became murderers. A brilliant general, who played a decisive part in our own recent Palestinian campaign, told me with a sort of grim humour that he hardly wondered at the story; for he himself had entered Jerusalem in a sort of fury of disappointment; "We went through such a hell to get there, and now it's spoilt for all of us." Such is the heavy irony that hangs over our human nature, making it enter the Holy City as if it were the Heavenly City, and more than any earthly city can be. But the struggle which led to the scaling of Jerusalem in the First Crusade was something much wilder and more incalculable than anything that can be conceived in modern war. We can hardly wonder that the crusading crowd saw the town in front of them as a sort of tower full of demons, and the hills around them as an enchanted and accursed land. For in one very real sense it really was so; for all the elements and expedients were alike unknown qualities. All their enemies' methods were secrets sprung upon them. All their own methods were new things made out of nothing. They wondered alike what would be done on the other side and what could be done on their own side; every movement against them was a stab out of the darkness and every movement they made was a leap in the dark. First, on the one side, we have Tancred trying to take the whole fortified city by climbing up a single slender ladder, as if a man tried to lasso the peak of a mountain. Then we have the flinging from the turrets of a strange and frightful fiery rain, as if water itself had caught fire. It was afterwards known as the Greek Fire and was probably petroleum; but to those who had never seen (or felt) it before it may well have seemed the flaming oil of witchcraft. Then Godfrey and the wiser of the warriors set about to build wooden siege-towers and found they had next to no wood to build them. There was scarcely anything in that rocky waste but the dwarf trees of olive; a poetic fantasy woven about that war in after ages described them as hindered even in their wood-cutting by the demons of that weird place. And indeed the fancy had an essential truth, for the very nature of the land fought against them; and each of those dwarf trees, hard and hollow and twisted, may well have seemed like a grinning goblin. It is said that they found timbers by accident in a cavern; they tore down the beams from ruined houses; at last they got into touch with some craftsmen from Genoa who went to work more successfully; skinning the cattle, who had died in heaps, and covering the timbers. They built three high towers on rollers, and men and beasts dragged them heavily against the high towers of the city. The catapults of the city answered them, the cataracts of devouring fire came down; the wooden towers swayed and tottered, and two of them suddenly stuck motionless and useless. And as the darkness fell a great flare must have told them that the third and last was in flames.

All that night Godfrey was toiling to retrieve the disaster. He took down the whole tower from where it stood and raised it again on the high ground to the north of the city which is now marked by the pine tree that grows outside Herod's gate. And all the time he toiled, it was said, sinister sorcerers sat upon the battlements, working unknown marvels for the undoing of the labour of man. If the great knight had a touch of such symbolism on his own side, he might have seen in his own strife with the solid timber something of the craft that had surrounded the birth of his creed, and the sacred trade of the carpenter. And indeed the very pattern of all carpentry is cruciform, and there is something more than an accident in the allegory. The transverse position of the timber does indeed involve many of those mathematical that are analogous to moral truths and almost every structural shape has the shadow of the mystic rood, as the three dimensions have a shadow of the Trinity. Here is the true mystery of equality; since the longer beam might lengthen itself to infinity, and never be nearer to the symbolic shape without the help of the shorter. Here is that war and wedding between two contrary forces, resisting and supporting each other; the meeting-place of contraries which we, by a sort of pietistic pun, still call the crux of the question. Here is our angular and defiant answer to the self-devouring circle of Asia. It may be improbable, though it is far from impossible (for the age was philosophical enough) that a man like Godfrey thus extended the mystical to the metaphysical; but the writer of a real romance about him would be well within his rights in making him see the symbolism of his own tower, a tower rising above him through the clouds of night as if taking hold on the heaven or showing its network of beams black against the daybreak; scaling the skies and open to all the winds, a ladder and a labyrinth, repeating till it was lost in the twilight the pattern of the sign of the cross.

When dawn was come all those starving peasants may well have stood before the high impregnable walls in the broad daylight of despair. Even their nightmares during the night, of unearthly necromancers looking down at them from the battlements and with signs and spells paralysing all their potential toils, may well have been a sort of pessimistic consolation, anticipating and accounting for failure. The Holy City had become for them a fortress full of fiends, when Godfrey de Bouillon again set himself sword in hand upon the wooden tower and gave the order once more to drag it tottering towards the towers on either side of the postern gate. So they crawled again across the fosse full of the slain, dragging their huge house of timber behind them, and all the blast and din of war broke again about their heads. A hail of bolts hammered such shields as covered them for a canopy, stones and rocks fell on them and crushed them like flies in the mire, and from the engines of the Greek Fire all the torrents of their torment came down on them like red rivers of hell. For indeed the souls of those peasants must have been sickened with something of the topsy-turvydom felt by too many peasants of our own time under the frightful flying batteries of scientific war; a blasphemy of inverted battle in which hell itself has occupied heaven. Something of the vapours vomited by such cruel chemistry may have mingled with the dust of battle, and darkened such light as showed where shattering rocks were rending a roof of shields, to men bowed and blinded as they are by such labour of dragging and such a hailstorm of death. They may have heard through all the racket of nameless noises the high minaret cries of Moslem triumph rising shriller like a wind in shrill pipes, and known little else of what was happening above or beyond them. It was most likely that they laboured and strove in that lower darkness, not knowing that high over their heads, and up above the cloud of battle, the tower of timber and the tower of stone had touched and met in mid-heaven; and great Godfrey, alone and alive, had leapt upon the wall of Jerusalem.

CHAPTER XII

THE FALL OF CHIVALRY

On the back of this book is the name of the New Jerusalem
and on the first page of it a phrase about the necessity of
going back to the old even to find the new, as a man
retraces his steps to a sign-post. The common sense of that
process is indeed most mysteriously misunderstood. Any
suggestion that progress has at any time taken the wrong
turning is always answered by the argument that men
idealise the past, and make a myth of the Age of Gold. If
my progressive guide has led me into a morass or a man-
trap by turning to the left by the red pillar-box, instead of
to the right by the blue palings of the inn called the Rising
Sun, my progressive guide always proceeds to soothe me by
talking about the myth of an Age of Gold. He says I am
idealising the right turning. He says the blue palings are not
so blue as they are painted. He says they are only blue with
distance. He assures me there are spots on the sun, even on
the rising sun. Sometimes he tells me I am wrong in my
fixed conviction that the blue was of solid sapphires, or the
sun of solid gold. In short he assures me I am wrong in
supposing that the right turning was right in every possible
respect; as if I had ever supposed anything of the sort. I
want to go back to that particular place, not because it was
all my fancy paints it, or because it was the best place my
fancy can paint; but because it was a many thousand times
better place than the man-trap in which he and his like
have landed me.

G. K. CHESTERTON

But above all I want to go back to it, not because I know it was the right place but because I think it was the right turning. And the right turning might possibly have led me to the right place; whereas the progressive guide has quite certainly led me to the wrong one.

Now it is quite true that there is less general human testimony to the notion of a New Jerusalem in the future than to the notion of a Golden Age in the past. But neither of those ideas, whether or no they are illusions, are any answer to the question of a plain man in the plain position of this parable; a man who has to find some guidance in the past if he is to get any good in the future. What he positively knows, in any case, is the complete collapse of the present. Now that is the exact truth about the thing so often rebuked as a romantic and unreal return of modern men to medieval things. They suppose they have taken the wrong turning, because they know they are in the wrong place. To know that, it is necessary not to idealise the medieval world, but merely to realise the modern world. It is not so much that they suppose the medieval world was above the average as that they feel sure the modern world is below the average. They do not start either with the idea that man is meant to live in a New Jerusalem of pearl and sapphire in the future, or that a man was meant to live in a picturesque and richly-painted tavern of the past; but with a strong inward and personal persuasion that a man was not meant to live in a man-trap.

For there is and will be more and more a turn of total change in all our talk and writing about history. Everything in the past was praised if it had led up to the present, and blamed if it would have led up to anything else. In short everybody has been searching the past for the secret of our success. Very soon everybody may be searching the past for the secret of our failure. They may be talking in such terms as they use after a motor smash or a bankruptcy; where was the blunder? They may be writing such books as generals write after a military defeat; whose was the fault? The failure will be assumed even in being explained.

For industrialism is no longer a vulgar success. On the contrary, it is now too tragic even to be vulgar. Under the cloud of doom the modern city has taken on something of the dignity of Babel or Babylon. Whether we call it the nemesis of Capitalism or the nightmare of Bolshevism makes no difference; the rich grumble as much as the poor; every one is discontented, and none more than those who are chiefly discontented with the discontent. About that discord we are in perfect harmony; about that disease we all think alike, whatever we think of the diagnosis or the cure. By whatever process in the past we might have come to the right place, practical facts in the present and future will prove more and more that we have come to the wrong place. And for many a premonition will grow more and more of a probability; that we may or may not await another century or another world to see the New Jerusalem rebuilt and shining on our fields; but in the flesh we shall see Babylon fall.

But there is another way in which that metaphor of the forked road will make the position plain. Medieval society was not the right place; it was only the right turning. It was only the right road; or perhaps only the beginning of the right road. The medieval age was very far from being the age in which everything went right. It would be nearer the truth I mean to call it the age in which everything went wrong. It was the moment when things might have developed well, and did develop badly. Or rather, to be yet more exact, it was the moment when they were developing well, and yet they were driven to develop badly. This was the history of all the medieval states and of none more than medieval Jerusalem; indeed there were signs of some serious idea of making it the model medieval state. Of this notion of Jerusalem as the New Jerusalem, of the Utopian aspect of the adventure of the Latin Kingdom, something may be said in a moment. But meanwhile there was a more important part played by Jerusalem, I think, in all that great progress and reaction which has left us the problem of modern Europe. And the suggestion of it is bound up with the former suggestion, about the difference between the goal and the right road that might have led to it. It is bound up with that quality of the civilisation in question, that it was potential rather than perfect; and there is no need to idealise it in order to regret it. This peculiar part played by Jerusalem I mention merely as a suggestion; I might almost say a suspicion. Anyhow, it is something of a guess; but I for one have found it a guide.

Medievalism died, but it died young. It was at once energetic and incomplete when it died, or very shortly before it died. This is not a matter of sympathy or antipathy, but of appreciation of an interesting historic comparison with other historic cases. When the Roman Empire finally failed we cannot of course say that it had done all it was meant to do, for that is dogmatism. We cannot even say it had done all that it might have done, for that is guesswork. But we can say that it had done certain definite things and was conscious of having done them; that it had long and even literally rested on its laurels. But suppose that Rome had fallen when she had only half defeated Carthage, or when she had only half conquered Gaul, or even when the city was Christian but most of the provinces still heathen. Then we should have said, not merely that Rome had not done what she might have done, but that she had not done what she was actually doing. And that is very much the truth in the matter of the medieval civilisation. It was not merely that the medievals left undone what they might have done, but they left undone what they were doing. This potential promise is proved not only in their successes but in their failures. It is shown, for instance, in the very defects of their art. All the crafts of which Gothic architecture formed the frame-work were developed, not only less than they should have been, but less than they would have been. There is no sort of reason why their sculpture should not have become as perfect as their architecture; there is no sort of reason why their sense of form should not have been as finished as their sense of colour. A statue like the St. George of Donatello would have stood more appropriately under a Gothic than under a Classic arch. The niches were already made for the statues. The same thing is true, of course, not only about the state of the crafts but about the status of the craftsman. The best proof that the system of the guilds had an undeveloped good in it is that the most advanced modern men are now going back five hundred years to get the good out of it. The best proof that a rich house was brought to ruin is that our very pioneers are now digging in the ruins to find the riches. That the new guildsmen add a great deal that never belonged to the old guildsmen is not only a truth, but is part of the truth I maintain here. The new guildsmen add what the old guildsmen would have added if they had not died young. When we renew a frustrated thing we do not renew the frustration. But if there are some things in the new that were not in the old, there were certainly some things in the old that are not yet visible in the new; such as individual humour in the handiwork. The point here, however, is not merely that the worker worked well but that he was working better; not merely that his mind was free but that it was growing freer. All this popular power and humour was increasing everywhere, when something touched it and it withered away. The frost had struck it in the spring.

Some people complain that the working man of our own day does not show an individual interest in his work. But it will be well to realise that they would be much more annoyed with him if he did. The medieval workman took so individual an interest in his work that he would call up devils entirely on his own account, carving them in corners according to his own taste and fancy. He would even reproduce the priests who were his patrons and make them as ugly as devils; carving anti-clerical caricatures on the very seats and stalls of the clerics. If a modern householder, on entering his own bathroom, found that the plumber had twisted the taps into the images of two horned and grinning fiends, he would be faintly surprised. If the householder, on returning at evening to his house, found the door-knocker distorted into a repulsive likeness of himself, his surprise might even be tinged with disapproval. It may be just as well that builders and bricklayers do not gratuitously attach gargoyles to our smaller residential villas. But well or ill, it is certainly true that this feature of a flexible popular fancy has never reappeared in any school of architecture or any state of society since the medieval decline. The great classical buildings of the Renascence were swept as bare of it as any villa in Balham. But those who best appreciate this loss to popular art will be the first to agree that at its best it retained a touch of the barbaric as well as the popular. While we can admire these matters of the grotesque, we can admit that their work was sometimes unintentionally as well as intentionally grotesque. Some of the carving did remain so rude that the angels were almost as ugly as the devils. But this is the very point upon which I would here insist; the mystery of why men who were so obviously only beginning should have so suddenly stopped.

Men with medieval sympathies are sometimes accused, absurdly enough, of trying to prove that the medieval period was perfect. In truth the whole case for it is that it was imperfect. It was imperfect as an unripe fruit or a growing child is imperfect. Indeed it was imperfect in that very particular fashion which most modern thinkers generally praise, more than they ever praise maturity. It was something now much more popular than an age of perfection; it was an age of progress. It was perhaps the one real age of progress in all history. Men have seldom moved with such rapidity and such unity from barbarism to civilisation as they did from the end of the Dark Ages to the times of the universities and the parliaments, the cathedrals and the guilds. Up to a certain point we may say that everything, at whatever stage of improvement, was full of the promise of improvement. Then something began to go wrong, almost equally rapidly, and the glory of this great culture is not so much in what it did as in what it might have done. It recalls one of these typical medieval speculations, full of the very fantasy of free will, in which the schoolmen tried to fancy the fate of every herb or animal if Adam had not eaten the apple. It remains, in a cant historical phrase, one of the great might-have-beens of history.

I have said that it died young; but perhaps it would be truer to say that it suddenly grew old. Like Godfrey and many of its great champions in Jerusalem, it was overtaken in the prime of life by a mysterious malady. The more a man reads of history the less easy he will find it to explain that secret and rapid decay of medieval civilisation from within. Only a few generations separated the world that worshipped St. Francis from the world that burned Joan of Arc. One would think there might be no more than a date and a number between the white mystery of Louis the Ninth and the black mystery of Louis the Eleventh. This is the very real historical mystery; the more realistic is our study of medieval things, the more puzzled we shall be about the peculiar creeping paralysis which affected things so virile and so full of hope. There was a growth of moral morbidity as well as social inefficiency, especially in the governing classes; for even to the end the guildsmen and the peasants remained much more vigorous. How it ended we all know; personally I should say that they got the Reformation and deserved it. But it matters nothing to the truth here whether the Reformation was a just revolt and revenge or an unjust culmination and conquest. It is common ground to Catholics and Protestants of intelligence that evils preceded and produced the schism; and that evils were produced by it and have pursued it down to our own day. We know it if only in the one example, that the schism begat the Thirty Years' War, and the Thirty Years' War begat the Seven Years' War, and the Seven Years' War begat the Great War, which has passed like a pestilence through our own homes. After the schism Prussia could relapse into heathenry and erect an ethical system external to the whole culture of Christendom. But it can still be reasonably asked what begat the schism; and it can still be reasonably answered; something that went wrong with medievalism. But what was it that went wrong?

When I looked for the last time on the towers of Zion I had a fixed fancy that I knew what it was. It is a thing that cannot be proved or disproved; it must sound merely an ignorant guess. But I believe myself that it died of disappointment. I believe the whole medieval society failed, because the heart went out of it with the loss of Jerusalem. Let it be observed that I do not say the loss of the war, or even the Crusade. For the war against Islam was not lost. The Moslem was overthrown in the real battle-field, which was Spain; he was menaced in Africa; his imperial power was already stricken and beginning slowly to decline. I do not mean the political calculations about a Mediterranean war. I do not even mean the Papal conceptions about the Holy War. I mean the purely popular picture of the Holy City. For while the aristocratic thing was a view, the vulgar thing was a vision; something with which all stories stop, something where the rainbow ends, something over the hills and far away. In Spain they had been victorious; but their castle was not even a castle in Spain. It was a castle east of the sun and west of the moon, and the fairy prince could find it no more. Indeed that idle image out of the nursery books fits it very exactly. For its mystery was and is in standing in the middle, or as they said in the very centre of the earth. It is east of the sun of Europe, which fills the world with a daylight of sanity, and ripens real and growing things. It is west of the moon of Asia, mysterious and archaic with its cold volcanoes, silver mirror for poets and a most fatal magnet for lunatics.

Anyhow the fall of Jerusalem, and in that sense the failure of the Crusades, had a widespread effect, as I should myself suggest, for the reason I have myself suggested. Because it had been a popular movement, it was a popular disappointment; and because it had been a popular movement, its ideal was an image; a particular picture in the imagination. For poor men are almost always particularists; and nobody has ever seen such a thing as a mob of pantheists. I have seen in some of that lost literature of the old guilds, which is now everywhere coming to light, a list of the stage properties required for some village play, one of those popular plays acted by the medieval trades unions, for which the guild of the shipwrights would build Noah's Ark or the guild of the barbers provide golden wigs for the haloes of the Twelve Apostles. The list of those crude pieces of stage furniture had a curious colour of poetry about it, like the impromptu apparatus of a nursery charade; a cloud, an idol with a club, and notably among the rest, the walls and towers of Jerusalem. I can imagine them patiently painted and gilded as a special feature, like the two tubs of Mr. Vincent Crummles. But I can also imagine that towards the end of the Middle Ages, the master of the revels might begin to look at those towers of wood and pasteboard with a sort of pain, and perhaps put them away in a corner, as a child will tire of a toy especially if it is associated with a disappointment or a dismal misunderstanding. There is noticeable in some of the later popular poems a disposition to sulk about the Crusades. But though the popular feeling had been largely poetical, the same thing did in its degree occur in the political realm that was purely practical. The Moslem had been checked, but he had not been checked enough. The whole story of what was called the Eastern Question, and three-quarters of the wars of the modern world, were due to the fact that he was not checked enough.

The only thing to do with unconquerable things is to conquer them. That alone will cure them of invincibility; or what is worse, their own vision of invincibility. That was the conviction of those of us who would not accept what we considered a premature peace with Prussia. That is why we would not listen either to the Tory Pro-Germanism of Lord Lansdowne or the Socialist Pro-Germanism of Mr. Macdonald. If a lunatic believes in his luck so fixedly as to feel sure be cannot be caught, he will not only believe in it still, but believe in it more and more, until the actual instant when he is caught. The longer the chase, the more certain he will be of escaping; the more narrow the escapes, the more certain will be the escape. And indeed if he does escape it will seem a miracle, and almost a divine intervention, not only to the pursued but to the pursuers. The evil thing will chiefly appear unconquerable to those who try to conquer it. It will seem after all to have a secret of success; and those who failed against it will hide in their hearts a secret of failure. It was that secret of failure, I fancy, that slowly withered from within the high hopes of the Middle Ages. Christianity and chivalry had measured their force against Mahound, and Mahound had not fallen; the shadow of his horned helmet, the crest of the Crescent, still lay across their sunnier lands; the Horns of Hattin. The streams of life that flowed to guilds and schools and orders of knighthood and brotherhoods of friars were strangely changed and chilled. So, if the peace had left Prussianism secure even in Prussia, I believe that all the liberal ideals of the Latins, and all the liberties of the English, and the whole theory of a democratic experiment in America, would have begun to die of a deep and even subconscious despair. A vote, a jury, a newspaper, would not be as they are, things of which it is hard to make the right use, or any use; they would be things of which nobody would even try to make any use. A vote would actually look like a vassal's cry of "haro," a jury would look like a joust; many would no more read headlines than blazon heraldic coats. For these medieval things look dead and dusty because of a defeat, which was none the less a defeat because it was more than half a victory.

A curious cloud of confusion rests on the details of that defeat. The Christian captains who acted in it were certainly men on a different moral level from the good Duke Godfrey; their characters were by comparison mixed and even mysterious. Perhaps the two determining personalities were Raymond of Tripoli, a skilful soldier whom his enemies seemed to have accused of being much too skilful a diplomatist; and Renaud of Chatillon, a violent adventurer whom his enemies seem to have accused of being little better than a bandit. And it is the irony of the incident that Raymond got into trouble for making a dubious peace with the Saracens, while Renaud got into trouble by making an equally dubious war on the Saracens. Renaud exacted from Moslem travellers on a certain road what he regarded as a sort of feudal toll or tax, and they regarded as a brigand ransom; and when they did not pay he attacked them. This was regarded as a breach of the truce; but probably it would have been easier to regard Renaud as waging the war of a robber, if many had not regarded Raymond as having made the truce of a traitor. Probably Raymond was not a traitor, since the military advice he gave up to the very instant of catastrophe was entirely loyal and sound, and worthy of so wise a veteran. And very likely Renaud was not merely a robber, especially in his own eyes; and there seems to be a much better case for him than many modern writers allow. But the very fact of such charges being bandied among the factions shows a certain fall from the first days under the headship of the house of Bouillon. No slanderer ever suggested that Godfrey was a traitor; no enemy ever asserted that Godfrey was only a thief. It is fairly clear that there had been a degeneration; but most people hardly realise sufficiently that there had been a very great thing from which to degenerate.

The first Crusades had really had some notion of Jerusalem as a New Jerusalem. I mean they had really had a vision of the place being not only a promised land but a Utopia or even an Earthly Paradise. The outstanding fact and feature which is seldom seized is this: that the social experiment in Palestine was rather in advance of the social experiments in the rest of Christendom. Having to begin at the beginning, they really began with what they considered the best ideas of their time; like any group of Socialists founding an ideal Commonwealth in a modern colony. A specialist on this period, Colonel Conder of the Palestine Exploration, has written that the core of the Code was founded on the recommendations of Godfrey himself in his "Letters of the Sepulchre"; and he observes concerning it: "The basis of these laws was found in Justinian's code, and they presented features as yet quite unknown in Europe, especially in their careful provision of justice for the bourgeois and the peasant, and for the trading communes whose fleets were so necessary to the king. Not only were free men judged by juries of their equals, but the same applied to those who were technically serfs and actually aborigines." The original arrangements of the Native Court seem to me singularly liberal, even by modern standards of the treatment of natives. That in many such medieval codes citizens were still called serfs is no more final than the fact that in many modern capitalist newspapers serfs are still called citizens. The whole point about the villein was that he was a tenant at least as permanent as a peasant. He "went with the land"; and there are a good many hopeless tramps starving in streets, or sleeping in ditches, who might not be sorry if they could go with a little land. It would not be very much worse than homelessness and hunger to go with a good kitchen garden of which you could always eat most of the beans and turnips; or to go with a good cornfield of which you could take a considerable proportion of the corn. There has been many a modern man would have been none the worse for "going" about burdened with such a green island, or dragging the chains of such a tangle of green living things. As a fact, of course, this system throughout Christendom was already evolving rapidly into a pure peasant proprietorship; and it will be long before industrialism evolves by itself into anything so equal or so free. Above all, there appears notably that universal mark of the medieval movement; the voluntary liberation of slaves. But we may willingly allow that something of the earlier success of all this was due to the personal qualities of the first knights fresh from the West; and especially to the personal justice and moderation of Godfrey and some of his immediate kindred. Godfrey died young; his successors had mostly short periods of power, largely through the prevalence of malaria and the absence of medicine. Royal marriages with the more oriental tradition of the Armenian princes brought in new elements of luxury and cynicism; and by the time of the disputed truce of Raymond of Tripoli, the crown had descended to a man named Guy of Lusignan who seems to have been regarded as a somewhat unsatisfactory character. He had quarrelled with Raymond, who was ruler of Galilee, and a curious and rather incomprehensible concession made by the latter, that the Saracens should ride in arms but in peace round his land, led to alleged Moslem insults to Nazareth, and the outbreak of the furious Templar, Gerard of Bideford, of which mention has been made already. But the most serious threat to them and their New Jerusalem was the emergence among the Moslems of a man of military genius, and the fact that all that land lay now under the shadow of the ambition and ardour of Saladin.

With the breach of the truce, or even the tale of it, the common danger of Christians was apparent; and Raymond of Tripoli repaired to the royal headquarters to consult with his late enemy the king; but he seems to have been almost openly treated as a traitor. Gerard of Bideford, the fanatic who was Grand Master of the Templars, forced the king's hand against the advice of the wiser soldier, who had pointed out the peril of perishing of thirst in the waterless wastes between them and the enemy. Into those wastes they advanced, and they were already weary and unfit for warfare by the time they came in sight of the strange hills that will be remembered for ever under the name of the

Horns of Hattin. On those hills, a few hours later, the last knights of an army of which half had fallen gathered in a final defiance and despair round the relic they carried in their midst, a fragment of the True Cross. In that hour fell, as I have fancied, more hopes than they themselves could number, and the glory departed from the Middle Ages. There fell with them all that New Jerusalem which was the symbol of a new world, all those great and growing promises and possibilities of Christendom of which this vision was the centre, all that "justice for the bourgeois and the peasant, and for the trading communes," all the guilds that gained their charters by fighting for the Cross, all the hopes of a happier transformation of the Roman Law wedded to charity and to chivalry. There was the first slip and the great swerving of our fate; and in that wilderness we lost all the things we should have loved, and shall need so long a labour to find again.

Raymond of Tripoli had hewn his way through the enemy and ridden away to Tyre. The king, with a few of the remaining nobles, including Renaud de Chatillon, were brought before Saladin in his tent. There occurred a scene strangely typical of the mingled strains in the creed or the culture that triumphed on that day; the stately Eastern courtesy and hospitality; the wild Eastern hatred and self-will. Saladin welcomed the king and gracefully gave him a cup of sherbet, which he passed to Renaud. "It is thou and not I who hast given him to drink," said the Saracen, preserving the precise letter of the punctilio of hospitality. Then he suddenly flung himself raving and reviling upon Renaud de Chatillon, and killed the prisoner with his own hands. Outside, two hundred Hospitallers and Templars were beheaded on the field of battle; by one account I have read because Saladin disliked them, and by another because they were Christian priests.

There is a strong bias against the Christians and in favour of the Moslems and the Jews in most of the Victorian historical works, especially historical novels. And most people of modern, or rather of very recent times got all their notions of history from dipping into historical novels. In those romances the Jew is always the oppressed where in reality he was often the oppressor. In those romances the Arab is always credited with oriental dignity and courtesy and never with oriental crookedness and cruelty. The same injustice is introduced into history, which by means of selection and omission can be made as fictitious as any fiction. Twenty historians mention the way in which the maddened Christian mob murdered the Moslems after the capture of Jerusalem, for one who mentions that the Moslem commander commanded in cold blood the murder of some two hundred of his most famous and valiant enemies after the victory of Hattin. The former cannot be shown to have been the act of Tancred, while the latter was quite certainly the act of Saladin. Yet Tancred is described as at best a doubtful character, while Saladin is represented as a Bayard without fear or blame. Both of them doubtless were ordinary faulty fighting men, but they are not judged by an equal balance. It may seem a paradox that there should be this prejudice in Western history in favour of Eastern heroes. But the cause is clear enough; it is the remains of the revolt among many Europeans against their own old religious organisation, which naturally made them hunt through all ages for its crimes and its victims. It was natural that Voltaire should sympathise more with a Brahmin he had never seen than with a Jesuit with whom he was engaged in a violent controversy; and should similarly feel more dislike of a Catholic who was his enemy than of a Moslem who was the enemy of his enemy. In this atmosphere of natural and even pardonable prejudice arose the habit of contrasting the intolerance of the Crusaders with the toleration shown by the Moslems. Now as there are two sides to everything, it would undoubtedly be quite possible to tell the tale of the Crusades, correctly enough in detail, and in such a way as entirely to justify the Moslems and condemn the Crusaders. But any such real record of the Moslem case would have very little to do with any questions of tolerance or intolerance, or any modern ideas about religious liberty and equality. As the modern world does not know what it means itself by religious liberty and equality, as the moderns have not thought out any logical theory of toleration at all (for their vague generalisations can always be upset by twenty tests from Thugs to Christian Science) it would obviously be unreasonable to expect the moderns to understand the much clearer philosophy of the Moslems. But some rough suggestion of what was really involved may be found convenient in this case.

Islam was not originally a movement directed against Christianity at all. It did not face westwards, so to speak; it faced eastwards towards the idolatries of Asia. But Mahomet believed that these idols could be fought more successfully with a simpler kind of creed; one might almost say with a simpler kind of Christianity. For he included many things which we in the West commonly suppose not only to be peculiar to Christianity but to be peculiar to Catholicism. Many things have been rejected by Protestantism that are not rejected by Mahometanism. Thus the Moslems believe in Purgatory, and they give at least a sort of dignity to the Mother of Christ. About such things as these they have little of the bitterness that rankles in the Jews and is said sometimes to become hideously vitriolic. While I was in Palestine a distinguished Moslem said to a Christian resident: "We also, as well as you, honour the Mother of Christ. Never do we speak of her but we call her the Lady Miriam. I dare not tell you what the Jews call her."

The real mistake of the Moslems is something much more modern in its application than any particular or passing persecution of Christians as such. It lay in the very fact that they did think they had a simpler and saner sort of Christianity, as do many modern Christians. They thought it could be made universal merely by being made uninteresting. Now a man preaching what he thinks is a platitude is far more intolerant than a man preaching what he admits is a paradox. It was exactly because it seemed self-evident, to Moslems as to Bolshevists, that their simple creed was suited to everybody, that they wished in that particular sweeping fashion to impose it on everybody. It was because Islam was broad that Moslems were narrow. And because it was not a hard religion it was a heavy rule. Because it was without a self-correcting complexity, it allowed of those simple and masculine but mostly rather dangerous appetites that show themselves in a chieftain or a lord. As it had the simplest sort of religion, monotheism, so it had the simplest sort of government, monarchy. There was exactly the same direct spirit in its despotism as in its deism. The Code, the Common Law, the give and take of charters and chivalric vows, did not grow in that golden desert. The great sun was in the sky and the great Saladin was in his tent, and he must be obeyed unless he were assassinated. Those who complain of our creeds as elaborate often forget that the elaborate Western creeds have produced the elaborate Western constitutions; and that they are elaborate because they are emancipated. And the real moral of the relations of the two great religions is something much more subtle and sincere than any mere atrocity tales against Turks. It is the same as the moral of the Christian refusal of a Pagan Pantheon in which Christ should rank with Ammon and Apollo. Twice the Christian Church refused what seemed like a handsome offer of a large latitudinarian sort; once to include Christ as a god and once to include him as a prophet; once by the admission of all idols and once by the abandonment of all idols. Twice the Church took the risk and twice the Church survived alone and succeeded alone, filling the world with her own children; and leaving her rivals in a desert, where the idols were dead and the iconoclasts were dying.

But all this history has been hidden by a prejudice more general than the particular case of Saracens and Crusaders.

The modern, or rather the Victorian prejudice against Crusaders is positive and not relative; and it would still desire to condemn Tancred if it could not acquit Saladin. Indeed it is a prejudice not so much against Crusaders as against Christians. It will not give to these heroes of religious war the fair measure it gives to the heroes of ordinary patriotic and imperial war. There never was a nobler hero than Nelson, or one more national or more normal. Yet Nelson quite certainly did do what Tancred almost certainly did not do; break his own word by giving up his own brave enemies to execution. If the cause of Nelson in other times comes to be treated as the creed of Tancred has often in recent times been treated, this incident alone will be held sufficient to prove not only that Nelson was a liar and a scoundrel, but that he did not love England at all, did not love Lady Hamilton at all, that he sailed in English ships only to pocket the prize money of French ships, and would as willingly have sailed in French ships for the prize money of English ships. That is the sort of dull dust of gold that has been shaken like the drifting dust of the desert over the swords and the relics, the crosses and the clasped hands of the men who marched to Jerusalem or died at Hattin. In these medieval pilgrims every inconsistency is a hypocrisy; while in the more modern patriots even an infamy is only an inconsistency. I have rounded off the story here with the ruin at Hattin because the whole reaction against the pilgrimage had its origin there; and because it was this at least that finally lost Jerusalem. Elsewhere in Palestine, to say nothing of Africa and Spain, splendid counter-strokes were still being delivered from the West, not the least being the splendid rescue by Richard of England. But I still think that with the mere name of that tiny town upon the hills the note of the whole human revolution had been struck, was changed and was silent. All the other names were only the names of Eastern towns; but that was nearer to a man than his neighbours; a village inside his village, a house inside his house.

There is a hill above Bethlehem of a strange shape, with a flat top which makes it look oddly like an island, habitable though uninhabited, when all Moab heaves about it and beyond it as with the curves and colours of a sea. Its stability suggests in some strange fashion what may often be felt in these lands with the longest record of culture; that there may be not only a civilisation but even a chivalry older than history. Perhaps the table-land with its round top has a romantic reminiscence of a round table. Perhaps it is only a fantastic effect of evening, for it is felt most when the low skies are swimming with the colours of sunset, and in the shadows the shattered rocks about its base take on the shapes of titanic paladins fighting and falling around it. I only know that the mere shape of the hill and vista of the landscape suggested such visions and it was only afterwards that I heard the local legend, which says it is here that some of the Christian knights made their last stand after they lost Jerusalem and which names this height The Mountain of the Latins.

They fell, and the ages rolled on them the rocks of scorn; they were buried in jests and buffooneries. As the Renascence expanded into the rationalism of recent centuries, nothing seemed so ridiculous as to butcher and bleed in a distant desert not only for a tomb, but an empty tomb. The last legend of them withered under the wit of Cervantes, though he himself had fought in the last Crusade at Lepanto. They were kicked about like dead donkeys by the cool vivacity of Voltaire; who went off, very symbolically, to dance attendance on the new drill-sergeant of the Prussians. They were dissected like strange beasts by the serene disgust of Gibbon, more serene than the similar horror with which he regarded the similar violence of the French Revolution. By our own time even the flippancy has become a platitude. They have long been the butt of every penny-a-liner who can talk of a helmet as a tin pot, of every caricaturist on a comic paper who can draw a fat man falling off a bucking horse; of every pushing professional politician who can talk about the superstitions of the Middle Ages. Great men and small have agreed to contemn them; they were renounced by their children and refuted by their biographers; they were exposed, they were exploded, they were ridiculed and they were right.

They were proved wrong, and they were right. They were judged finally and forgotten, and they were right. Centuries after their fall the full experience and development of political discovery has shown beyond question that they were right. For there is a very simple test of the truth; that the very thing which was dismissed, as a dream of the ages of faith, we have been forced to turn into a fact in the ages of fact. It is now more certain than it ever was before that Europe must rescue some lordship, or overlordship, of these old Roman provinces. Whether it is wise for England alone to claim Palestine, whether it would be better if the Entente could do so, I think a serious question. But in some form they are reverting for the Roman Empire. Every opportunity has been given for any other empire that could be its equal, and especially for the great dream of a mission for Imperial Islam. If ever a human being had a run for his money, it was the Sultan of the Moslems riding on his Arab steed. His empire expanded over and beyond the great Greek empire of Byzantium; a last charge of the chivalry of Poland barely stopped it at the very gates of Vienna. He was free to unfold everything that was in him, and he unfolded the death that was in him. He reigned and he could not rule; he was successful and he did not succeed. His baffled and retreating enemies left him standing, and he could not stand. He fell finally with that other half-heathen power in the North, with which he had made an alliance against the remains of Roman and Byzantine culture. He fell because barbarism cannot stand; because even when it succeeds it rather falls on its foes and crushes them. And after all these things, after all these ages, with a wearier philosophy, with a heavier heart, we have been forced to do again the very thing that the Crusaders were derided for doing. What Western men failed to do for the faith, other Western men have been forced to do even without the faith. The sons of Tancred are again in Tripoli. The heirs of Raymond are again in Syria. And men from the Midlands or the Northumbrian towns went again through a furnace of thirst and fever and furious fighting, to gain the same water-courses and invest the same cities as of old. They trod the hills of Galilee and the Horns of Hattin threw no shadow on their souls; they crossed dark and disastrous fields whose fame had been hidden from them, and avenged the fathers they had forgotten. And the most cynical of modern diplomatists, making their settlement by the most sceptical of modern philosophies, can find no practical or even temporary solution for this sacred land, except to bring it again under the crown of Coeur de Lion and the cross of St. George.

There came in through the crooked entry beside the great gap in the wall a tall soldier, dismounting and walking and wearing only the dust-hued habit of modern war. There went no trumpet before him, neither did he enter by the Golden Gate; but the silence of the deserts was full of a phantom acclamation, as when from far away a wind brings in a whisper the cheering of many thousand men. For in that hour a long-lost cry found fulfilment, and something counted irrational returned in the reason of things. And at last even the wise understood, and at last even the learned were enlightened on a need truly and indeed international, which a mob in a darker age had known by the light of nature; something that could be denied and delayed and evaded, but not escaped for ever. *Id Deus vult.*

CHAPTER XIII

THE PROBLEM OF ZIONISM

There is an attitude for which my friends and I were for a long period rebuked and even reviled; and of which at the present period we are less likely than ever to repent. It was always called Anti-Semitism; but it was always much more true to call it Zionism. At any rate it was much nearer to the nature of the thing to call it Zionism, whether or no it can find its geographical concentration in Zion. The substance of this heresy was exceedingly simple. It consisted entirely in saying that Jews are Jews; and as a logical consequence that they are not Russians or Roumanians or Italians or Frenchmen or Englishmen. During the war the newspapers commonly referred to them as Russians; but the ritual wore so singularly thin that I remember one news-paper paragraph saying that the Russians in the East End complained of the food regulations, because their religion forbade them to eat pork. My own brief contact with the Greek priests of the Orthodox Church in Jerusalem did not permit me to discover any trace of this detail of their discipline; and even the Russian pilgrims were said to be equally negligent in the matter. The point for the moment, however, is that if I was violently opposed to anything, it was not to Jews, but to that sort of remark about Jews; or rather to the silly and craven fear of making it a remark about Jews. But my friends and I had in some general sense a policy in the matter; and it was in substance the desire to give Jews the dignity and status of a separate nation. We desired that in some fashion, and so far as possible, Jews should be represented by Jews, should live in a society of Jews, should be judged by Jews and ruled by Jews. I am an Anti-Semite if that is Anti-Semitism. It would seem more rational to call it Semitism.

Of this attitude, I repeat, I am now less likely than ever to repent. I have lived to see the thing that was dismissed as a fad discussed everywhere as a fact; and one of the most menacing facts of the age. I have lived to see people who accused me of Anti-Semitism become far more Anti-Semitic than I am or ever was. I have heard people talking with real injustice about the Jews, who once seemed to think it an injustice to talk about them at all. But, above all, I have seen with my own eyes wild mobs marching through a great city, raving not only against Jews, but against the English for identifying themselves with the Jews. I have seen the whole prestige of England brought into peril, merely by the trick of talking about two nations as if they were one. I have seen an Englishman arriving in Jerusalem with somebody he had been taught to regard as his fellow countryman and political colleague, and received as if he had come arm-in-arm with a flaming dragon. So do our frosty fictions fare when they come under that burning sun.

Twice in my life, and twice lately, I have seen a piece of English pedantry bring us within an inch of an enormous English peril. The first was when all the Victorian historians and philosophers had told us that our German cousin was a cousin german and even germane; something naturally near and sympathetic. That also was an identification; that also was an assimilation; that also was a union of hearts. For the second time in a few short years, English politicians and journalists have discovered the dreadful revenge of reality. To pretend that something is what it is not is business that can easily be fashionable and sometimes popular. But the thing we have agreed to regard as what it is not will always abruptly punish and pulverise us, merely by being what it is. For years we were told that the

Germans were a sort of Englishman because they were Teutons; but it was all the worse for us when we found out what Teutons really were. For years we were told that Jews were a sort of Englishman because they were British subjects. It is all the worse for us now we have to regard them, not subjectively as subjects, but objectively as objects; as objects of a fierce hatred among the Moslems and the Greeks. We are in the absurd position of introducing to these people a new friend whom they instantly recognise as an old enemy. It is an absurd position because it is a false position; but it is merely the penalty of falsehood.

Whether this Eastern anger is reasonable or not may be discussed in a moment; but what is utterly unreasonable is not the anger but the astonishment; at least it is our astonishment at their astonishment. We might believe ourselves in the view that a Jew is an Englishman; but there was no reason why they should regard him as an Englishman, since they already recognised him as a Jew. This is the whole present problem of the Jew in Palestine; and it must be solved either by the logic of Zionism or the logic of purely English supremacy and, impartiality; and not by what seems to everybody in Palestine a monstrous muddle of the two. But of course it is not only the peril in Palestine that has made the realisation of the Jewish problem, which once suffered all the dangers of a fad, suffer the opposite dangers of a fashion. The same journalists who politely describe Jews as Russians are now very impolitely describing certain Russians who are Jews. Many who had no particular objection to Jews as Capitalists have a very great objection to them as Bolshevists. Those who had an innocent unconsciousness of the nationality of Eckstein, even when he called himself Eckstein, have managed to discover the nationality of Braunstein, even, when he calls, himself Trotsky. And much of this peril also might easily have been lessened, by the simple proposal to call men and things by their own names.

I will confess, however, that I have no very full sympathy with the new Anti-Semitism which is merely Anti-Socialism. There are good, honourable and magnanimous Jews of every type and rank, there are many to whom I am greatly attached among my own friends in my own rank; but if I have to make a general choice on a general chance among different types of Jews, I have much more sympathy with the Jew who is revolutionary than the Jew who is plutocratic. In other words, I have much more sympathy for the Israelite we are beginning to reject, than for the Israelite we have already accepted. I have more respect for him when he leads some sort of revolt, however narrow and anarchic, against the oppression of the poor, than when he is safe at the head of a great money-lending business oppressing the poor himself. It is not the poor aliens, but the rich aliens I wish we had excluded. I myself wholly reject Bolshevism, not because its actions are violent, but because its very thought is materialistic and mean. And if this preference is true even of Bolshevism, it is ten times truer of Zionism. It really seems to me rather hard that the full storm of fury should have burst about the Jews, at the very moment when some of them at least have felt the call of a far cleaner ideal; and that when we have tolerated their tricks with our country, we should turn on them precisely when they seek in sincerity for their own.

But in order to judge this Jewish possibility, we must understand more fully the nature of the Jewish problem. We must consider it from the start, because there are still many who do not know that there is a Jewish problem. That problem has its proof, of course, in the history of the Jew, and the fact that he came from the East. A Jew will sometimes complain of the injustice of describing him as a man of the East; but in truth another very real injustice may be involved in treating him as a man of the West. Very often even the joke against the Jew is rather a joke against those who have made the joke; that is, a joke against what they have made out of the Jew. This is true especially, for

G. K. CHESTERTON

instance, of many points of religion and ritual. Thus we cannot help feeling, for instance, that there is something a little grotesque about the Hebrew habit of putting on a top-hat as an act of worship. It is vaguely mixed up with another line of humour, about another class of Jew, who wears a large number of hats; and who must not therefore be credited with an extreme or extravagant religious zeal, leading him to pile up a pagoda of hats towards heaven. To Western eyes, in Western conditions, there really is something inevitably fantastic about this formality of the synagogue. But we ought to remember that we have made the Western conditions which startle the Western eyes. It seems odd to wear a modern top-hat as if it were a mitre or a biretta; it seems quainter still when the hat is worn even for the momentary purpose of saying grace before lunch. It seems quaintest of all when, at some Jewish luncheon parties, a tray of hats is actually handed round, and each guest helps himself to a hat as a sort of *hors d'oeuvre*. All this could easily be turned into a joke; but we ought to realise that the joke is against ourselves. It is not merely we who make fun of it, but we who have made it funny. For, after all, nobody can pretend that this particular type of head-dress is a part of that uncouth imagery "setting painting and sculpture at defiance" which Renan remarked in the tradition of Hebrew civilisation. Nobody can say that a top-hat was among the strange symbolic utensils dedicated to the obscure service of the Ark; nobody can suppose that a top-hat descended from heaven among the wings and wheels of the flying visions of the Prophets. For this wild vision the West is entirely responsible. Europe has created the Tower of Giotto; but it has also created the topper. We of the West must bear the burden, as best we may, both of the responsibility and of the hat. It is solely the special type and shape of hat that makes the Hebrew ritual seem ridiculous. Performed in the old original Hebrew fashion it is not ridiculous, but rather if anything sublime. For the original fashion was an oriental fashion; and the Jews are orientals; and the mark of all such orientals is the wearing of long and loose draperies. To throw those loose draperies over the head is decidedly a dignified and even poetic gesture. One can imagine something like justice done to its majesty and mystery in one of the great dark drawings of William Blake. It may be true, and personally I think it is true, that the Hebrew covering of the head signifies a certain stress on the fear of God, which is the beginning of wisdom, while the Christian uncovering of the head suggests rather the love of God that is the end of wisdom. But this has nothing to do with the taste and dignity of the ceremony; and to do justice to these we must treat the Jew as an oriental; we must even dress him as an oriental.

I have only taken this as one working example out of many that would point to the same conclusion. A number of points upon which the unfortunate alien is blamed would be much improved if he were, not less of an alien, but rather more of an alien. They arise from his being too like us, and too little like himself. It is obviously the case, for instance, touching that vivid vulgarity in clothes, and especially the colours of clothes, with which a certain sort of Jews brighten the landscape or seascape at Margate or many holiday resorts. When we see a foreign gentleman on Brighton Pier wearing yellow spats, a magenta waistcoat, and an emerald green tie, we feel that he has somehow missed certain fine shades of social sensibility and fitness. It might considerably surprise the company on Brighton Pier, if he were to reply by solemnly unwinding his green necktie from round his neck, and winding it round his head. Yet the reply would be the right one; and would be equally logical and artistic. As soon as the green tie had become a green turban, it might look as appropriate and even attractive as the green turban of any pilgrim of Mecca or any descendant of Mahomet, who walks with a stately air through the streets of Jaffa or Jerusalem. The bright colours that make the Margate Jews hideous are no brighter than those that make the Moslem crowd picturesque. They are only worn in the wrong place, in the wrong way, and in

G. K. CHESTERTON

conjunction with a type and cut of clothing that is meant to be more sober and restrained. Little can really be urged against him, in that respect, except that his artistic instinct is rather for colour than form, especially of the kind that we ourselves have labelled good form.

This is a mere symbol, but it is so suitable a symbol that I have often offered it symbolically as a solution of the Jewish problem. I have felt disposed to say: let all liberal legislation stand, let all literal and legal civic equality stand; let a Jew occupy any political or social position which he can gain in open competition; let us not listen for a moment to any suggestions of reactionary restrictions or racial privilege. Let a Jew be Lord Chief justice, if his exceptional veracity and reliability have clearly marked him out for that post. Let a Jew be Archbishop of Canterbury, if our national religion has attained to that receptive breadth that would render such a transition unobjectionable and even unconscious. But let there be one single-clause bill; one simple and sweeping law about Jews, and no other. Be it enacted, by the King's Most Excellent Majesty, by and with the advice of the Lords Spiritual and Temporal and the Commons in Parliament assembled, that every Jew must be dressed like an Arab. Let him sit on the Woolsack, but let him sit there dressed as an Arab. Let him preach in St. Paul's Cathedral, but let him preach there dressed as an Arab. It is not my point at present to dwell on the pleasing if flippant fancy of how much this would transform the political scene; of the dapper figure of Sir Herbert Samuel swathed as a Bedouin, or Sir Alfred Mond gaining a yet greater grandeur from the gorgeous and trailing robes of the East. If my image is quaint my intention is quite serious; and the point of it is not personal to any particular Jew. The point applies to any Jew, and to our own recovery of healthier relations with him. The point is that we should know where we are; and he would know where he is, which is in a foreign land.

This is but a parenthesis and a parable, but it brings us to the concrete controversial matter which is the Jewish problem. Only a few years ago it was regarded as a mark of a blood-thirsty disposition to admit that the Jewish problem was a problem, or even that the Jew was a Jew. Through much misunderstanding certain friends of mine and myself have persisted in disregarding the silence thus imposed; but facts have fought for us more effectively than words. By this time nobody is more conscious of the Jewish problem than the most intelligent and idealistic of the Jews. The folly of the fashion by which Jews often concealed their Jewish names, must surely be manifest by this time even to those who concealed them. To mention but one example of the way in which this fiction falsified the relations of everybody and everything, it is enough to note that it involved the Jews themselves in a quite new and quite needless unpopularity in the first years of the war. A poor little Jewish tailor, who called himself by a German name merely because he lived for a short time in a German town, was instantly mobbed in Whitechapel for his share in the invasion of Belgium. He was cross-examined about why he had damaged the tower of Rheims; and talked to as if he had killed Nurse Cavell with his own pair of shears. It was very unjust; quite as unjust as it would be to ask Bethmann-Hollweg why he had stabbed Eglon or hewn Agag in pieces. But it was partly at least the fault of the Jew himself, and of the whole of that futile and unworthy policy which had led him to call himself Bernstein when his name was Benjamin.

In such cases the Jews are accused of all sorts of faults they have not got; but there are faults that they have got. Some of the charges against them, as in the cases I have quoted concerning religious ritual and artistic taste, are due merely to the false light in which they are regarded. Other faults may also be due to the false position in which they are placed. But the faults exist; and nothing was ever more dangerous to everybody concerned than the recent fashion of denying or ignoring them. It was done simply by the snobbish habit of suppressing the experience and evidence of the majority of people, and especially of the majority of poor people. It was done by confining the controversy to a small world of wealth and refinement, remote from all the real facts involved. For the rich are the most ignorant people on earth, and the best that can be said for them, in cases like these, is that their ignorance often reaches the point of innocence.

I will take a typical case, which sums up the whole of this absurd fashion. There was a controversy in the columns of an important daily paper, some time ago, on the subject of the character of Shylock in Shakespeare. Actors and authors of distinction, including some of the most brilliant of living Jews, argued the matter from the most varied points of view. Some said that Shakespeare was prevented by the prejudices of his time from having a complete sympathy with Shylock. Some said that Shakespeare was only restrained by fear of the powers of his time from expressing his complete sympathy with Shylock. Some wondered how or why Shakespeare had got hold of such a queer story as that of the pound of flesh, and what it could possibly have to do with so dignified and intellectual a character as Shylock. In short, some wondered why a man of genius should be so much of an Anti-Semite, and some stoutly declared that he must have been a Pro-Semite. But all of them in a sense admitted that they were puzzled as to what the play was about. The correspondence filled column after column and went on for weeks. And from one end of that correspondence to the other, no human being even so much as mentioned the word "usury." It is exactly as if twenty clever critics were set down to talk for a month about the play of Macbeth, and were all strictly forbidden to mention the word "murder."

The play called *The Merchant of Venice* happens to be about usury, and its story is a medieval satire on usury. It is the fashion to say that it is a clumsy and grotesque story; but as a fact it is an exceedingly good story. It is a perfect and pointed story for its purpose, which is to convey the moral of the story. And the moral is that the logic of usury is in its nature at war with life, and might logically end in breaking into the bloody house of life. In other words, if a creditor can always claim a man's tools or a man's home, he might quite as justly claim one of his arms or legs. This principle was not only embodied in medieval satires but in very sound medieval laws, which set a limit on the usurer who was trying to take away a man's livelihood, as the usurer in the play is trying to take away a man's life. And if anybody thinks that usury can never go to lengths wicked enough to be worthy of so wild an image, then that person either knows nothing about it or knows too much. He is either one of the innocent rich who have never been the victims of money-lenders, or else one of the more powerful and influential rich who are money-lenders themselves.

All this, I say, is a fact that must be faced, but there is another side to the case, and it is this that the genius of Shakespeare discovered. What he did do, and what the medieval satirist did not do, was to attempt to understand Shylock; in the true sense to sympathise with Shylock the money-lender, as he sympathised with Macbeth the murderer. It was not to deny that the man was an usurer, but to assert that the usurer was a man. And the Elizabethan dramatist does make him a man, where the medieval satirist made him a monster. Shakespeare not only makes him a man but a perfectly sincere and self-respecting man. But the point is this: that he is a sincere man who sincerely believes in usury. He is a self-respecting man who does not despise himself for being a usurer. In one word, he regards usury as normal. In that word is the whole problem of the popular impression of the Jews. What Shakespeare suggested about the Jew in a subtle and sympathetic way, millions of plain men everywhere would suggest about him in a rough and ready way. Regarding the Jew in relation to his ideas about interest, they think either that he is simply immoral; or that if he is moral, then he has a different

G. K. CHESTERTON

morality. There is a great deal more to be said about how far this is true, and about what are its causes and excuses if it is true. But it is an old story, surely, that the worst of all cures is to deny the disease.

To recognise the reality of the Jewish problem is very vital for everybody and especially vital for Jews. To pretend that there is no problem is to precipitate the expression of a rational impatience, which unfortunately can only express itself in the rather irrational form of Anti-Semitism. In the controversies of Palestine and Syria, for instance, it is very common to hear the answer that the Jew is no worse than the Armenian. The Armenian also is said to be unpopular as a money-lender and a mercantile upstart; yet the Armenian figures as a martyr for the Christian faith and a victim of the Moslem fury. But this is one of those arguments which really carry their own answer. It is like the sceptical saying that man is only an animal, which of itself provokes the retort, "What an animal!" The very similarity only emphasises the contrast. Is it seriously suggested that we can substitute the Armenian for the Jew in the study of a world-wide problem like that of the Jews? Could we talk of the competition of Armenians among Welsh shop-keepers, or of the crowd of Armenians on Brighton Parade? Can Armenian usury be a common topic of talk in a camp in California and in a club in Piccadilly? Does Shakespeare show us a tragic Armenian towering over the great Venice of the Renascence? Does Dickens show us a realistic Armenian teaching in the thieves' kitchens of the slums? When we meet Mr. Vernon Vavasour, that brilliant financier, do we speculate on the probability of his really having an Armenian name to match his Armenian nose? Is it true, in short, that all sorts of people, from the peasants of Poland to the peasants of Portugal, can agree more or less upon the special subject of Armenia? Obviously it is not in the least true; obviously the Armenian question is only a local question of certain Christians, who may be more avaricious than other Christians. But it is the truth about the Jews. It is only half the truth, and one which by itself would be very unjust to the Jews. But it is the truth, and we must realise it as sharply and clearly as we can. The truth is that it is rather strange that the Jews should be so anxious for international agreements. For one of the few really international agreements is a suspicion of the Jews.

A more practical comparison would be one between the Jews and gipsies; for the latter at least cover several countries, and can be tested by the impressions of very different districts. And in some preliminary respects the comparison is really useful. Both races are in different ways landless, and therefore in different ways lawless. For the fundamental laws are land laws. In both cases a reasonable man will see reasons for unpopularity, without wishing to indulge any task for persecution. In both cases he will probably recognise the reality of a racial fault, while admitting that it may be largely a racial misfortune. That is to say, the drifting and detached condition may be largely the cause of Jewish usury or gipsy pilfering; but it is not common sense to contradict the general experience of gipsy pilfering or Jewish usury. The comparison helps us to clear away some of the cloudy evasions by which modern men have tried to escape from that experience. It is absurd to say that people are only prejudiced against the money methods of the Jews because the medieval church has left behind a hatred of their religion. We might as well say that people only protect the chickens from the gipsies because the medieval church undoubtedly condemned fortune-telling. It is unreasonable for a Jew to complain that Shakespeare makes Shylock and not Antonio the ruthless money-lender; or that Dickens makes Fagin and not Sikes the receiver of stolen goods. It is as if a gipsy were to complain when a novelist describes a child as stolen by the gipsies, and not by the curate or the mothers' meeting. It is to complain of facts and probabilities. There may be good gipsies; there may be good qualities which specially belong to them as gipsies; many students of the strange race have, for instance, praised a certain dignity and self-respect among the women of the Romany. But no student ever praised them for an exaggerated respect for private property, and the whole argument about gipsy theft can be roughly repeated about Hebrew usury. Above all, there is one other respect in which the comparison is even more to the point. It is the essential fact of the whole business, that the Jews do not become national merely by becoming a political part of any nation. We might as well say that the gipsies had villas in Clapham, when their caravans stood on Clapham Common.

But, of course, even this comparison between the two wandering peoples fails in the presence of the greater problem. Here again even the attempt at a parallel leaves the primary thing more unique. The gipsies do not become municipal merely by passing through a number of parishes, and it would seem equally obvious that a Jew need not become English merely by passing through England on his way from Germany to America. But the gipsy not only is not municipal, but he is not called municipal. His caravan is not immediately painted outside with the number and name of 123 Laburnam Road, Clapham. The municipal authorities generally notice the wheels attached to the new cottage, and therefore do not fall into the error. The gipsy may halt in a particular parish, but he is not as a rule immediately made a parish councillor. The cases in which a travelling tinker has been suddenly made the mayor of an important industrial town must be comparatively rare. And if the poor vagabonds of the Romany blood are bullied by mayors and magistrates, kicked off the land by landlords, pursued by policemen and generally knocked about from pillar to post, nobody raises an outcry that *they* are the victims of religious persecution; nobody summons meetings in public halls, collects subscriptions or sends petitions to parliament; nobody threatens anybody else with the organised indignation of the gipsies all over the world. The case of the Jew in the nation is very different from that of the tinker in the town. The moral elements that can be appealed to are of a very different style and scale. No gipsies are millionaires.

In short, the Jewish problem differs from anything like the gipsy problem in two highly practical respects. First, the Jews already exercise colossal cosmopolitan financial power. And second, the modern societies they live in also grant them vital forms of national political power. Here the vagrant is already as rich as a miser and the vagrant is actually made a mayor. As will be seen shortly, there is a Jewish side of the story which leads really to the same ending of the story; but the truth stated here is quite independent of any sympathetic or unsympathetic view of the race in question. It is a question of fact, which a sensible Jew can afford to recognise, and which the most sensible Jews do very definitely recognise. It is really irrational for anybody to pretend that the Jews are only a curious sect of Englishmen, like the Plymouth Brothers or the Seventh Day Baptists, in the face of such a simple fact as the family of Rothschild. Nobody can pretend that such an English sect can establish five brothers, or even cousins, in the five great capitals of Europe. Nobody can pretend that the Seventh Day Baptists are the seven grandchildren of one grandfather, scattered systematically among the warring nations of the earth. Nobody thinks the Plymouth Brothers are literally brothers, or that they are likely to be quite as powerful in Paris or in Petrograd as in Plymouth.

The Jewish problem can be stated very simply after all. It is normal for the nation to contain the family. With the Jews the family is generally divided among the nations. This may not appear to matter to those who do not believe in nations, those who really think there ought not to be any nations. But I literally fail to understand anybody who does believe in patriotism thinking that this state of affairs can be consistent with it. It is in its nature intolerable, from a national standpoint, that a man admittedly powerful in one nation should be bound to a man equally powerful in another nation, by ties more private and personal even than nationality. Even when the purpose is not any sort of treachery, the very position is a sort of treason. Given the passionately patriotic peoples of the west of Europe especially, the state of things cannot conceivably be satisfactory to a patriot. But least of all can it conceivably be satisfactory to a Jewish patriot; by which I do not mean a sham Englishman or a sham Frenchman, but a man who is sincerely patriotic for the historic and highly civilised nation of the Jews.

For what may be criticised here as Anti-Semitism is only the negative side of Zionism. For the sake of convenience I have begun by stating it in terms of the universal popular impression which some call a popular prejudice. But such a truth of differentiation is equally true on both its different sides. Suppose somebody proposes to mix up England and America, under some absurd name like the Anglo-Saxon Empire. One man may say, "Why should the jolly English inns and villages be swamped by these priggish provincial Yankees?" Another may say, "Why should the real democracy of a young country be tied to your snobbish old squirarchy?" But both these views are only versions of the same view of a great American: "God never made one people good enough to rule another."

The primary point about Zionism is that, whether it is right or wrong, it does offer a real and reasonable answer both to Anti-Semitism and to the charge of Anti-Semitism. The usual phrases about religious persecution and racial hatred are not reasonable answers, or answers at all. These Jews do not deny that they are Jews; they do not deny that Jews may be unpopular; they do not deny that there may be other than superstitious reasons for their unpopularity. They are not obliged to maintain that when a Piccadilly dandy talks about being in the hands of the Jews he is moved by the theological fanaticism that prevails in

Piccadilly; or that when a silly youth on Derby Day says he was done by a dirty Jew, he is merely conforming to that Christian orthodoxy which is one of the strict traditions of the Turf. They are not, like some other Jews, forced to pay so extravagant a compliment to the Christian religion as to suppose it the ruling motive of half the discontented talk in clubs and public-houses, of nearly every business man who suspects a foreign financier, or nearly every working man who grumbles against the local pawn-broker. Religious mania, unfortunately, is not so common. The Zionists do not need to deny any of these things; what they offer is not a denial but a diagnosis and a remedy. Whether their diagnosis is correct, whether their remedy is practicable, we will try to consider later, with something like a fair summary of what is to be said on both sides. But their theory, on the face of it, is perfectly reasonable. It is the theory that any abnormal qualities in the Jews are due to the abnormal position of the Jews. They are traders rather than producers because they have no land of their own from which to produce, and they are cosmopolitans rather than patriots because they have no country of their own for which to be patriotic. They can no more become farmers while they are vagrant than they could have built the Temple of Solomon while they were building the Pyramids of Egypt. They can no more feel the full stream of nationalism while they wander in the desert of nomadism than they could bathe in the waters of Jordan while they were weeping by the waters of Babylon. For exile is the worst kind of bondage. In insisting upon that at least the Zionists have insisted upon a profound truth, with many applications to many other moral issues. It is true that for any one whose heart is set on a particular home or shrine, to be locked out is to be locked in. The narrowest possible prison for him is the whole world.

It will be well to notice briefly, however, how the principle applies to the two Anti-Semitic arguments already considered. The first is the charge of usury and unproductive loans, the second the charge either of treason or of unpatriotic detachment. The charge of usury is regarded, not unreasonably, as only a specially dangerous development of the general charge of uncreative commerce and the refusal of creative manual exercise; the unproductive loan is only a minor form of the unproductive labour. It is certainly true that the latter complaint is, if possible, commoner than the former, especially in comparatively simple communities like those of Palestine. A very honest Moslem Arab said to me, with a singular blend of simplicity and humour, "A Jew does not work; but he grows rich. You never see a Jew working; and yet they grow rich. What I want to know is, why do we not all do the same? Why do we not also do this and become rich?" This is, I need hardly say, an over-simplification. Jews often work hard at some things, especially intellectual things. But the same experience which tells us that we have known many industrious Jewish scholars, Jewish lawyers, Jewish doctors, Jewish pianists, chess-players and so on, is an experience which cuts both ways. The same experience, if carefully consulted, will probably tell us that we have not known personally many patient Jewish ploughmen, many laborious Jewish blacksmiths, many active Jewish hedgers and ditchers, or even many energetic Jewish hunters and fishermen. In short, the popular impression is tolerably true to life, as popular impressions very often are; though it is not fashionable to say so in these days of democracy and self-determination. Jews do not generally work on the land, or in any of the handicrafts that are akin to the land; but the Zionists reply that this is because it can never really be their own land. That is Zionism, and that has really a practical place in the past and future of Zion.

Patriotism is not merely dying for the nation. It is dying with the nation. It is regarding the fatherland not merely as a real resting-place like an inn, but as a final resting-place, like a house or even a grave. Even the most Jingo of the Jews do not feel like this about their adopted country; and I doubt if the most intelligent of the Jews would pretend that they did. Even if we can bring ourselves to believe that Disraeli lived for England, we cannot think that he would have died with her. If England had sunk in the Atlantic he would not have sunk with her, but easily floated over to America to stand for the Presidency. Even if we are profoundly convinced that Mr. Beit or Mr. Eckstein had patriotic tears in his eyes when he obtained a gold concession from Queen Victoria, we cannot believe that in her absence he would have refused a similar concession from the German Emperor. When the Jew in France or in England says he is a good patriot he only means that he is a good citizen, and he would put it more truly if he said he was a good exile. Sometimes indeed he is an abominably bad citizen, and a most exasperating and execrable exile, but I am not talking of that side of the case. I am assuming that a man like Disraeli did really make a romance of England, that a man like Dernburg did really make a romance of Germany, and it is still true that though it was a romance, they would not have allowed it to be a tragedy. They would have seen that the story had a happy ending, especially for themselves. These Jews would not have died with any Christian nation.

But the Jews did die with Jerusalem. That is the first and last great truth in Zionism. Jerusalem was destroyed and Jews were destroyed with it, men who cared no longer to live because the city of their faith had fallen. It may be questioned whether all the Zionists have all the sublime insanity of the Zealots. But at least it is not nonsense to suggest that the Zionists might feel like this about Zion. It is nonsense to suggest that they would ever feel like this about Dublin or Moscow. And so far at least the truth both in Semitism and Anti-Semitism is included in Zionism.

It is a commonplace that the infamous are more famous than the famous. Byron noted, with his own misanthropic moral, that we think more of Nero the monster who killed his mother than of Nero the noble Roman who defeated Hannibal. The name of Julian more often suggests Julian the Apostate than Julian the Saint; though the latter crowned his canonisation with the sacred glory of being the patron saint of inn-keepers. But the best example of this unjust historical habit is the most famous of all and the most infamous of all. If there is one proper noun which has become a common noun, if there is one name which has been generalised till it means a thing, it is certainly the name of Judas. We should hesitate perhaps to call it a Christian name, except in the more evasive form of Jude. And even that, as the name of a more faithful apostle, is another illustration of the same injustice; for, by comparison with the other, Jude the faithful might almost be called Jude the obscure. The critic who said, whether innocently or ironically, "What wicked men these early Christians were!" was certainly more successful in innocence than in irony; for he seems to have been innocent or ignorant of the whole idea of the Christian communion. Judas Iscariot was one of the very earliest of all possible early Christians. And the whole point about him was that his hand was in the same dish; the traitor is always a friend, or he could never be a foe. But the point for the moment is merely that the name is known everywhere merely as the name of a traitor. The name of Judas nearly always means Judas Iscariot; it hardly ever means Judas Maccabeus. And if you shout out "Judas" to a politician in the thick of a political tumult, you will have some difficulty in soothing him afterwards, with the assurance that you had merely traced in him something of that splendid zeal and valour which dragged down the tyranny of Antiochus, in the day of the great deliverance of Israel.

Those two possible uses of the name of Judas would give us yet another compact embodiment of the case for Zionism. Numberless international Jews have gained the bad name of Judas, and some have certainly earned it. If you have gained or earned the good name of Judas, it can quite fairly and intelligently be affirmed that this was not the fault of the Jews, but of the peculiar position of the Jews. A man can betray like Judas Iscariot in another man's house; but a man cannot fight like Judas Maccabeus for another man's temple. There is no more truly rousing revolutionary story amid all the stories of mankind, there is no more perfect type of the element of chivalry in rebellion, than that magnificent tale of the Maccabee who stabbed from underneath the elephant of Antiochus and died under the fall of that huge and living castle. But it would be unreasonable to ask Mr. Montagu to stick a knife into the elephant on which Lord Curzon, let us say, was riding in all the pomp of Asiatic imperialism. For Mr. Montagu would not be liberating his own land; and therefore he naturally prefers to interest himself either in operations in silver or in somewhat slower and less efficient methods of liberation. In short, whatever we may think of the financial or social services such as were rendered to England in the affair of Marconi, or to France in the affair of Panama, it must be admitted that these exhibit a humbler and more humdrum type of civic duty, and do not remind us of the more reckless virtues of the Maccabees or the Zealots. A man may be a good citizen of anywhere, but he cannot be a national hero of nowhere; and for this particular type of patriotic passion it is necessary to have a *patria*. The Zionists therefore are maintaining a perfectly reasonable proposition, both about the charge of usury and the charge of treason, if they claim that both could be cured by the return to a national soil as promised in Zionism.

Unfortunately they are not always reasonable about their own reasonable proposition. Some of them have a most unlucky habit of ignoring, and therefore implicitly denying, the very evil that they are wisely trying to cure. I have already remarked this irritating innocence in the first of the two questions; the criticism that sees everything in Shylock except the point of him, or the point of his knife. How in the politics of Palestine at this moment this first question is in every sense the primary question. Palestine has hardly as yet a patriotism to be betrayed; but it certainly has a peasantry to be oppressed, and especially to be oppressed as so many peasantries have been with usury and forestalling. The Syrians and Arabs and all the agricultural and pastoral populations of Palestine are, rightly or wrongly, alarmed and angered at the advent of the Jews to power; for the perfectly practical and simple reason of the reputation which the Jews have all over the world. It is really ridiculous in people so intelligent as the Jews, and especially so intelligent as the Zionists, to ignore so enormous and elementary a fact as that reputation and its natural results. It may or may not in this case be unjust; but in any case it is not unnatural. It may be the result of persecution, but it is one that has definitely resulted. It may be the consequence of a misunderstanding; but it is a misunderstanding that must itself be understood. Rightly or wrongly, certain people in Palestine fear the coming of the Jews as they fear the coming of the locusts; they regard them as parasites that feed on a community by a thousand methods of financial intrigue and economic exploitation. I could understand the Jews indignantly denying this, or eagerly disproving it, or best of all, explaining what is true in it while exposing what is untrue. What is strange, I might almost say weird, about the attitude of some quite intelligent and sincere Zionists, is that they talk, write and apparently think as if there were no such thing in the world.

I will give one curious example from one of the best and most brilliant of the Zionists. Dr. Weizmann is a man of large mind and human sympathies; and it is difficult to believe that any one with so fine a sense of humanity can be entirely empty of anything like a sense of humour. Yet, in the middle of a very temperate and magnanimous address on "Zionist Policy," he can actually say a thing like this, "The Arabs need us with our knowledge, and our experience and our money. If they do not have us they will fall into the hands of others, they will fall among sharks."

One is tempted for the moment to doubt whether any one else in the world could have said that, except the Jew with his strange mixture of brilliancy and blindness, of subtlety and simplicity. It is much as if President Wilson were to say, "Unless America deals with Mexico, it will be dealt with by some modern commercial power, that has trust-magnates and hustling millionaires." But would President Wilson say it? It is as if the German Chancellor had said, "We must rush to the rescue of the poor Belgians, or they may be put under some system with a rigid militarism and a bullying bureaucracy." But would even a German Chancellor put it exactly like that? Would anybody put it in the exact order of words and structure of sentence in which Dr. Weizmann has put it? Would even the Turks say, "The Armenians need us with our order and our discipline and our arms. If they do not have us they will fall into the hands of others, they will perhaps be in danger of massacres." I suspect that a Turk would see the joke, even if it were as grim a joke as the massacres themselves. If the Zionists wish to quiet the fears of the Arabs, surely the first thing to do is to discover what the Arabs are afraid of. And very little investigation will reveal the simple truth that they are very much afraid of sharks; and that in their book of symbolic or heraldic zoology it is the Jew who is adorned with the dorsal fin and the crescent of cruel teeth. This may be a fairy-tale about a fabulous animal; but it is one which all sorts of races believe, and certainly one which these races believe.

But the case is yet more curious than that. These simple tribes are afraid, not only of the dorsal fin and dental arrangements which Dr. Weizmann may say (with some justice) that he has not got; they are also afraid of the other things which he says he has got. They may be in error, at the first superficial glance, in mistaking a respectable professor for a shark. But they can hardly be mistaken in attributing to the respectable professor what he himself considers as his claims to respect. And as the imagery about the shark may be too metaphorical or almost mythological, there is not the smallest difficulty in stating in plain words what the Arabs fear in the Jews. They fear, in exact terms, their knowledge and their experience and their money. The Arabs fear exactly the three things which he says they need. Only the Arabs would call it a knowledge of financial trickery and an experience of political intrigue, and the power given by hoards of money not only of their own but of other peoples. About Dr. Weizmann and the true Zionists this is self-evidently unjust; but about Jewish influence of the more visible and vulgar kind it has to be proved to be unjust. Feeling as I do the force of the real case for Zionism, I venture most earnestly to implore the Jews to disprove it, and not to dismiss it. But above all I implore them not to be content with assuring us again and again of their knowledge and their experience and their money. That is what people dread like a pestilence or an earthquake; their knowledge and their experience and their money. It is needless for Dr. Weizmann to tell us that he does not desire to enter Palestine like a Junker or drive thousands of Arabs forcibly out of the land; nobody supposes that Dr. Weizmann looks like a Junker; and nobody among the enemies of the Jews says that they have driven their foes in that fashion since the wars with the Canaanites. But for the Jews to reassure us by insisting on their own economic culture or commercial education is exactly like the Junkers reassuring us by insisting on the unquestioned supremacy of their Kaiser or the unquestioned obedience of their soldiers. Men bar themselves in their houses, or even hide themselves in their cellars, when such virtues are abroad in the land.

In short the fear of the Jews in Palestine, reasonable or unreasonable, is a thing that must be answered by reason. It is idle for the unpopular thing to answer with boasts, especially boasts of the very quality that makes it unpopular. But I think it could be answered by reason, or at any rate tested by reason; and the tests by consideration.

The principle is still as stated above; that the tests must not merely insist on the virtues the Jews do show, but rather deal with the particular virtues which they are generally accused of not showing. It is necessary to understand this more thoroughly than it is generally understood, and especially better than it is usually stated in the language of fashionable controversy. For the question involves the whole success or failure of Zionism. Many of the Zionists know it; but I rather doubt whether most of the Anti-Zionists know that they know it. And some of the phrases of the Zionists, such as those that I have noted, too often tend to produce the impression that they ignore when they are not ignorant. They are not ignorant; and they do not ignore in practice; even when an intellectual habit makes them seem to ignore in theory. Nobody who has seen a Jewish rural settlement, such as Rishon, can doubt that some Jews are sincerely filled with the vision of sitting under their own vine and fig-tree, and even with its accompanying lesson that it is first necessary to grow the fig-tree and the vine.

The true test of Zionism may seem a topsy-turvy test. It will not succeed by the number of successes, but rather by the number of failures, or what the world (and certainly not least the Jewish world) has generally called failures. It will be tested, not by whether Jews can climb to the top of the ladder, but by whether Jews can remain at the bottom; not by whether they have a hundred arts of becoming important, but by whether they have any skill in the art of remaining insignificant. It is often noted that the intelligent Israelite can rise to positions of power and trust outside Israel, like Witte in Russia or Rufus Isaacs in England. It is generally bad, I think, for their adopted country; but in any case it is no good for the particular problem of their own country. Palestine cannot have a population of Prime Ministers and Chief Justices; and if those they rule and judge are not Jews, then we have not established a commonwealth but only an oligarchy. It is said again that the ancient Jews turned their enemies into hewers of wood and drawers of water. The modern Jews have to turn themselves into hewers of wood and drawers of water. If they cannot do that, they cannot turn themselves into citizens, but only into a kind of alien bureaucrats, of all kinds the most perilous and the most imperilled. Hence a Jewish state will not be a success when the Jews in it are successful, or even when the Jews in it are statesmen. It will be a success when the Jews in it are scavengers, when the Jews in it are sweeps, when they are dockers and ditchers and porters and hodmen. When the Zionist can point proudly to a Jewish navvy who has *not* risen in the world, an under-gardener who is not now taking his ease as an upper-gardener, a yokel who is still a yokel, or even a village idiot at least sufficiently idiotic to remain in his village, then indeed the world will come to blow the trumpets and lift up the heads of the everlasting gates; for God will have turned the captivity of Zion.

Zionists of whose sincerity I am personally convinced, and of whose intelligence anybody would be convinced, have told me that there really is, in places like Rishon, something like a beginning of this spirit; the love of the peasant for his land. One lady, even in expressing her conviction of it, called it "this very un-Jewish characteristic." She was perfectly well aware both of the need of it in the Jewish land, and the lack of it in the Jewish race. In short she was well aware of the truth of that seemingly topsy-turvy test I have suggested; that of whether men are worthy to be drudges. When a humorous and humane Jew thus accepts the test, and honestly expects the Jewish people to pass it, then I think the claim is very serious indeed, and one not lightly to be set aside. I do certainly think it a very serious responsibility under the circumstances to set it altogether aside. It is our whole complaint against the Jew that he does not till the soil or toil with the spade; it is very hard on him to refuse him if he really says, "Give me a soil and I will till it; give me a spade and I will use it." It is our whole reason for distrusting him that he cannot really love any of the lands in which he wanders; it seems rather indefensible to be deaf to him if he really says, "Give me a land and I will love it." I would certainly give him a land or some instalment of the land, (in what general sense I will try to suggest a little later) so long as his conduct on it was watched and tested according to the principles I have suggested. If he asks for the spade he must use the spade, and not merely employ the spade, in the sense of hiring half a hundred men to use spades. If he asks for the soil he must till the soil; that is he must belong to the soil and not merely make the soil belong to him. He must have the simplicity, and what many would call the stupidity of the peasant. He must not only call a spade a spade, but regard it as a spade and not as a speculation. By some true conversion the urban and modern man must be not only on the soil, but of the soil, and free from our urban trick of inventing the word dirt for the dust to which we shall return. He must be washed in mud, that he may be clean.

How far this can really happen it is very hard for anybody, especially a casual visitor, to discover in the present crisis. It is admitted that there is much Arab and Syrian labour employed; and this in itself would leave all the danger of the Jew as a mere capitalist. The Jews explain it, however, by saying that the Arabs will work for a lower wage, and that this is necessarily a great temptation to the struggling colonists. In this they may be acting naturally as colonists, but it is none the less clear that they are not yet acting literally as labourers. It may not be their fault that they are not proving themselves to be peasants; but it is none the less clear that this situation in itself does not prove them to be peasants. So far as that is concerned, it still remains to be decided finally whether a Jew will be an agricultural labourer, if he is a decently paid agricultural labourer. On the other hand, the leaders of these local experiments, if they have not yet shown the higher materialism of peasants, most certainly do not show the lower materialism of capitalists. There can be no doubt of the patriotic and even poetic spirit in which many of them hope to make their ancient wilderness blossom like the rose. They at least would still stand among the great prophets of Israel, and none the less though they prophesied in vain.

I have tried to state fairly the case for Zionism, for the reason already stated; that I think it intellectually unjust that any attempt of the Jews to regularise their position should merely be rejected as one of their irregularities. But I do not disguise the enormous difficulties of doing it in the particular conditions Of Palestine. In fact the greatest of the real difficulties of Zionism is that it has to take place in Zion. There are other difficulties, however, which when they are not specially the fault of Zionists are very much the fault of Jews. The worst is the general impression of a business pressure from the more brutal and businesslike type of Jew, which arouses very violent and very just indignation. When I was in Jerusalem it was openly said that Jewish financiers had complained of the low rate of interest at which loans were made by the government to the peasantry, and even that the government had yielded to them. If this were true it was a heavier reproach to the government even than to the Jews. But the general truth is that such a state of feeling seems to make the simple and solid patriotism of a Palestinian Jewish nation practically impossible, and forces us to consider some alternative or some compromise. The most sensible statement of a compromise I heard among the Zionists was suggested to me by Dr. Weizmann, who is a man not only highly intelligent but ardent and sympathetic. And the phrase he used gives the key to my own rough conception of a possible solution, though he himself would probably, not accept that solution.

Dr. Weizmann suggested, if I understood him rightly, that he did not think Palestine could be a single and simple national territory quite in the sense of France; but he did not see why it should not be a commonwealth of cantons after the manner of Switzerland. Some of these could be Jewish cantons, others Arab cantons, and so on according to the type of population. This is in itself more reasonable than much that is suggested on the same side; but the point of it for my own purpose is more particular. This idea, whether it correctly represents Dr. Weizmann's meaning or no, clearly involves the abandonment of the solidarity of Palestine, and tolerates the idea of groups of Jews being separated from each other by populations of a different type. Now if once this notion be considered admissible, it seems to me capable of considerable extension. It seems possible that there might be not only Jewish cantons in Palestine but Jewish cantons outside Palestine, Jewish colonies in suitable and selected places in adjacent parts or in many other parts of the world. They might be affiliated to some official centre in Palestine, or even in Jerusalem, where there would naturally be at least some great religious headquarters of the scattered race and religion. The nature of that religious centre it must be for Jews to decide; but I think if I were a Jew I would build the Temple without bothering about the site of the Temple. That they should have the old site, of course, is not to be thought of; it would raise a Holy War from Morocco to the marches of China. But seeing that some of the greatest of the deeds of Israel were done, and some of the most glorious of the songs of Israel sung, when their only temple was a box carried about in the desert, I cannot think that the mere moving of the situation of the place of sacrifice need even mean so much to that historic tradition as it would to many others. That the Jews should have some high place of dignity and ritual in Palestine, such as a great building like the Mosque of Omar, is certainly right and reasonable; for upon no theory can their historic connection be dismissed. I think it is sophistry to say, as do some Anti-Semites, that the Jews have no more right there than the Jebusites. If there are Jebusites they are Jebusites without knowing it. I think it sufficiently answered in the fine phrase of an English priest,

G. K. CHESTERTON

in many ways more Anti-Semitic than I: "The people that remembers has a right." The very worst of the Jews, as well as the very best, do in some sense remember. They are hated and persecuted and frightened into false names and double lives; but they remember. They lie, they swindle, they betray, they oppress; but they remember. The more we happen to hate such elements among the Hebrews the more we admire the manly and magnificent elements among the more vague and vagrant tribes of Palestine, the more we must admit that paradox. The unheroic have the heroic memory; and the heroic people have no memory.

But whatever the Jewish nation might wish to do about a national shrine or other supreme centre, the suggestion for the moment is that something like a Jewish territorial scheme might really be attempted, if we permit the Jews to be scattered no longer as individuals but as groups. It seems possible that by some such extension of the definition of Zionism we might ultimately overcome even the greatest difficulty of Zionism, the difficulty of resettling a sufficient number of so large a race on so small a land. For if the advantage of the ideal to the Jews is to gain the promised land, the advantage to the Gentiles is to get rid of the Jewish problem, and I do not see why we should obtain all their advantage and none of our own. Therefore I would leave as few Jews as possible in other established nations, and to these I would give a special position best described as privilege; some sort of self-governing enclave with special laws and exemptions; for instance, I would certainly excuse them from conscription, which I think a gross injustice in their case. A Jew might be treated as respectfully as a foreign ambassador, but a foreign ambassador is a foreigner. Finally, I would give the same privileged position to all Jews everywhere, as an alternative policy to Zionism, if Zionism failed by the test I have named; the only true and the only tolerable test; if the Jews had not so much failed as peasants as succeeded as capitalists.

There is one word to be added; it will be noted that inevitably and even against some of my own desires, the argument has returned to that recurrent conclusion, which was found in the Roman Empire and the Crusades. The European can do justice to the Jew; but it must be the European who does it. Such a possibility as I have thrown out, and any other possibility that any one can think of, becomes at once impossible without some idea of a general suzerainty of Christendom over the lands of the Moslem and the Jew. Personally, I think it would be better if it were a general suzerainty of Christendom, rather than a particular supremacy of England. And I feel this, not from a desire to restrain the English power, but rather from a desire to defend it. I think there is not a little danger to England in the diplomatic situation involved; but that is a diplomatic question that it is neither within my power or duty to discuss adequately. But if I think it would be wiser for France and England together to hold Syria and Palestine together rather than separately, that only completes and clinches the conclusion that has haunted me, with almost uncanny recurrence, since I first saw Jerusalem sitting on the hill like a turreted town in England or in France; and for one moment the dark dome of it was again the Templum Domini, and the tower on it was the Tower of Tancred.

Anyhow with the failure of Zionism would fall the last and best attempt at a rationalistic theory of the Jew. We should be left facing a mystery which no other rationalism has ever come so near to providing within rational cause and cure. Whatever we do, we shall not return to that insular innocence and comfortable unconsciousness of Christendom, in which the Victorian agnostics could suppose that the Semitic problem was a brief medieval insanity. In this as in greater things, even if we lost our faith we could not recover our agnosticism. We can never recover agnosticism, any more than any other kind of ignorance. We know that there is a Jewish problem; we only hope that there is a

G. K. CHESTERTON

Jewish solution. If there is not, there is no other. We cannot believe again that the Jew is an Englishman with certain theological theories, any more than we can believe again any other part of the optimistic materialism whose temple is the Albert Memorial. A scheme of guilds may be attempted and may be a failure; but never again can we respect mere Capitalism for its success. An attack may be made on political corruption, and it may be a failure; but never again can we believe that our politics are not corrupt. And so Zionism may be attempted and may be a failure; but never again can we ourselves be at ease in Zion. Or rather, I should say, if the Jew cannot be at ease in Zion we can never again persuade ourselves that he is at ease out of Zion. We can only salute as it passes that restless and mysterious figure, knowing at last that there must be in him something mystical as well as mysterious; that whether in the sense of the sorrows of Christ or of the sorrows of Cain, he must pass by, for he belongs to God.

CONCLUSION

To have worn a large scallop shell in my hat in the streets of London might have been deemed ostentatious, to say nothing of carrying a staff like a long pole; and wearing sandals might have proclaimed rather that I had not come from Jerusalem but from Letchworth, which some identify with the New Jerusalem descending out of heaven from God. Lacking such attributes, I passed through South England as one who might have come from Ramsgate or from anywhere; and the only symbol left to me of my pilgrimage was a cheap ring of metal coloured like copper and brass. For on it was written in Greek characters the word "Jerusalem," and though it may be less valuable than a brass nail, I do not think you can buy it in the Strand. All those enormous and everlasting things, all those gates of bronze and mosaics of purple and peacock colouring, all those chapels of gold and columns of crimson marble, had all shrivelled up and dwindled down to that one small thread of red metal round my finger. I could not help having a feeling, like Aladdin, that if I rubbed the ring perhaps all those towers would rise again. And there was a sort of feeling of truth in the fancy after all. We talk of the changeless East; but in one sense the impression of it is really rather changing, with its wandering tribes and its shifting sands, in which the genii of the East might well build the palace or the paradise of a day. As I saw the low and solid English cottages rising around me amid damp delightful thickets under rainy skies, I felt that in a deeper sense it is rather we who build for permanence or at least for a sort of peace. It is something more than comfort; a

G. K. CHESTERTON

relative and reasonable contentment. And there came back on me like a boomerang a rather indescribable thought which had circled round my head through most of my journey; that Christendom is like a gigantic bronze come out of the furnace of the Near East; that in Asia is only the fire and in Europe the form. The nearest to what I mean was suggested in that very striking book *Form and Colour*, by Mr. March Philips. When I spoke of the idols of Asia, many moderns may well have murmured against such a description of the ideals of Buddha or Mrs. Besant. To which I can only reply that I do know a little about the ideals, and I think I prefer the idols. I have far more sympathy with the enthusiasm for a nice green or yellow idol, with nine arms and three heads, than with the philosophy ultimately represented by the snake devouring his tail; the awful sceptical argument in a circle by which everything begins and ends in the mind. I would far rather be a fetish worshipper and have a little fun, than be an oriental pessimist expected always to smile like an optimist. Now it seems to me that the fighting Christian creed is the one thing that has been in that mystical circle and broken out of it, and become something real as well. It has gone westward by a sort of centrifugal force, like a stone from a sling; and so made the revolving Eastern mind, as the Franciscan said in Jerusalem, do something at last.

Anyhow, although I carried none of the trappings of a pilgrim I felt strongly disposed to take the privileges of one. I wanted to be entertained at the firesides of total strangers, in the medieval manner, and to tell them interminable tales of my travels. I wanted to linger in Dover, and try it on the citizens of that town. I nearly got out of the train at several wayside stations, where I saw secluded cottages which might be brightened by a little news from the Holy Land. For it seemed to me that all my fellow-countrymen must be my friends; all these English places had come much closer together after travels that seemed in comparison as vast as the spaces between the stars. The hop-fields of Kent seemed to me like outlying parts of my own kitchen garden; and London itself to be really situated at London End. London was perhaps the largest of the suburbs of Beaconsfield. By the time I came to Beaconsfield itself, dusk was dropping over the beechwoods and the white cross-roads. The distance seemed to grow deeper and richer with darkness as I went up the long lanes towards my home; and in that distance, as I drew nearer, I heard the barking of a dog.

Choose from Thousands of 1stWorldLibrary Classics By

Adolphus WilliamWard
Aesop
Agatha Christie
Alexander Aaronsohn
Alexander Kielland
Alexandre Dumas
Alfred Gatty
Alfred Ollivant
Alice Duer Miller
Alice Turner Curtis
Alice Dunbar
Ambrose Bierce
Amelia E. Barr
Andrew Lang
Andrew McFarland Davis
Anna Sewell
Annie Besant
Annie Hamilton Donnell
Annie Payson Call
Anton Chekhov
Arnold Bennett
Arthur Conan Doyle
Arthur Ransome
Atticus
B. M. Bower
Basil King
Bayard Taylor
Ben Macomber
Booth Tarkington
Bram Stoker
C. Collodi
C. E. Orr
C. M. Ingleby
Carolyn Wells
Catherine Parr Traill
Charles A. Eastman
Charles Dickens
Charles Dudley Warner
Charles Farrar Browne
Charles Ives
Charles Kingsley
Charles Lathrop Pack
Charles Whibley
Charles Willing Beale
Charlotte M. Braeme
Charlotte M.Yonge
Clair W. Hayes
Clarence Day Jr.
Clarence E. Mulford

Clemence Housman
Confucius
Cornelis DeWitt Wilcox
Cyril Burleigh
D. H. Lawrence
Daniel Defoe
David Garnett
Don Carlos Janes
Donald Keyhole
Dorothy Kilner
Dougan Clark
E. Nesbit
E.P.Roe
E. Phillips Oppenheim
Edgar Allan Poe
Edgar Rice Burroughs
Edith Wharton
Edward J. O'Biren
John Cournos
Edwin L. Arnold
Eleanor Atkins
Elizabeth Cleghorn
Gaskell
Elizabeth Von Arnim
Ellem Key
Emily Dickinson
Erasmus W. Jones
Ernie Howard Pie
Ethel Turner
Ethel Watts Mumford
Eugenie Foa
Eugene Wood
Evelyn Everett-Green
Everard Cotes
F. J. Cross
Federick Austin Ogg
Ferdinand Ossendowski
Francis Bacon
Francis Darwin
Frances Hodgson Burnett
Frank Gee Patchin
Frank Harris
Frank Jewett Mather
Frank L. Packard
Frederick Trevor Hill
Frederick Winslow Taylor
Friedrich Kerst
Friedrich Nietzsche
Fyodor Dostoyevsky

Gabrielle E. Jackson
Garrett P. Serviss
Gaston Leroux
George Ade
Geroge Bernard Shaw
George Ebers
George Eliot
George MacDonald
George Orwell
George Tucker
George W. Cable
George Wharton James
Gertrude Atherton
Grace E. King
Grant Allen
Guillermo A. Sherwell
Gulielma Zollinger
Gustav Flaubert
H. A. Cody
H. B. Irving
H. G. Wells
H. H. Munro
H. Irving Hancock
H. Rider Haggard
H. W. C. Davis
Hamilton Wright Mabie
Hans Christian Andersen
Harold Avery
Harold McGrath
Harriet Beecher Stowe
Harry Houidini
Helent Hunt Jackson
Helen Nicolay
Hendy David Thoreau
Henrik Ibsen
Henry Adams
Henry Ford
Henry Frost
Henry James
Henry Jones Ford
Henry Seton Merriman
Henry Wadsworth
Longfellow
Henry W Longfellow
Herbert A. Giles
Herbert N. Casson
Herman Hesse
Homer
Honore De Balzac

Horace Walpole
Horatio Alger, Jr.
Howard Pyle
Howard R. Garis
Hugh Lofting
Hugh Walpole
Humphry Ward
Ian Maclaren
Israel Abrahams
J.G.Austin
J. Henri Fabre
J. M. Barrie
J. Macdonald Oxley
J. S. Knowles
J. Storer Clouston
Jack London
Jacob Abbott
James Allen
James Lane Allen
James Andrews
James Baldwin
James DeMille
James Joyce
James Oliver Curwood
James Oppenheim
James Otis
Jane Austen
Jens Peter Jacobsen
Jerome K. Jerome
John Burroughs
John F. Kennedy
John Gay
John Glasworthy
John Habberton
John Joy Bell
John Milton
John Philip Sousa
Jonathan Swift
Joseph Carey
Joseph Conrad
Joseph Jacobs
Julian Hawthrone
Julies Vernes
Justin Huntly McCarthy
Kakuzo Okakura
Kenneth Grahame
Kate Langley Bosher
L. A. Abbot
L. T. Meade
L. Frank Baum
Laura Lee Hope

Laurence Housman
Leo Tolstoy
Leonid Andreyev
Lewis Carroll
Lilian Bell
Lloyd Osbourne
Louis Tracy
Louisa May Alcott
Lucy Fitch Perkins
Lucy Maud Montgomery
Lydia Miller Middleton
Lyndon Orr
M. H. Adams
Margaret E. Sangster
Margaret Vandercook
Maria Edgeworth
Maria Thompson Daviess
Mariano Azuela
Marion Polk Angellotti
Mark Overton
Mark Twain
Mary Austin
Mary Cole
Mary Rowlandson
Mary Wollstonecraft
  Shelley
Max Beerbohm
Myra Kelly
Nathaniel Hawthrone
O. F. Walton
Oscar Wilde
Owen Johnson
P.G.Wodehouse
Paul and Mable Thorn
Paul G. Tomlinson
Paul Severing
Peter B. Kyne
Plato
R. Derby Holmes
R. L. Stevenson
Rabindranath Tagore
Rahul Alvares
Ralph Waldo Emmerson
Rene Descartes
Rex E. Beach
Richard Harding Davis
Richard Jefferies
Robert Barr
Robert Frost
Robert Gordon Anderson
Robert L. Drake

Robert Lansing
Robert Michael Ballantyne
Robert W. Chambers
Rosa Nouchette Carey
Ross Kay
Rudyard Kipling
Samuel B. Allison
Samuel Hopkins Adams
Sarah Bernhardt
Selma Lagerlof
Sherwood Anderson
Sigmund Freud
Standish O'Grady
Stanley Weyman
Stella Benson
Stephen Crane
Stewart Edward White
Stijn Streuvels
Swami Abhedananda
Swami Parmananda
T. S. Ackland
The Princess Der Ling
Thomas A. Janvier
Thomas A Kempis
Thomas Anderton
Thomas Bailey Aldrich
Thomas Bulfinch
Thomas De Quincey
Thomas H. Huxley
Thomas Hardy
Thomas More
Thornton W. Burgess
U. S. Grant
Valentine Williams
Victor Appleton
Virginia Woolf
Walter Scott
Washington Irving
Wilbur Lawton
Wilkie Collins
Willa Cather
Willard F. Baker
William Makepeace
  Thackeray
William W. Walter
Winston Churchill
Yei Theodora Ozaki
Young E. Allison
Zane Grey